Personnel P

Accessible and engaging, this textbook introduces students to the field of personnel psychology, also known as industrial psychology.

Based on their years of teaching in this area, Luong, Sprung, and Zickar survey core topics in the field, including job analysis, recruitment, selection, assessment, and performance evaluation. Throughout, they emphasize a psychological – rather than management – approach, explaining the key psychological principles that underpin human resources practices. Supported by plentiful examples, review questions, and discussion questions, this comprehensive overview shows how personnel psychologists endeavor toward a better workplace.

Written in a clear and captivating style, this book introduces students to the most recent and pertinent scientific research in personnel psychology and inspires future study in industrial-organizational psychology and related fields.

Alexandra Luong is Associate Professor, Department of Psychology, University of Minnesota Duluth, USA.

Justin M. Sprung is Associate Professor, Department of Psychology, Luther College, USA.

Michael J. Zickar is Sandman Professor, Department of Psychology, Bowling Green State University, USA.

Personnel Psychology

Alexandra Luong, Justin M. Sprung, and Michael J. Zickar

Cover image: © Getty Images

First published 2024
by Routledge
605 Third Avenue, New York, NY 10158

and by Routledge
4 Park Square, Milton Park, Abingdon, Oxon, OX14 4RN

Routledge is an imprint of the Taylor & Francis Group, an informa business

© 2024 Alexandra Luong, Justin M. Sprung, and Michael J. Zickar

The right of Alexandra Luong, Justin M. Sprung, and Michael J. Zickar to be identified as authors of this work has been asserted in accordance with sections 77 and 78 of the Copyright, Designs and Patents Act 1988.

All rights reserved. No part of this book may be reprinted or reproduced or utilised in any form or by any electronic, mechanical, or other means, now known or hereafter invented, including photocopying and recording, or in any information storage or retrieval system, without permission in writing from the publishers.

Trademark notice: Product or corporate names may be trademarks or registered trademarks, and are used only for identification and explanation without intent to infringe.

Library of Congress Cataloging-in-Publication Data
Names: Luong, Alexandra, author. | Sprung, Justin M., author. | Zickar, Michael J., author.
Title: Personnel psychology / Alexandra Luong, Justin M. Sprung and Michael J. Zickar.
Description: New York, NY : Routledge, 2024. | Includes bibliographical references and index. |
Identifiers: LCCN 2023010284 (print) | LCCN 2023010285 (ebook) |
ISBN 9781138842212 (hardback) | ISBN 9781138842229 (paperback) |
ISBN 9781315731735 (ebook)
Subjects: LCSH: Psychology, Industrial. | Personnel management.
Classification: LCC HF5548.8 .L78 2024 (print) | LCC HF5548.8 (ebook) |
DDC 158.7--dc23/eng/20230302
LC record available at https://lccn.loc.gov/2023010284
LC ebook record available at https://lccn.loc.gov/2023010285

ISBN: 978-1-138-84221-2 (hbk)
ISBN: 978-1-138-84222-9 (pbk)
ISBN: 978-1-315-73173-5 (ebk)

DOI: 10.4324/9781315731735

Typeset in Optima
by KnowledgeWorks Global Ltd.

Contents

1 Overview of personnel psychology	1
2 Discrimination and employment law	18
3 Job analysis	39
4 Recruitment	67
5 Validity	86
6 Criterion terms, concepts, and measures	104
7 Applicant reactions and fairness perceptions	115
8 Judgment and decision-making in selection	132
9 Ability tests	143
10 Non-cognitive tests	155
11 Behavioral and observational measures	173
12 New waves of assessment	191
13 Performance evaluation	202
14 Training	214
15 Summary and review	235
Index	245

Overview of personnel psychology

LEARNING OBJECTIVES

- Understand the differences between Industrial and Organizational (I-O) psychology and the fields of human resources (HR) and business management
- Be able to distinguish the two branches (industrial and organizational) of I-O psychology
- Know key people and events that shaped the history of personnel psychology
- Understand what career options are available within personnel psychology
- Know some of the current trends of interest to personnel psychologists

What is personnel psychology?

All three of us (Alexandra, Mike, and Justin) have spent our professional careers studying what makes people successful at their jobs, helping companies design and validate selection procedures to help companies make better decisions, and investigating these selection and promotion tools for bias to ensure that individual decisions are fair and unrelated to legally protected characteristics. We have worked with companies to identify potential star performers and designed tests to identify people who were likely to quit early on their jobs. In short, we have spent our careers working in the area of *personnel psychology*, the topic of this textbook and your class. We have trained students who work as corporate recruiters and managers in HR departments, as well as other students who have gone on to work as consultants to help organizations solve personnel problems. We love helping people succeed at their jobs, hence helping organizations succeed as well.

Before defining personnel psychology, it is important to first explain what *Industrial-Organizational Psychology* is, as this is the broader subfield of psychology in which personnel psychology resides. Industrial-Organizational Psychology (I-O Psychology or just *I-O* for short) is the study of how workers think, feel, and behave. The Society for Industrial-Organizational Psychology (SIOP), the professional association for I-O psychologists, states that I-O "tries to understand and measure human behavior to improve employees' satisfaction in their work, employers' ability to select and promote the best people, and to generally make the workplace better for the [people] who work there. They do this by creating tests and by designing products such as training courses, selection procedures and surveys."[1] I-O follows the **scientist-practitioner model**, in which our understanding of and solutions to workplace issues are grounded in theory, based upon the scientific method, and utilizes statistics to make conclusions of empirical data. In short, I-O psychology applies findings and theories from the larger field of psychology to address any and all topics within the workplace. Over the years, I-O psychologists have studied a diverse set of topics, including how to motivate employees to work harder, how to reduce job-related stress, how to predict which applicants will be successful on the job, and what personality traits are shared by successful managers and leaders.

> **Scientist-Practitioner Approach:** A model emphasizing that psychologists are both practitioners and scientists who base their practice and activities on sound empirical research.

Given the focus of I-O psychology on the workplace, it is not surprising that I-O is sometimes confused with other fields such as HR or business management. Whereas HR is more concerned with the administration of policies and procedures, I-O is focused more on the *psychology* behind any HR issues. Compared to business management, which involves broad and technical functions of an organization, including areas such as finance and accounting, I-O psychology differs in that our focus is primarily on the people in the workplace and the psychology of how these employees perform, relate to others, feel about their job, and so forth. In short, what differentiates I-O psychology from other related fields lies first and foremost in our namesake: *psychological* principles drive our understanding of how workers think, feel, and behave. As a social *science*, our practices are based upon empirical research, rather than case studies, clinical judgment, or intuition. In an ideal world, research findings from I-O psychology would inform the practice of HR and business management. In reality, sometimes HR practitioners follow our guidance and other times they are influenced by management fads that have little research support. We believe that businesses benefit by following the evidence-based approach espoused by I-O.

I and O

For convenience sake, the field of I-O psychology has been separated into two branches: industrial psychology (the *I* side) and organizational psychology (the *O* side). Personnel psychology is synonymous with the *I* side, with an emphasis on the individual as the micro unit, and on productivity and efficiency as outcomes. In contrast, the *O* side is focused more on the processes involved in the workplace, either between individuals as in teams or leadership, or intra-individually, such as what may motivate workers. The focus of the *O* side is also more macro, including the topics of organizational culture and development. Of course, this dichotomy is really one of convenience, as many *I* and *O* topics blend together in various ways. Although the material in this book will focus on the *I* side (i.e., personnel psychology), we will at times reference research on the *O* side because to understand individual performance (an *I* side topic), we will need to have a good understanding of the organizational influence (the *O* side).

Most of personnel psychology is focused on issues related to the selection and evaluation of employees. Personnel psychology relies heavily on quantitative methodology to evaluate the reliability and validity of pre-applicant hiring tests and the testing of theories related to human performance. If you have ever reflected on which activities would be best suited for your individual talents, evaluated your performance at a given task, or contemplated how you might perform a job better in the future, you have informally engaged in activities relevant to the topics presented in this book. Personnel psychologists strive to answer these same questions, albeit in a more formal manner, by relying on careful and objective measurement of people, jobs, and performance. A few general premises that serve as the foundation for personnel psychology theory and research are (1) jobs differ in their content, (2) people differ in their knowledge, skills, and abilities, and (3) we should capitalize on these variations in order to enhance the performance and work experiences of individuals and organizations.

History of personnel psychology

Before exploring the various topics within personnel psychology, we felt it is essential to provide a brief overview of the history of the field as we see a lot of truth to the age-old saying that understanding the past is essential to understanding the present. The world of work has changed significantly over the years and will continue to do so in the future. Therefore, an appreciation of the past will help to ground your comprehension of the tools, methods, and theories used within the field today.

The inception of personnel psychology as a discipline occurred in the early 1900s. Although not yet formally recognized as a sub-discipline within psychology, the zeitgeist of the early 20th century helped instigate the need for and promise of personnel psychology as a worthy enterprise. At that time, psychology was maturing as a scientific discipline, the industrialization of the American workforce led to larger organizations and a separation of the manager class from front-line workers (i.e., the emergence of the middle class), and labor unions were advocating for fair compensation and adequate working conditions.[2,3,4] Furthermore, the United States' involvement in World War I (WWI) and World War II (WWII) brought about several personnel concerns that needed to be resolved in a timely manner. The time was right to take psychology to work. In this section, we will review some of the people and events that shaped the field of personnel psychology.

Early pioneers

Within a few decades after Wilhelm Wundt established the first psychological research laboratory in Leipzig, Germany in 1879, several psychologists and business leaders developed an interest in applying psychology to the business realm in order to maximize efficiency.[5] Lying at the heart of the intersection between business and psychology was the study and application of individual differences (i.e., differential psychology), which remains a central theme in personnel psychology to this day.[4] A handful of psychologists, in particular, were especially influential in laying the groundwork for the blending of psychology and industry.

One of the most notable figures in the early days of personnel psychology was Hugo Munsterberg. After studying under Wundt in Germany, Munsterberg was brought to Harvard University in 1892 in order to oversee Harvard's psychological laboratory. Munsterberg was initially a strict experimental psychologist, as were most psychologists of the time. In 1907, however, Munsterberg's focus shifted from experimentation in the lab to the *application* of psychology to address practical problems in the realms of industry, law, education, and psychiatric practice.[6] It may seem counterintuitive now looking back, but at the time, practical application of psychology beyond the lab setting was a novel idea. Accordingly, Munsterberg is not only considered a founder of personnel psychology, but also of applied psychology more broadly.

As for his specific influence on personnel psychology, Munsterberg was one of the first psychologists to measure individual differences in worker abilities and link those differences to work performance. Perhaps the most distinguishing accomplishment for Munsterberg is being credited with publishing the first personnel psychology textbook – *Psychology and*

Industrial Efficiency. This book was published in German in 1910 and in English in 1913. Although he did not have a long career (due to an untimely death), many of the subsequent books and publications in personnel psychology built on the structure provided by Munsterberg in his initial textbook. In fact, Landy (1997) even noted that "this book was the bible for the application of differential psychology in industry" (p. 470).[6] Thus, Munsterberg's contribution to the field of personnel psychology cannot be understated.

Like Munsterberg, Walter Dill Scott was an influential figure in promoting the application of psychology to the business setting. Scott also studied under Wundt, subsequently taking a position at Northwestern University in 1900. Shortly thereafter, he published multiple books on the significance of psychology in advertising: *The Theory of Advertising* in 1903 and *The Psychology of Advertising* in 1908. After his venture into advertising, Scott then sought to explore the application of psychological principles to several areas of industry more broadly, including concerns related to leadership, efficiency, selection, and motivation.[6] This work culminated in the publication of the book *Increasing Human Efficiency in Business* in 1910, which served as a counterpart to Munsterberg's text.

Even more so than his publications, Scott is well known for his work as a practitioner. In 1916, Scott took a leave of absence from Northwestern to join the Carnegie Institute as a professor of applied psychology. There, along with Walter Bingham, he assisted in the development and application of various selection tests and methods, some of which are still used today.[5] Scott was also the driving force in establishing the first personnel **consulting firm** in 1919 – the Scott Company – which provided various forms of personnel assistance to private organizations. This began the longstanding tradition of I-O psychologists working as consultants in private industry. Moreover, Scott was a prominent force in showcasing the value of personnel psychology within the military. Scott's work in the testing and placement of recruits during WWI (discussed further later in this chapter) not only earned him a Distinguished Service Medal from the army, but also helped to establish personnel psychology as a reputable field more broadly.[3] As can be seen by his many accomplishments in both research and practice, Scott truly embodied the scientist-practitioner approach.

> **Consulting Firm:** A business providing expert advice and strategies to assist companies with personnel issues.

Two additional figures – James McKeen Cattell and Walter Bingham – also played critical roles in the movement toward application of psychology within the work setting. Cattell, similar to Munsterberg, trained under Wundt and was one of the first researchers to explore the importance of individual differences in relation to behavior. Cattell was a forerunner in early research on mental ability testing, spending the majority of his career in this area and setting the stage for the vast amount of research that would follow. His most lasting accomplishment was the establishment of the Psychological Corporation in 1921, which marketed psychological tests to clients in the realm of education, industry, and government.[6]

Walter Bingham was another early advocate of mental testing. In 1916, Bingham served as the head of Carnegie Institute's Division of Applied Psychology (the first of its kind) and was instrumental in promoting the value of psychology in industry. Bingham supervised Walter Dill Scott's work at the Carnegie Institute, and also worked closely with Scott in the personnel evaluation effort during WWI. Bingham eventually took over the Psychological Corporation from Cattell in 1926, increasing the organization's success and reach in the decades that followed.[6]

All four of these individuals – Munsterberg, Scott, Cattell, and Bingham – sought to apply principles of psychology to the work setting before it was commonplace to do so. The practical application of psychology is so commonplace today that we often take it for granted, but this was not always the case. As a result of their trailblazing work, many other psychologists followed in their footsteps. Now that you know a few of the early pioneers within the field, let's take a look at some of the events that were instrumental in the development of personnel psychology.

Scientific management

Around the same time pioneers of personnel psychology were doing their work, Frederick Taylor, an industrial engineer, sought to establish a scientific approach to managing workers. In the early 1900s, Taylor proposed the theory of **scientific management**. Taylor presumed that simplifying jobs and optimizing worker actions would maximize productivity. The central tenet of scientific management is that there is "one best way" to perform every work task, and that each worker should be trained to perform the task in this specified manner.[7] A second key element to scientific management was piece-rate incentive systems, where workers would get paid for the amount they accomplished during the day. Taylor's goal with scientific management was to remove all inefficiency from the work place by regulating worker activity.

> **Scientific Management:** A theory of management focusing on optimizing worker efficiency and productivity through use of the scientific method.

At this point, you may be wondering how Taylor went about finding that "one best way" to perform job tasks. As part of his theory, Taylor advocated for the use of time studies. Time studies entailed breaking each task down into its component parts, timing each movement needed to perform the task with a stopwatch, and determining the most efficient movement(s) for increasing productivity. According to Taylor, time studies would determine the best way to execute a job. For example, in his book, *The Principles of Scientific Management*, Taylor describes, in detail, the "science of shoveling." Specifically, he overviews the process of experimentation used to discover the ideal shovel capacity (in pounds) to ensure maximum performance for a shovel worker over the course of a workday. Based on the results of his time studies with several different shovel sizes and many clicks of his stopwatch, he concluded that a 21-pound shovel would lead to the most efficient body movements, and, in turn, the highest productivity for shovel workers.[7]

Taylor believed that scientific management would lead to happier employees, not only because they would be more efficient, but also because they would get paid more (due to his emphasis on piece-rate incentive systems). However, many workers felt alienated because they were deprived of any control over their work. The sole focus on efficiency served the purpose of dehumanizing the work process, making many workers feel more like machines than actual people. To put Taylor's practice into context, imagine you were taking a college exam, and during that exam your professor stood next to you with a stopwatch recording how long it took you to answer each question. How would that make you feel? Chances are, you would not be too fond of that process. Although scientific management did not lead to happier employees, Taylor's work was influential in that it served as one of the foundations for modern ergonomics and human factors psychology. These two fields, sometimes referred to interchangeably, strive to design work tasks and environments in a way that is best suited to workers' sensory and perceptual capacities. Rather than being focused primarily on efficiency, as was scientific management, these fields expanded on Taylor's ideas by prioritizing human-centered design and consideration of the physical, psychological, and social nature of the work setting.

Early advocates of scientific management included Lillian and Frank Gilbreth. Lillian was the first person to receive a PhD in industrial psychology. Her husband, Frank, was an industrial engineer. The Gilbreths extended Taylor's work by performing motion studies, which sought to maximize efficiency in work processes by reducing the motions involved in the task. Through the removal of unnecessary movements, this would also serve the purpose of lessening worker fatigue. Lillian applied these studies in order to improve processes in the workplace and at home. For example, Lillian Gilbreth is responsible for the foot-operated trash can, as this would allow for efficient opening of the trash can while also eliminating the need to wash one's hands after touching the lid. She is also responsible for coming up with the concept of adjustable shelves in refrigerator doors.[8] While Lillian Gilbreth understood the importance of efficiency, what set her apart from Taylor was the emphasis she placed on the human element of work. She sought to apply psychological principles to Taylor's scientific management in order to compensate for his lack of concern for how workers felt about their tasks. Combining their two approaches, Taylor and the Gilbreths are responsible for the development of **time and motion studies**, which were commonly used by industrial engineers and personnel psychologists at that time. An additional fun fact about the Gilbreths, the book (and movie) *Cheaper by the Dozen* was written about Frank and Lillian Gilbreth and their 12 children. Given the large demands that come along with 12 children, it makes sense that the Gilbreths were concerned with efficiency!

> **Time and Motion Study:** An analysis of the time and movements required by a job or task.

WWI

Perhaps the most pivotal single event in the history of personnel psychology was WWI. Upon entering WWI in 1917, the United States' military had to process and place over one million recruits, a large personnel problem if there ever was one! This provided early personnel psychologists with the opportunity to demonstrate the practical value of their field. Walter Dill Scott and Walter Bingham, along with a team of psychologists, worked to develop cognitive ability tests that could be used to assist in the selection and classification of army recruits. The end product was the Army Alpha, developed to assess army recruits who were able to read, and the Army Beta, developed to assess army recruits who were illiterate. This process demonstrated the viability of a large-scale testing and selection program.[2] Scott and Bingham extended this work by establishing the Committee on Classification of Personnel, a committee designed to address various Army personnel needs. As part of their duties, this committee crafted job descriptions, performance rating systems, and standardized tests for the Army. In fact, the work that was done by this committee set the stage for modern-day job analysis, a fundamental topic within personnel psychology.[2]

The effort of many applied psychologists during WWI served as the precursor to the ensuing permeation of ability testing in the realms of government, industry, and education. Shortly after the war, Walter Dill Scott founded the Scott Company consulting firm, followed by Cattell's Psychological Corporation. Indeed, WWI proved to be a monumental boon to the growing field of personnel psychology.

The Human Relations Movement

Have you ever worked at a job where you felt like your work was not appreciated, or even went unnoticed? Or that your company was preoccupied with productivity at the expense of your overall work experience? Prior to the **Human Relations Movement**, many organizations prioritized efficiency at the expense of workers' attitudes and morale. This is best evidenced by the theory of scientific management discussed earlier. The Human Relations Movement brought to light the idea that monetary incentives and maximizing efficiency were not the only strategies for improving worker performance. Rather, positive treatment, improved working conditions, and an interest in employees' attitudes can go a long way toward increasing productivity.[3] As a result of this movement, researchers began to place more emphasis on topics such as employee motivation, emotions, and job satisfaction.

> **Human Relations Movement:** A movement focused on the social, motivational, and emotional experience of the worker.

One of the driving forces of the Human Relations Movement was Elton Mayo, an Australian psychologist who took a job at Harvard in 1926. Rather than focusing solely on efficiency within the workplace, Mayo was more interested in worker emotions. Mayo is largely known for his role in the **Hawthorne studies**, a series of studies conducted at the Western Electric Corporation in Hawthorne, Illinois. These studies were originally designed to examine how changes in the work environment – such as lighting levels, work schedules, and temperature – may impact performance.[9] When the studies yielded some counterintuitive results, showing that productivity may increase under worse working conditions (e.g., decreased lighting) and decrease under better working conditions (e.g., increased lighting), researchers interviewed employees to explore what was going on. Conclusions from the studies revealed that simply paying attention to workers may change their attitudes and behaviors, and, in turn, their performance. This notion, that being watched may lead to behavior change, is commonly referred to as the **Hawthorne Effect**.[3]

> **Hawthorne Studies:** A series of studies demonstrating the important role that worker attitudes play in predicting worker behavior.
>
> **Hawthorne Effect:** When workers change their behavior simply due to the fact that they are being observed.

By highlighting the fact that social aspects of the work setting may be just as important to performance as physical work conditions, the Hawthorne studies kick-started the Human Relations Movement and served as the birth of the O side of I-O psychology. Psychological principles and theories would now not only be used to improve worker efficiency, but also to enhance worker well-being. This expanded focus added to the building momentum for personnel psychology.

WWII

Like WWI, WWII proved to be an important opportunity for psychologists to further establish the credibility of their field in the applied setting. Walter Bingham served as the chief psychologist for the United States Department of War, working with hundreds of psychologists to build on the foundation of assessment techniques established in WWI. Moreover, WWII allowed for a much wider application of psychological principles to wartime efforts. Psychologists were not only able to implement useful ability testing and selection techniques within the Army, but also developed performance appraisal procedures, training methods, strategies for team development, methods for morale and attitude change, and recommendations for equipment design.[2] Two specific examples of the advancements that came from applied psychologists during the WWII wartime effort include (1) the standardization of aircraft cockpits in order to increase ease of use and reduce accidents among pilots (often referred to as the birth of human factors psychology) and (2) the development of the assessment center to evaluate candidates for spy positions. Assessment centers – an in-depth evaluation method based on several ability tests and behavioral exercises – are still used today and will be reviewed more fully in Chapter 11. The positive showing from applied psychologists in WWII served as the catalyst for additional opportunities within industry, government, and education after the war.

Title VII of the 1964 Civil Rights Act

The use of ability tests in industry increased substantially after WWII. Prior to 1964, these tests could be used in the workplace without any evidence demonstrating their relation to job performance. Title VII of the 1964 Civil Rights Act changed this, prohibiting employment discrimination based on race, color, sex, religion, and national origin (i.e., protected classes). The general purpose of the act was to ensure equal employment opportunity. According to this legislation, if an employment test was found to be discriminatory against one or more of the protected classes (i.e., one group was selected at a lesser ratio as a result of scores on the employment test), that test may be deemed illegal if the organization does not have evidence to demonstrate the validity of the test. Thus, employment tests were now regulated. To ensure fairness in the selection process and to protect from lawsuits, organizations had to demonstrate evidence to show that any tests they used to make workplace decisions were valid predictors of job performance. The issue of discrimination will be discussed further in Chapter 2, and a detailed exploration of validity will be provided in Chapter 5. For personnel psychologists, this simply meant another opportunity to demonstrate their value as a science.

Modern era

It goes without saying that advances in technology have had a massive impact on society as a whole, let alone work processes. Throughout the history of personnel psychology, technology has been a constant force in changing the nature of the work setting via improvements in tools, machines, work environments, and social processes. The advent of the internet, in particular, monumentally expanded the avenues for communication within and between organizations. To list just a few examples, most job applications are now completed online, computer adaptive testing is a common practice, virtual training and instruction methods have increased rapidly in recent years, and telecommuting is a common practice for many organizational workers. As the internet and its various applications have expanded, so have the opportunities for both workers and organizations. Given that there are often many pros and cons associated with technology advancements, particularly with regard to their ramifications for the work setting, this continues to be a focal point for personnel psychologists. Chapter 12 will explore this topic in more depth.

Increasingly sophisticated quantitative methodology has also greatly enhanced personnel psychologists' ability to measure people and jobs more effectively. It is easier to examine complex psychological phenomena today than ever before. Given the wealth of research already conducted in the field, many studies now include **mediator** and/or **moderator** variables to examine and explain *how*, *why*, or *when* simple relationships occur.

> **Mediator Variable:** A variable examined in a research study, above and beyond the X and Y variables, which explains why there is a relationship between the two.
>
> **Moderator Variable:** A variable examined in a research study, above and beyond the X and Y variables, which explains the conditions under which there is a relationship between the two.

To illustrate the importance of mediators and moderators, consider the following example. If we find a positive relationship between customer service friendliness and customer satisfaction, we do not know exactly how or why this relationship exists. Based on emotional contagion theory, we can propose that when customer service employees display friendliness, customers will themselves feel positive emotions, which, in turn, influences their higher ratings of the employee and their shopping experience. Hence, we can include a mediator variable in this study by measuring customer emotions after they have interacted with the service employee. The mediator variable is an intervening variable that explains an otherwise indirect relationship between the X (service friendliness) and Y (customer satisfaction) variables. In other words, when we observe a significant mediator variable, we can conclude that X does not directly lead to Y; rather, X leads to the mediator variable, which then leads to Y.

A moderator variable helps us understand when there may be a relationship between X and Y. For example, is there always a positive relationship between customer service employee friendliness and customer satisfaction? Research shows that it depends on a number of other factors, from the type of product being purchased to how busy the store is. Hence, the moderator variable is referred to as the "it depends" variable. It is also referred to as the variable that turns up or down the volume of the relationship between the X and Y variables. Let's say that for female service employees, displaying friendliness is critical to getting higher customer satisfaction, but for male employees, there is a weaker relationship, or even a negative relationship. The sex of the service employee is the moderator variable in this example; in other words, the relationship between friendliness and satisfaction depends upon whether the employee is male or female. See Figure 1.1 for a depiction of the moderator and mediator variables. The ability to examine and test for mediators and moderators is valuable for personnel psychologists in that it allows for a more fine-tuned analysis of various workplace issues.

Theory, research, and practice within personnel psychology have come a long way, with many people and events influencing the trajectory of the field. Although personnel psychology looks a lot different today than it did back in the early 20th century, the fundamental tenets of the field have stayed the same: jobs differ, people differ, and we should carefully and objectively measure those differences to maximize the performance and well-being of all workers.

Overview of personnel psychology

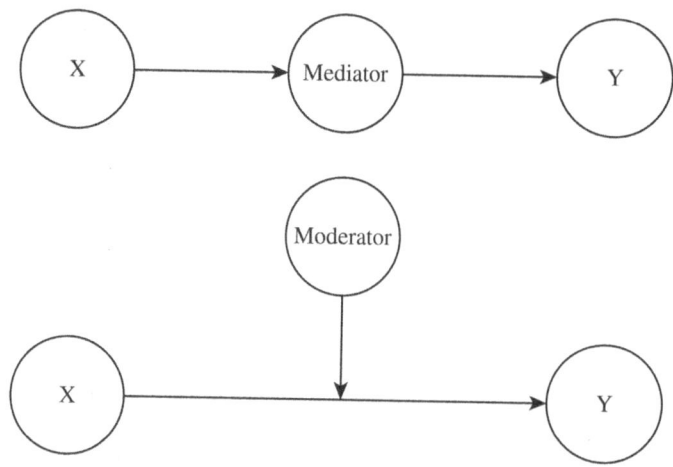

Figure 1.1 Mediator and moderator variables

Personnel psychology today

Today, personnel psychology encompasses a wide range of topics. Professionals in the field engage in research and practice in the areas of job analysis, recruitment, selection, performance appraisal, and employee training and development. To conclude this chapter, we provide an overview of some current workplace trends impacting the profession, career opportunities for those with a degree in personnel psychology, and some professional organizations related to the field.

Workplace trends

Now that you've been exposed to a brief history of personnel psychology, let's take a look at some of the current and emerging concerns within the field. Each year, SIOP surveys its members to determine which workplace issues will be of most concern to researchers and practitioners. Below is a list of the top ten workplace trends as indicated by the most recent survey (trends for 2022).[10]

#10: Enabling organizational culture in a changing workplace environment
#9: Employer's role in employees' mental health
#8: Creating effective diversity, equity, and inclusion interventions
#7: Stress and burnout
#6: The great resignation
#5: Caring for employee well-being
#4: Candidate attraction and retention in a candidate-driven market
#3: Managing the transition into post-pandemic work
#2: Ensuring inclusive environments and cultures
#1: Employee engagement and organizational commitment of remote workers

Although several of these trends slant more heavily toward the O side (e.g., #5, #7, and #9), this list demonstrates the somewhat arbitrary nature of separating I and O research topics. In reality, all of these trends are relevant to personnel psychologists and organizational psychologists. Take #7, stress and burnout, for example. Although reducing stress and burnout is a primary concern for organizational psychologists, this topic has some large implications for personal psychologists as well. Will an employee's stress and burnout impact the performance appraisal process? Will it impact their likelihood of applying for (and/or receiving) a promotion? Will training be as effective for employees experiencing burnout? Can we link the stress and burnout employees are experiencing to some of the job requirements outlined by a job analysis? As mentioned earlier in this chapter, although thinking about topics as I or O focused is convenient for broadly conceptualizing the field of I-O psychology, it is less practical when trying to solve work-related issues. Rather, we encourage you to think about how personnel psychology can contribute to addressing each of these ten issues. For some topics, it will be pretty easy. For others, it may take a bit more effort.

This list also demonstrates the large influence of the recent COVID-19 pandemic. Although telecommuting and remote work were on the rise for the past few decades, the pandemic led to a huge shift toward remote work due to the necessity of social distancing and quarantining. As organizations seek to move beyond the pandemic, it will be interesting to observe the long-term influence it has had on personnel issues, remote work in particular. The pandemic also serves as a general reminder of the importance of adaptability for personnel psychologists, and workplaces in general. Although events like this are rare, when they do occur, it is important to explore what can be learned and how organizations can best adapt moving forward. Research and practice within personnel psychology is continuously advancing, and the pandemic represents both a challenge and an opportunity to push the field further.

Finally, diversity, equity, and inclusion initiatives have been gaining steam in the last decade and will continue to be a focal issue for personnel psychologists in the future. What strategies can organizations use to attract a more diverse candidate pool? How is equity established in the selection process and beyond? What does it mean to be inclusive? These are questions that will drive a great deal of research and practice in personnel psychology in the years to come.

Career opportunities

You may be wondering what types of work and career opportunities are available for those interested in personnel psychology. True to the scientist-practitioner model, there are many prospects available in the areas of research and practice. Personnel psychologists may be found working in colleges and universities (i.e., academia), consulting firms, or public and private industry. Taking a look back at the top workplace trends presented previously, it's easy to see the wide variety of issues one may tackle as a personnel psychologist. Although many professionals tend to focus their efforts primarily on either research or practice, it is not uncommon for a personnel psychologist to have their foot in both worlds to some degree.

Regarding academia, you can find personnel psychologists working in psychology and business departments. Their primary duties include teaching, research, and service within their academic institution. Graduate programs in personnel psychology may also have an in-house consulting group where professors collaborate with students to provide consulting services to private industry. Although academic positions constitute the bulk of research-oriented positions available to personnel psychologists, private and public organizations may also seek a personnel psychologist to serve in a research role for their institution.

Outside the realm of academia, the majority of personnel psychologists work as consultants in private and public industry. Broadly speaking, consultants provide expert advice on various personnel issues. Consulting might entail working as an **internal consultant** or an **external consultant**. Although both types of consultants engage in similar work, the primary difference lies in the nature of their employment. An internal consultant is employed by an organization (public or private) and will assist that company with any or all of their internal personnel needs. An external consultant is employed by a consulting firm, which contracts out their consulting services to a variety of external organizations. While both types of consultants may be working on a variety of projects at any given time, the internal consultant's projects will all pertain to a single organization (their employer). The external consultant's projects, on the other hand, may be spread across multiple external organizations that have decided to partner with their employing company.

> **Internal Consultant:** A personnel psychologist employed by an organization for the purpose of addressing that company's inner personnel needs.
>
> **External Consultant:** A personnel psychologist employed by a consulting firm who works on various personnel projects for a variety of outside organizations.

There are also several opportunities outside the realms of academia and consulting. Given that personnel psychology lies at the intersection of psychology, business management, and HR, people within the field can provide valuable contributions in many areas. There are a variety of job titles and work positions in which personnel psychologists are employed, from typical HR positions to top-level administration and CEOs.

Professional organizations and resources

The field of I-O was formally recognized as a discipline in 1982 with the establishment of SIOP. SIOP represents Division 14 of the American Psychological Association and is the primary professional organization for personnel psychologists, including student members and working professionals. Being a member provides several benefits. For example, members of SIOP receive a quarterly newsletter and journal – *The Industrial-Organizational Psychologist* and *Industrial and Organizational Psychology: Perspectives on Science and Practice*, respectively – and a weekly e-newsletter. SIOP also hosts an annual conference where its members can network, share ideas, and keep up-to-date on current research and practice. In addition to SIOP, there are several other professional organizations to which personnel psychologists may belong:

- Society for Human Resource Management
- Academy of Management
- Society of Psychologists in Leadership
- American Management Association
- Human Factors and Ergonomics Society
- American Psychological Association

If interested in any of these organizations, we encourage you to check out the resources available on their website, as this will provide general details about the nature of the organization and the benefits available to its members. Some professional organizations are smaller than others, but all provide a network of individuals with similar interests and goals. Whether a researcher or practitioner, being a member in a professional organization is a good way to keep current in your career. It is not uncommon for personnel psychologists to be a member of more than one of the organizations listed above.

Summary

In this chapter, we introduced the field of personnel psychology, provided an overview of its historical roots, and reviewed career opportunities and current trends within the profession. Although similar to the fields of HR and business management, personnel psychology is more grounded in the scientist-practitioner model and the field of psychology more broadly. In the remaining chapters, we will focus on the specifics of how personnel psychologists use the tools of science to solve practical problems within organizations.

REVIEW QUESTIONS

1. What is the difference between I-O psychology and the fields of HR and business management?
2. Compare and contrast the I and O branches of I-O psychology.
3. Who are the pioneers of early personnel psychology? What are their accomplishments?

4. What is scientific management and how did it impact the working class?
5. Why were WWI and WWII important events for the field of personnel psychology?
6. What is the significance of the Hawthorne studies and the Human Relations Movement?
7. Compare and contrast moderator and mediator variables.
8. What career opportunities are available for those interested in personnel psychology?
9. Compare and contrast internal and external consulting.
10. What are some current workplace trends within the field of personnel psychology?

DISCUSSION QUESTIONS

1. If you were to be an I-O psychologist working in private industry, would you be more interested in working on I-related or O-related projects? Explain your answer.
2. Which historical people/events stood out to you most in terms of their contributions to personnel psychology? Why did they resonate with you?
3. Would you be more interested in a career path related to research (e.g., academia) or practice (e.g., consulting)? Why?
4. What would be some pros and cons associated with internal and/or external consulting?
5. Of the workplace trends listed, which do you find most interesting and why?

Notes

1 Society for Industrial and Organizational Psychology. (2022, June 4). *What are SIOP and I-O psychologists?* https://www.siop.org/Media-Resources/I-O-Psychology-Explained
2 Katzell, R. A., & Austin, J. T. (1992). From then to now: The development of industrial-organizational psychology in the United States. *Journal of Applied Psychology, 77*(6), 803–835.
3 Vinchur, A. J., & Koppes, L. L. (2011). A historical survey of research and practice in industrial and organizational psychology. In S. Zedeck (Ed.), *APA handbook of industrial and organizational psychology, Vol. 1. Building and developing the organization* (pp. 3–36). American Psychological Association.
4 Zickar, M. J., & Gibby, R. E. (2007). Four persistent themes throughout the history of I-O psychology in the United States. In L. Koppes Bryan (Ed.), *Historical perspectives in Industrial and Organizational Psychology* (pp. 42–62). Routledge.

5 Vinchur, A. J., & Koppes Bryan, L. (2007). Early contributors to the science and practice of industrial psychology. In L. Koppes Bryan (Ed.), *Historical perspectives in Industrial and Organizational Psychology* (pp. 42–62). Routledge.
6 Landy, F. J. (1997). Early influences on the development of industrial and organizational psychology. *Journal of Applied Psychology, 82*(4), 467–477.
7 Taylor, F. W. (1911). *The principles of scientific management*. Harper & Brothers.
8 Koppes, L. L. (1997). American female pioneers of industrial and organizational psychology during the early years. *Journal of Applied Psychology, 82*(4), 500–515.
9 Roethlisberger, F. J., & Dickson, W. J. (1939). *Management and the worker. An account of a research program conducted by the Western Electric Company, Hawthorne Works.* Wiley.
10 Society for Industrial and Organizational Psychology. (2022, June 4). *What are SIOP and I-O psychologists?* https://www.siop.org/Business-Resources/Top-10-Work-Trends

2 Discrimination and employment law

> **LEARNING OBJECTIVES**
>
> - Understand definitions of discrimination
> - Understand the psychology of discrimination
> - Know the major federal laws, statutes, and enforcement agencies
> - Know the current state of discrimination practices
> - Identify ways to reduce discrimination in the workplace
> - Understand the relationship between discrimination and diversity management

Imagine you have your hard-earned diploma in hand and are pounding the pavement (or more likely, clicking on the internet) in search of a job. You come across the following ads:

- Bookkeeper – A young lady, thoroughly familiar with bookkeeping methods, who can calculate costs and who has some knowledge of the conduct of business, to act as general bookkeeper in a newly organized manufacturing establishment; this is a very desirable opportunity for a thoroughly competent and intelligent young lady.
- Wanted – Bright, trustworthy Christian American boy to take charge of advertising department and do general office work; must be well educated, neat, and thoroughly trustworthy; references required.

What would you think if you ran across these ads? We suspect your first reaction would be disgust or outrage. Being female and young are not necessary to be a bookkeeper, and neither is being of any religious affiliation nor national origin a requirement for a job in advertising! You likely think these ads are discriminatory, but what does it mean to discriminate? What does this mean in psychological terms, and under employment law?

Defining *discrimination*

Let us begin with a definition from the psychological literature. **Discrimination** is the differential treatment of individuals, based upon their membership in a particular group. Discrimination is different from *prejudice*, which refers to negative *attitudes* toward members of a particular group. Although prejudice implies dislike toward members of a particular group, discrimination need not be preceded by negative affect. One could treat members of one's group more favorably than those of another, not because of animosity toward the other group, but because of favoritism toward one's own in-group. Discrimination is also distinguished from *stereotypes*, which refers to generalized beliefs about characteristics of a particular group. These beliefs may be negative (e.g., "female managers are too emotional") or positive (e.g., "female managers are democratic and caring").

> **Discrimination:** The differential treatment of individuals, based upon their membership in a particular group.

In employment law terms, *discrimination* also refers to the negative or unfavorable treatment of members of a particular group. As relevant to personnel psychology, employment discrimination refers to unfavorable treatment of members of a particular group in any employment-related decision or procedure. Types of employment decisions and procedures that are often scrutinized for potential discrimination include recruitment, hiring, promotion, termination, evaluation, and training. This legal definition stipulates that the particular group must be protected by a law or statute in order for an act to be considered discriminatory. In legal terms, members of a group protected by the law are referred to as a **protected class.**

> **Employment Discrimination:** Unfavorable treatment of members of a particular group in any employment-related decision or procedure.

> **Protected Class:** A group of people with a common characteristic who are legally protected from employment discrimination on the basis of that characteristic.

For example, in the job ads provided above, these would be discriminatory under current employment law as sex, national origin, and religion are all protected classes under the Civil Rights Act of 1964. However, posted more than 50 years prior to the Civil Rights Act, these job ads from a help-wanted section of *The New York Times* from the early 1900s were not unlawful for their time. Employers were able to specify any requirements for a job, even those that are not job-related, thereby denying individuals of many protected classes from gainful employment. In other words, denying the opportunity to anyone other than American Christian males from applying for the position in advertisement or prohibiting older, male applicants to pursue the job of the bookkeeper is, generally speaking, discriminatory. However, if there is not an existing law covering a protected class, negative treatment of members of that class is not discriminatory under terms of employment law.

As a more contemporary example, consider the case of Cheryl Summerville, a former employee of Cracker Barrel.[1] A cook for three and half years at one of their restaurants, Summerville was called into her manager's office and asked if she was a lesbian. Summerville answered truthfully regarding her sexual orientation and then was fired. Her termination record, filed by the manager with the state department of labor, had stated: *This employee is being terminated due to violation of company policy. The employee is gay.* In addition to Summerville, as many as 15 other employees were also terminated due to a new company policy, stating that it was "inconsistent with [Cracker Barrel's] concept and values and ... with those of [its] customer base, to continue to employ individuals ... whose sexual preferences fail to demonstrate normal heterosexual values which have been the foundation of families in our society."

In general terms, Summerville and these other employees were discriminated against as they were negatively treated based upon their membership in a particular group. In employment law terms, however, these individuals had no legal recourse. At the time of these terminations in the early 1990s, there was no federal law which specified sexual orientation as a protected class. In order for a claim of employment discrimination to be made, the targeted group must first be covered as a protected class by a particular employment law or statute. While anti-discrimination laws and statues existed in various state and local jurisdictions, none of these firings occurred in those states, cities, or counties.

Under employment law terms, discrimination takes two forms. The first is *disparate treatment*, which refers to intentional or blatant unfavorable treatment of members of a protected class.

> **Disparate Treatment:** Intentional or blatant unfavorable treatment of members of a protected class.

For example, denying males the opportunity to apply for the job of a bookkeeper is disparate treatment. Below are a few more examples of disparate treatment cases:

- In 2011, clothing retailer Abercrombie & Fitch was sued by a Muslim applicant for disparate treatment on the basis of religion, as she claimed that she was not hired due to the fact that she wore a *hijab* (head scarf) during the job interview.[2]
- In 1997, a group of applicants sued the restaurant chain Hooter's for disparate treatment on the basis of sex. They claimed that they were denied the right to work as restaurant servers because they were males.
- In 1992, female flight attendants sued United Airlines for enforcing more stringent weight policies for female employees than for male employees.

The second form of employment discrimination is *adverse impact*. Here, members of a protected class are on the surface treated equally. That is, there is no policy or overt behavior that forbids a member of the protected class from applying for a job or promotion. Despite the lack of overt discrimination, under adverse impact, the outcome of a hiring process produces different outcomes, thereby adversely affecting a particular group.

> **Adverse (Disparate) Impact:** Members of a protected class are treated equally but the outcome of a hiring process produces different outcomes.

The landmark case of **Griggs versus Duke Power** (1971) set the precedent for using adverse impact as a method for determining discrimination. Prior to the passage of the Civil Rights Act of 1964, Duke Power had a policy of only allowing Black employees to work in its Labor Department, which had the lowest paying jobs. After the Civil Rights Act was passed, such a policy would clearly have been found to be illegal and so Duke Power instituted a requirement that all employees outside of the Labor Department must have a high school diploma or pass an aptitude test. In the communities where Duke Power existed, there was a large difference in prevalence of obtaining a high school diploma between Whites and Blacks, and so such a requirement, although on its face might appear to be race-neutral, in actuality resulted in a large barrier to hiring for Black individuals. In addition, as the United States Supreme Court noted, because there had been segregated schools in the regions and the schools where Black students attended were generally judged to be inferior, the aptitude test could be considered discriminatory. Even without proving intent to discriminate, the employer's practices were found to be discriminatory as they failed to demonstrate the job-relatedness of the test and degree requirement. The company had no evidence that a high school diploma or high aptitude test scores were necessary for most of the jobs for which they were hiring. More than 40 years later, employers such as Bayerische Motoren Werke (BMW) and Dollar General have faced lawsuits due to adverse impact charges. In the case of BMW, workers had to reapply for jobs as the warehouse for which they were working switched companies. Part of the reapplication process required criminal background checks, although the employer did not clearly demonstrate how this requirement had relevance to the job. According to the lawsuit, a disproportionate number of Black employees were adversely affected by the hiring process.

Numerous other Supreme Court cases have clarified the definitions of employment discrimination as the methods used to identify it. In these legal cases, I-O psychologists have often played a key role in providing expert witness testimony to help the legal community. In addition, key agencies within the government as well as professional testing agencies have helped provide guidance and best practices on how to implement law and legal precedents. In an initial way to standardize implementation and to provide guidance to confused employers, in 1978, a group of government agencies (The Equal Employment Opportunity Commission, the Civil Service Commission, the Department of Labor, and the Department of Justice) provided the Uniform Guidelines on Employee Selection Procedures. These guidelines specified what *disproportionate* hiring means for adverse impact to exist. To determine adverse impact, the selection ratios of the minority group and of the majority group are calculated. Selection ratio is calculated by dividing the number of those hired by the number of those who applied for a particular job. If the selection ratio for the minority group is less than 80% of the selection ratio for the majority group, then adverse impact exists. Hence, adverse impact is also referred to as the four-fifths rule or the 80% rule.

> **Four-fifths or 80% Rule:** Adverse impact calculated by comparing the selection ratio for the minority group versus the selection ratio for the majority group.

Suppose there were 100 Black individuals applying for a particular job and 40 were hired. At the same time, there were also 1,000 White individuals who applied for the same job and 600 were hired. In this case, the selection ratio for Blacks would be 40/100 or 40% and the selection ratio for Whites would be 60%. Given that the Black selection ratio is two-thirds of the White selection ratio, it would fall below the four-fifths standard and hence adverse impact would be judged to exist. When there is adverse impact, the employer would have to demonstrate that the test is valid (that is, test scores are related to job performance). If an employer demonstrates test validity, the plaintiff may still win an adverse impact case by showing there were other tests that could have been used that were equally valid but that demonstrated less adverse impact. At each step of the way, I-O psychologists are often employed to demonstrate and evaluate a test's adverse impact as well as its validity. One of us (Mike) has been employed as an expert witness to judge tests' validity and level of adverse impact in the court system. In this role, he has worked with lawyers, written reports, been deposed, and testified in the courtroom.

Since the adoption of the four-fifths rule, there have been numerous critiques of its utility. For example, in small samples, the change in just one of two hiring decisions may have tipped the adverse impact ratio above or below the four-fifths criteria. In addition, the four-fifths criteria have been critiqued as arbitrary and statistically simple.

Another popular method for assessing adverse impact uses a Z-test to investigate whether there are statistically significant differences between selection ratios. These statistical tests have advantages over the four-fifths rule in that they use the standard logic of null hypothesis testing to test whether differences in selection ratios are statistically different from each other. This approach is preferred by many I-O psychologists because it does not rely on an arbitrary cut-off like the four-fifths rule (though some would argue that using a p-value to determine whether something is significant is itself arbitrary). However, a problem with using this particular test is that with large sample sizes, using a statistical method will almost always result in significant differences even if the differences are practically not meaningful. With large sample sizes, assessing the practical significance of any difference in selection ratios would be important.

The psychology of stereotypes, prejudice, and discrimination

Having defined discrimination and investigated some of the roles that I-O psychologists play in determining whether using a particular test can be considered discriminatory, let us probe why we harbor negative attitudes toward others and act and behave in ways that result in their negative treatment. Various psychological explanations come from the cognitive, social, and evolutionary perspectives. The cognitive explanation rests on the well-founded assumption that stereotypes (i.e., social categorizations) arise from basic processes of categorization. Furthermore, distinctive stimuli receive more enhanced processing than non-distinctive stimuli, and are more likely to be noticed and remembered. Members of a minority group are more distinctive than those of the majority group, and negative behaviors are more distinctive than positive ones. Hence, we will notice and remember more negative behavior of a member of a minority group than that of a member of a majority, which we then associate strongly with each other. This results in **illusory correlations** between negative behaviors and minority groups. Additionally, we will look for information that confirms our existing beliefs, rather than information that disconfirms such beliefs; this **confirmation bias** continues to perpetuate stereotypes and prejudices.

From a social perspective, psychologists propose that we are influenced by our social groups (e.g., family and peers) and institutions (e.g., education, the media, and the legal system) and stereotypes and prejudices are created and propagated by these environmental factors. Additionally, we observe the **unequal status** between groups to rationalize our prior beliefs. In a list published by Fortune 500, only 4.6% of Fortune 500 CEOs are females and only 14.2% are top executives. We then think that this is the case because "females are too emotional to make good leaders."

Social psychological explanations rely on social identity theory, which is the idea that our self-concept is based upon our membership in various groups (e.g., family, gender, and social class).[3] This membership is a source of pride and self-esteem; therefore, to enhance our individual self-image, we think of members of our own "in-group" as superior to those of the "out-group." By harboring prejudice and holding negative stereotypes of members of the out-group, we are also able to boost our own self-esteem. Relatedly, we tend to prefer others who are similar to ourselves, which is referred to as the **similarity effect**.

Evolutionary psychologists argue that stereotypes and prejudice are hard-wired into our brains as an adaptive feature that has allowed our species to survive. Imagine being a caveman faced with a real threat, such as an animal about to attack. By quickly and unconsciously categorizing a large and hairy creature as "dangerous" versus a friendly, fellow cave-dweller, our ancestors were able to flee such life-threatening situations, survived, mated, and then passed this ability to their offspring. Although this ability to quickly distinguish real threats to life and safety has enabled our survival, its evolution has resulted in often erroneous negative categorizations of out-group members.

Regardless of perspective, psychologists agree on several conclusions regarding stereotypes and prejudice. First, categorizing others helps us navigate an otherwise complex social world, and is a natural, prevalent human tendency. Second, these categorizations that give rise to stereotypes and prejudice frequently occur automatically, often without the individual's awareness and control. Third, it is well understood that stereotypes and prejudice influence our judgment and decision-making. Finally, stereotypes and prejudice may not necessarily manifest in discrimination. Social norms and standards may motivate individuals to not allow their prejudice to be expressed in how they behave toward others.[4]

Empirical research on employment discrimination

Research shows that discrimination occurs in all aspects of life, from education to housing to criminal justice. Of interest to industrial-organizational psychology is discrimination in the workplace, with the areas of recruitment, hiring, and employee evaluation of relevance to personnel psychology. Below is a discussion of the scientific research on these forms of discrimination against members of particular groups.

Sex and gender

Research shows evidence of sex discrimination, although its occurrence depends upon several factors, including the sex-type of the job and gender of the applicant. In a 2000 meta-analysis of research covering the years 1964–1994, researchers found that female and male applicants received lower ratings when being considered for an opposite-sex-type job.[5] Similarly, in a

2015 meta-analysis of 111 experimental studies, researchers found that males were preferred over females for masculine-type jobs.[6] **Gender role theory** helps us understand these findings. According to this theory, we hold stereotypes about males and females and the roles they should assume. For instance, we may stereotype men to be aggressive and domineering, and women to be nurturing. What happens when members of a stereotyped group aspire to occupy a role that is incongruent with the group to which they belong? For example, how will women be evaluated in leadership roles, when being an effective leader is often associated with masculine-type characteristics? According to **role congruity theory,** this inconsistency between our stereotype of females as "nurturing" and our expectation of leaders as "aggressive" and "domineering" would lower our evaluation of the female.[7] It is notable, as summarized above, that the 2015 meta-analysis did *not* show a bias in favor of women in feminine-type jobs, as would be expected by this theory. Although not a strong preference, both male and female decision-makers favored male versus female applicants for feminine-type jobs.

Research on sex discrimination in performance evaluation shows inconsistent results. In a 2000 meta-analysis of field studies,[8] researchers concluded that there was little evidence of overall gender bias in performance evaluation. However, in a more recent meta-analysis,[9] researchers found an overall small bias in favor of females in ratings of performance and a pro-male bias in ratings of promotion potential.

Research findings regarding the similarity effect in sex discrimination have been quite mixed. In one study, female recruiters favored female applicants over male applicants, while male recruiters did not exhibit a pro-male bias.[10] In another study, the opposite was found, with female decision-makers biased in favor of male applicants.[11] In explaining their results, the researchers proposed that this occurred because male applicants occupied a higher-status category to which females aspired. In yet another study, male recruiters favored female applicants, with this relationship being mediated by interpersonal attraction.[12] In a 2015 meta-analysis, male decision-makers tended to be biased in favor of male applicants, while female decision-makers did not show biases in favor of male or female applicants.[13]

Race

An employer receives resumes from otherwise equivalently qualified applicants but is more likely to call the applicants with White-sounding names for interviews than those with Black-sounding names. This is the finding from a study conducted in 2004, in which the researchers sent out nearly 5,000 resumes in response to 1,300 real-life help-wanted ads spanning a variety of job categories.[14] They manipulated the names of applicants on the resume to reflect race. For the White applicant, names such as "Emily" or "Greg" were used; for the Black applicant, names such as "Lakisha" or "Jamal" were used. Results indicated statistically significant racial differences in callback rates. To receive one callback, job applicants with White-sounding names needed to send about 10 resumes, whereas those with Black-sounding names needed to send around 15 to achieve the same result.

Research suggests that a hiring manager's perceived similarity to the applicant may influence the selection decision. Laboratory studies have found similarities in recruiter-applicant race to be positively correlated with selection decisions.[15] Field studies, however, have found race-similarity bias only when the recruiter is White.[16]

Age

Age is a protected class under the 1967 Age Discrimination in Employment Act (ADEA), although it is only illegal to discriminate against people age 40 and over. Workers under the age of 40 may be discriminated against and would have no legal recourse under federal legislation. Therefore, if you are denied a job because you are too young, you could not turn to the courts to sue, at least under federal law. Research in psychology, however, suggests that the young are rarely discriminated against, while older people face numerous prejudices. Finkelstein and colleagues found that young raters rate older applicants to be less favorable than younger applicants, especially when comparing a mixture of old and young workers side-by-side.[17] This finding might explain why in the technology industry, there is a predominance of younger employees and older applicants claim that they are not given serious consideration. When young raters are making hiring decisions, they tend to rate older applicants worse. Posthuma and Campion reviewed specific stereotypes that are often held about older employees.[18] Most of these stereotypes are negative (e.g., older employees have poor performance, have lower ability to learn, and are resistant to change), although some are positive (e.g., older people are more dependable and trustworthy). They provide suggestions for HR practices, including using training and development to help avoid relying on inaccurate stereotypes, focusing on job-related information, and using older workers as a competitive advantage.

Religion

In a field experiment,[19] researchers found discrimination against applicants with Arabic names. In another similar field study,[20] researchers sent out fictitious resumes in response to real-life job ads; additionally, they created applicant profiles on popular social network sites (i.e., LinkedIn and Facebook) and manipulated whether the applicant identified as being Muslim or Christian. Although the study did not result in the large differences seen in the race experiment, the researchers note possible discrimination toward Muslim applicants, especially in more conservative states. Religious discrimination claims have risen the most in recent years compared to other types of discrimination claims,[21] often attributed to an increase in religious diversity as well as increased norms for religious expression. Compared to other types of discrimination, there has been relatively less research on religious discrimination, especially as it relates to hiring decisions.

Disability

The Americans with Disabilities Act of 1990 was groundbreaking legislation that forbade discrimination against employees with disabilities, physical and/or mental, and required employers to provide reasonable accommodations to help those with disabilities perform their jobs. In terms of hiring procedures, employers are forbidden to ask about information about disabilities until they have made a particular hiring decision. Then, the law allows the new employee to disclose their disability and work with the employer on a reasonable accommodation and demonstrate their capacity for completing work-related tasks with the accommodation. Subsequent court cases have adjudicated the limits of reasonable accommodation. Relatively little research has been conducted on disabilities within the I-O psychology community, while more work in this area has been done by vocational counselors and rehabilitation psychologists. The Americans with Disabilities Act forbids discrimination based on physical and mental disabilities. There has been significant discussion within the personnel testing domain on whether many personality tests might be judged to be discriminatory against individuals with mental illnesses such as depression.

Weight

One of the most prevalent discriminations is against individuals who are obese. In a creative study, King and colleagues had relatively obese confederate shoppers interact in stores and compared their treatment to non-obese customers, finding that obese confederate shoppers were discriminated in subtle and covert manners.[22] Some of this discrimination is based on the belief that obesity is controllable and revealing of personal limitations and failures. They suggest that reminding individuals of the uncontrollability of obesity (e.g., the high genetic predisposition to obesity) is helpful in removing this stigma. Bartels and Nordstrom, in an experiment where identical resumes were paired with photographs that varied based on sex and weight, found that obese women were much less likely to be given high ratings compared to non-obese women, holding all other things constant on their resumes.[23] There was no difference between obese men and non-obese men, suggesting that obesity may exacerbate sex discrimination by penalizing obese women but not penalizing men. As obesity rates continue to rise in the United States and the world, there needs to be much more work in this area to provide guidance on how to enact policies to reduce this bias. The Bartels and Nordstrom study is also a good reminder on why it is important to exclude physical appearance as much as possible from the hiring process when how a person looks is not related to doing the job. This is one reason why many employers forbid googling candidates or checking their social media as you might be more influenced by perceived attractiveness or other irrelevant information compared to work-related information.

Sexual orientation

Up until fairly recently, there has been no federal legislation forbidding discrimination based on sexual orientation, although many states and local municipalities have had this legislation. However, in 2020, the United States Supreme Court ruled that discriminating against employees because of their sexual orientation or transgender status violates Title

VII. In addition, 91% of Fortune 500 companies explicitly forbid such discrimination and 83% forbid discrimination based on gender identity. The role of I-O psychologists, however, should not be limited to studying legally protected classes. We should be at the forefront of ending discrimination in the workplace and helping employers make better decisions by focusing only on work-related characteristics. There has been significant research suggesting that lesbian, gay, bisexual, and transgendered (LGBT) applicants are rated lower than heterosexual employees,[24] though it should be noted that attitudes toward LGBT individuals are changing rapidly, based partially on the historic Supreme Court decision legalizing gay marriage as well as the U.S. military removing its discriminatory policies. More current research needs to be conducted. King and Cortina argue that LGBT-supportive policies need to be expanded and I-O psychologists should continue to conduct research showing that harassment at work can contribute to negative consequences to LGBT employees.[25]

Major employment laws and statutes

As we see from the research literature reviewed above, discrimination against members of certain groups is alive and well in hiring and evaluation decisions. Fortunately, laws and statutes have been enacted and enforced to prohibit such discrimination. All those who work in the area of human resource management should be well aware of the legal context in employment. I-O psychologists, for example, need to be cognizant of employment law to ensure that the tools they develop do not unfairly disadvantage any particular group of people. Human resource professionals need to understand employment law so they do not violate the rights of applicants and employees, and also they can help managers and the organization uphold such rights. Hiring managers themselves need to know employment law so they do not knowingly impede on these rights. Although the potential legal, financial, and business ramifications of failing to comply with the law may be compelling enough, it is important to note that there is a noble central tenet to the establishment and enforcement of these laws – to protect the civil rights of individuals.

In the most obvious sense, employment law serves applicants and employees by requiring (though not guaranteeing) fair and equal treatment. The law also serves to benefit society by alleviating historical workplace inequality. Employment law also benefits the organization, by requiring, for example, that its hiring practices are relevant to the job. Recruitment, selection, and other HR processes cost a company money, and it behooves the employer to ensure that, for example, a test it is using to hire new employees actually does predict later job performance.

The employment legal landscape is vast, complex, and ever-changing. Therefore, it is beyond the scope of this chapter to cover laws that govern international companies, let alone all the jurisdictions within the United States. Our focus is on employment law within the United States only, as well as only major laws and statutes at the federal level. Rather than providing fine details regarding the provisions and amendments of each law or statute, below we specify the law, its major provisions, and protected classes.

Title VII of the Civil Rights Act of 1964

Signed into law by President Lyndon Johnson on July 2, 1964, the Civil Rights Act is the most important civil rights legislation since Reconstruction. Most pertinent to employment law is Title VII of the Civil Rights Act, which prohibited employment discrimination based **on race, color, religion, sex, and national origin**. All employers with at least 15 employees, including state and local governments, are covered by this law. The only exceptions are religious organizations, Native American reservations, and certain departments and corporations owned by the U.S. government.

Title VII and other federal employment laws presented below are enforced by the **Equal Employment Opportunity Commission (EEOC)**, a government body appointed by the President of the United States.

Below are some recent or ongoing Title VII cases filed by the EEOC:

- A transgender woman, while still presenting as a man, applies for a job in the crime lab of the Bureau of Alcohol, Tobacco, Firearms and Explosives (Agency) in Walnut Creek, California. Trained and certified as a National Integrated Ballistic Information Network (NIBIN) operator and a BrassTrax ballistics investigator, the applicant is qualified for the job. After an interview, the candidate was offered the position, pending a clear criminal background check. However, after informing the employer of her transition from male to female, her job offer was revoked.
- The Director of Hearing Services at Lakeland Clinic Eye Clinic in Tampa, Florida, a transgender employee, is fired after she began to present as a woman, despite a record of satisfactory performance throughout her employment.
- In 2015, Bass Pro Outdoor World, LLC (Bass Pro) was charged with failing to hire Black and Hispanic applicants for positions in its retail stores nationwide. According to the EEOC's suit, qualified Black and Hispanic employees were routinely denied retail, supervisory, managerial, and other positions at many Bass Pro stores nationwide.
- Rotten Ralph's, a popular Philadelphia restaurant, is charged with religious discrimination by refusing to allow a server to wear a religious headscarf as a reasonable accommodation of her religious beliefs and fired her because of her Muslim religion.

The first two cases presented above are the first ever filed by the EEOC on behalf of transgender individuals. Evoking Title VII, the EEOC has held that discrimination against an individual because that person is transgender (also known as gender identity discrimination) is discrimination on the basis of sex. Plaintiffs won in both these cases, which have been marked as landmark cases for transgender discrimination.

Americans with Disabilities Act (ADA) 1990

The Americans with Disabilities Act prohibits employers with 15 or more employees from discriminating against qualified individuals with disabilities in all employment processes, from application and hiring, to firing, promotion, and training. As defined by the ADA, a disability is a physical or mental impairment that substantially limits one or more major life activities. In order to be regarded as part of this protected class, the individual must demonstrate a record of impairment and that s/he is regarded as having such impairment. Furthermore, the individual must also meet job-related requirements of the position (i.e., be qualified). Once these stipulations are met, the employer must provide reasonable accommodations to enable the individual to perform the job. Let's break this down with an example to help you understand the various stipulations of this statute.

In Chapter 3, we will discuss a job analysis that one of us (Alexandra) conducted on the job of an estate investigator. Following the job analysis, I used the information gathered to create selection tools in order to hire applicants. After months of work, I was ready to screen and select applicants for several open positions. One week before the test administration, I received a phone call from one of the applicants who had passed the screening process. The individual informed me that he had a disability and requested accommodation on the selection tests. As this was the first time I had encountered a real ADA request, you can imagine my antennae went up! Recalling what I read in textbooks and learned in graduate school, I asked the applicant if he had documentation of his disability; indeed, he said he was able to provide documentation from his physician. In other words, there was record of and regard of impairment. My review of this documentation also allowed me to ascertain the nature of his impairment and that it would "limit major life activities."

The next step I took was to ask the applicant what type of accommodation he requested. Recall that ADA requires employers to provide reasonable accommodation to qualified applicants unless doing so would cause "undue hardship." According to general principles provided by the EEOC (http://www.eeoc.gov/policy/docs/accommodation.html), reasonable accommodation falls in three categories:

i. modifications or adjustments to a job application process that enable a qualified applicant with a disability to be considered for the position such qualified applicant desires; or
ii. modifications or adjustments to the work environment, or to the manner or circumstances under which the position held or desired is customarily performed, that enable a qualified individual with a disability to perform the essential functions of that position; or
iii. modifications or adjustments that enable a covered entity's employee with a disability to enjoy equal benefits and privileges of employment as are enjoyed by its other similarly situated employees without disabilities.

The applicant's request for accommodation fell in category (i) as he requested that any written tests be provided in larger-point font (the applicant had a visual disability). In terms of undue hardship, the EEO specifies undue hardship as significant expense or difficulty for the employer, as well as accommodations that would fundamentally alter the nature or operation of the business. What I did was provide him a written test in a larger font

(16-point) than that provided to other applicants. This was possible because this was not an "undue hardship" to the employer, in that it did not cost the company any money and did not alter the job nor the operations of the business. This applicant actually ended up doing quite well on the selection tests and was hired!

Age Discrimination in Employment Act (1967)

The Age Discrimination in Employment Act (ADEA) prohibits employment discrimination against those aged 40 and older in all aspects of employment, including "hiring, firing, pay, job assignments, promotions, layoff, training, fringe benefits, and any other term or condition of employment" (EEOC). Below are some examples of cases filed under ADEA:

- Strategic Legal Solutions, a New York-based legal employment agency, agreed to pay $85,000 to settle an age discrimination and retaliation suit. In the suit filed by the EEOC, the employer withdrew an offer for work from a 70-year-old attorney after learning of her date of birth.
- In *Meacham v. Knolls Atomic Power Laboratory*, the employer was charged with age discrimination when laying off employees after a voluntary buyout; of the 31 who were laid off, 30 were at least 40 years old.
- Josephine Mora, a 62-year-old fundraiser for Jackson Memorial Hospital, sued the employer for age discrimination after she was discharged from her position. She alleged that the CEO stated he "need[ed] someone younger" that he could "pay less."

Genetic Information Non-discrimination Act of 2008 (GINA)

In the 1997 movie *Gattaca*, Ethan Hawke and Jude Law play the characters in a future when eugenics rules a society in which parents are able to manipulate genes to choose the best traits their children will inherit. In this society, one's occupational fate is predetermined by one's genes. The character played by Hawke dreams of a career in outer space but, having been conceived outside of a eugenics program, is fated with the possibility of future diseases and relegated to jobs that involve only menial tasks. Although this science fictional vision may seem far-fetched, current reproductive technologies allow us to screen babies before they are born for a variety of diseases, and to choose their gender, or even eye and hair color. The Human Genome Project, completed in 2003, has successfully mapped the entire human genetic blueprint. Although few companies report using genetic tests in making employment decisions, the technology is there. Genetic screening allows an employer to detect the predisposition of applicants and employees to various diseases.

Genetic screening has raised a lot of controversy. Whether you are on the side of proponents, who argue that this could save employers a lot of money, or opponents, who argue that this violates employee right to privacy, note that effective November 21, 2009, Title II of GINA makes it illegal to discriminate against employees or applicants because of genetic information. Specifically, employers are prohibited from the use of "information about an individual's genetic tests and the genetic tests of an individual's family members, as well as information about the manifestation of a disease or disorder in an individual's family members" in making employment decisions. The first suit filed by the EEOC in regard to this act occurred in 2012 when Fabricut, Inc., a distributor of decorative fabrics, required an applicant to fill out a questionnaire regarding her family's medical history. The applicant was asked to disclose the existence of numerous disorders, including heart disease, hypertension, cancer, tuberculosis, diabetes, arthritis, and mental disorders, in her family history. The employer ended up paying $50,000 and had to agree to take specific actions to prevent further discrimination in its company. In a more recent case (2014), BNV healthcare violated the same law by requiring job applicants to complete a health assessment form which included numerous questions regarding family health history.

GINA differs from ADA in that it protects applicants and employees from discrimination in terms of possible *future* diseases. For example, an applicant denied employment because she *currently* has breast cancer would not be covered by GINA; this individual may be covered by ADA, depending upon the nature of her disability, qualifications, and nature of the job (see stipulations of the ADA discussed earlier). Because GINA refers to the *possibility* of future diseases, unlike ADA, there are no circumstances under which an employer may use genetic information or family medical history to make employment decisions.

Contemporary issues

Social media

The rise of social media has raised additional I-O-related concerns related to discrimination and mistreatment. As mentioned in this chapter, the rise of public information on the internet might make discrimination more prevalent and harder to detect. In one survey, 70% of HR hiring managers report using social media and web searches to learn information about applicants. There are no laws forbidding such practice, though we are concerned that the possibility of learning irrelevant information that might influence your decisions about an applicant is quite high. Some may be relatively innocent. For example, you may learn that an applicant is a University of Illinois graduate and a St. Louis Cardinals baseball fan (Mike is both!) and have a more favorable reaction to the candidate than otherwise. In a sense, this might just be adding random error into a decision, favoring a candidate based on information that has nothing to do with likelihood of success on the job. On the other hand, you may learn information about a candidate that would never come up in an interview, such as their strong religious beliefs, their sexual orientation, or a disability that they might have. Also, you might see the race of the applicant or the obesity of an applicant and this information may unconsciously influence your impressions.

HR managers like to use internet-related information because they hope that it may uncover information that they deem to be job-relevant, such as that somebody got fired from their last job for showing up drunk or they verbally abuse individuals on the internet.

Such information may be useful to consider and might be analogous to a background check conducted by many employers. One best practice might be to have an independent person conduct the internet and a social media background check and only provide relevant information to the hiring manager, perhaps using a standardized form. That way, hiring decisions will not be influenced by irrelevant information such as a person's embarrassing high school yearbook picture, silly Halloween costume, or obsession with Taylor Swift.

Other challenges occur when using social media for selection results in misidentification. It is relatively easy to identify Mike on the internet as there is only one other Michael Zickar that we are aware of (fortunately, his doppelganger has a PhD in mathematics and he wouldn't mind this confusion at times). However, if you google the other authors of this textbook, there appear to be many more people with their names. And if your name is John Scott (a prominent I-O psychologist), good luck untangling all of the people out there! Other concerns include the duration of information on the internet. Should someone be penalized for something they posted when they were 15? How much time should elapse before internet-related information should be judged irrelevant. Finally, some people have invisible social media profiles, making sure that they hide their personal information via pseudonyms. Alternatively, others opt out of social media altogether to avoid its hassles. One concern is that companies may view an invisible presence on the web as having something to hide.

International considerations

This chapter and textbook focus on employment laws and practices within the United States. For most large companies, though, the reality is that they are multinational organizations and subject to a variety of laws from different jurisdictions. I-O psychologists who work for multinational organizations need to learn about the local laws and practices of all of the countries in which their company has a presence. In the case of multinational corporations, much of the work that I-O psychologists do is train and prepare workers for expatriate assignments, as well as facilitate training to promote cultural understanding among workers from different countries and cultures. There is a whole research literature on cross-cultural psychology and I-O psychology that should be considered.

Where are we headed?

At this point, you may be thinking that with the passage of Title VII of the Civil Rights Act of 1964 and subsequent laws and statutes, employment discrimination no longer exists in the 21st century. Indeed, we have come a long way from the type of explicit discriminatory job ads that were presented at the top of this chapter. However, as lamented by Lindsey and colleagues (2013),[26] we still have a way to go in fulfilling the mission of the EEOC to "eradicate employment discrimination at the workplace." To fulfill this mission, industrial-organizational psychologists propose moving beyond merely abiding by employment law in the hope of preventing discrimination; instead, employers should proactively manage diversity in their workforce.

> **Diversity Management:** Organizational actions to include employees of various backgrounds in its formal and informal structures through deliberate programs, policies, and practices.

Diversity management is broad and may span many aspects of an organization. Of relevance to personnel psychology are actions that are related to hiring process (i.e., recruitment and selection, especially). The psychological research which helps us understand why discrimination occurs may be drawn upon to help create effective strategies toward eradicating discrimination. Below are some major psychological tenets we have garnered from decades of research, and actions an employer can take in managing diversity by drawing upon these principles:

We prefer those who are similar to ourselves

One equal opportunity officer I (Alexandra) know always begins her training sessions with the question, "Who do we see when we think of the ideal employee?" Her answer was to hold up a mirror in front of her face. I have always found this compelling. First, because she did this with such flair and humorously reminded me of the wicked Queen from *Snow White in the Seven Dwarves* declaring, *Mirror, mirror on the wall, who is the fairest of them all?* Second, her answer "our own self!" concurs with all we know from research on the similarity effect. As written by Frank Landy in a letter to the editor of the *Atlantic Monthly*,[27] the quest for diversity is an uphill battle:

> A founder or CEO surrounds himself or herself with people who share his or her values. These deputies, in turn, recruit and hire people who are similar to them (and, by extension, to the founder/CEO). Thus the organization becomes populated by people with the same interests and values, who tend to think alike (the "groupthink" phenomenon). While paying lip service to "diversity," the organization sets about creating and maintaining homogeneity.

As cynical as the above statements are, the good news for organizations striving for diversity is that they can capitalize on the fact that we are attracted to similar others. First, employers could use recruiters who reflect the characteristics of the desired applicant pool. Research suggests that diverse applicants' initial attraction to an organization may be increased when recruiters themselves are diverse. In one study, female participants who observe female employees during onsite visits found these organizations to be more welcoming of diversity. In another study, researchers found that female applicants were more attracted to job ads that contained wording that corresponded to their gender. Finally, as discussed in Chapter 4 on recruitment, we are attracted to organizations that have values that reflect our own. Therefore, an organization that wants to attract a certain pool of applicants may communicate values they know are held by applicants. However, such communication should be authentic, or the employer will be perceived as deceiving and any future efforts toward diversity may backfire.

We like those who like us

Across the numbers of studies that have examined what recruiter characteristics most influence the perceptions of applicants, personableness (along with being informative) stands out. In short, organizations should ensure via hiring and/or training that the front face of their hiring system is someone who exhibits warmth toward applicants from diverse backgrounds.

We rely on mental shortcuts and can make errors in judging others

As will be discussed in greater depth in Chapter 8, human judgment and decision-making can be flawed with biases. Therefore, one organizational action is to train hiring decision-makers. They may be trained, for example, in conducting structured job interviews that assess only job-relevant knowledge, skills, and ability. Organizations should also ensure that hiring processes involve only the use of objective, selection tools that have been found to be related to job performance (to be discussed in Chapter 5). Finally, the selection processes could be designed to limit the amount of information that could bias decision-making. For example, a third neutral party could screen resumes and forward only job-relevant information to actual decision-makers. Information such as applicant name or indicators of the individual's age, religion, and sex, for instance, could actually be removed from the resume if these are not relevant to the job. As noted earlier, this has particular relevance to the use of social media in recruitment and hiring. A survey shows that over 70% of employers google applicants to learn more about their job applicants.[28]

We want to be treated fairly

I-O psychologists play a key role in working to reduce adverse impact in selection tools. We do this by working to eliminate items that might be biased against individuals of a particular class and working to assess a broad range of knowledge, skills, and abilities to provide applicants with a fair chance of being hired. For example, using video-based items might result in less adverse impact than items that are text-based. In addition, focusing only on cognitive ability measures might result in perpetuating differences that exist because of our educational system. Including non-cognitive measures, in addition to cognitive measures, might assess other work-related aspects such as motivation and integrity. Finally, we work to remove barriers in the application process, helping organizations have a wider group of applicants to consider. By attracting more diverse individuals to apply, we can help organizations increase diversity.

We want to affirm our self-esteem

It is important that our HR practices help affirm our individual employees' self-esteem so that employees can be happier at work and so that we can unlock their highest potential.

A whole body of research on inclusive leadership is now emerging that emphasizes that leaders are important in setting the tone for developing an inclusive culture within their organization. This is an exciting new direction for I-O psychologists to pursue and is one in which we are excited to take part!

Summary

This chapter has covered the psychology of discrimination and provided a broad overview of legal issues that affect personnel psychology, with a focus on selection. Coverage of major federal laws, statutes, and enforcement agencies has been offered, as well as a review of current research on discrimination practices and ways to reduce discrimination in the workplace.

REVIEW QUESTIONS

1. Compare and contrast prejudice and discrimination.
2. Compare and contrast disparate treatment and adverse impact.
3. Define "protected class" and give an example of several with reference to the law or statute which specifies that protected class.
4. Compare and contrast the four-fifths rule and the Z-test to determine whether adverse impact exists.
5. What does the research tell us about discrimination based on sex, race, age, and weight?

DISCUSSION QUESTIONS

1. What protected classes are not included in employment law that you think will or should be included in the future?
2. What are your views on genetic screening to make employment decisions? Are you in favor of it? Why or why not?
3. Have you ever faced discrimination when applying for a job? What occurred and what was the outcome?
4. What is your view on using social media for hiring purposes? Do you think this will help organizations select better workers? Do you think it would be fair or accurate for your social media profile to be included in your own hiring decision if you are an applicant?
5. What are some current employment legal cases you have read about on the news? What are the protected classes, claims, and outcomes of the cases?

Notes

1 https://www.csub.edu/~kcarpenter/Cracker%20Barrel.pdf
2 http://www.nytimes.com/2015/06/02/us/supreme-court-rules-in-samantha-elauf-abercrombie-fitch-case.html?_r=0
3 Tajfel, H., & Turner, J. C. (1979). An integrative theory of intergroup conflict. In W. G. Austin, & S. Worchel (Eds.), *The social psychology of intergroup relations* (pp. 33–37). Brooks/Cole.
4 Dunton, B. C., & Fazio, R. H. (1997). An individual difference measure of motivation to control prejudiced reactions. *Personality and Social Psychology Bulletin, 23*(3), 316–326. Klonis, S. C., Plant, E. A., & Devine, P. G. (2005). Internal and external motivation to respond without sexism. *Personality and Social Psychology Bulletin, 31*(9), 1237–1249. Plant, E. A., & Devine, P. G. (1998). Internal and external motivation to respond without prejudice. *Journal of Personality and Social Psychology, 75*(3), 811.
5 Davison, H. K., & Burke, M. J. (2000). Sex discrimination in simulated employment contexts: A meta-analytic investigation. *Journal of Vocational Behavior, 56*(2), 225–248.
6 Koch, A. J., D'Mello, S. D., & Sackett, P. R. (2015). A meta-analysis of gender stereotypes and bias in experimental simulations of employment decision making. *Journal of Applied Psychology, 100*(1), 128–161.
7 Eagly, A. H., & Karau, S. J. (2002). Role congruity theory of prejudice toward female leaders. *Psychological Review, 109*(3), 573.
8 Bowen, C., Swim, J. K., & Jacobs, R. R. (2000). Evaluating gender biases on actual job performance of real people: A meta-analysis. *Journal of Applied Social Psychology, 30*(10), 2194–2215.
9 Roth, P. L., Purvis, K. L., & Bobko, P. (2012). A meta-analysis of gender group differences for measures of job performance in field studies. *Journal of Management, 38*(2), 719–739.
10 Graves, L. M., & Powell, G. N. (1996). Sex similarity, quality of the employment interview and recruiters' evaluation of actual applicants. *Journal of Occupational and Organizational Psychology, 69*, 243.
11 Graves, L. M., & Powell, G. N. (1995). The effect of sex similarity on recruiters' evaluations of actual applicants: A test of the similarity-attraction paradigm. *Personnel Psychology, 48*(1), 85–98.
12 Goldberg, C. B. (2005). Relational demography and similarity-attraction in interview assessments and subsequent offer decisions: Are we missing something? *Group & Organization Management, 30*(6), 597–624.
13 Koch, A. J., D'Mello, S. D., & Sackett, P. R. (2015). A meta-analysis of gender stereotypes and bias in experimental simulations of employment decision making. *Journal of Applied Psychology, 100*(1), 128–161.
14 Bertrand, M., & Mullainathan, S. (2004). Are Emily and Greg more employable than Lakisha and Jamal? A field experiment on labor market discrimination. *American Economic Review, 94*, 991–1013.
15 Rand, T. M., & Wexley, K. N. (1975). Demonstration of the effect, "similar to me," in simulated employment interviews. *Psychological Reports, 36*(2), 535–544. Wiley, M. G., & Eskilson, A. (1985). Speech style, gender stereotypes, and corporate success: What if women talk more like men? *Sex Roles, 12*(9), 993–1007. Heilman, M. E., Martell, R. F., & Simon, M. C. (1988). The vagaries of sex bias: Conditions regulating the undervaluation, equivaluation, and overvaluation of female job applicants. *Organizational Behavior and Human Decision Processes, 41*(1), 98–110.
16 Goldberg, C. B. (2005). Relational demography and similarity-attraction in interview assessments and subsequent offer decisions: Are we missing something? *Group & Organization Management, 30*(6), 597–624.

17 Finkelstein, L. M., Burke, M. J., & Raju, M. S. (1995). Age discrimination in simulated employment contexts: An integrative analysis. *Journal of Applied Psychology, 80*(6), 652.
18 Posthuma, R. A., & Campion, M. A. (2009). Age stereotypes in the workplace: Common stereotypes, moderators, and future research directions. *Journal of Management, 35*(1), 158–188.
19 Derous, E., Ryan, A. M., & Nguyen, H. D. (2012). Multiple categorization in resume screening: Examining effects on hiring discrimination against Arab applicants in field and lab settings. *Journal of Organizational Behavior, 33*(4), 544.
20 Acquisti, A., & Fong, C. (2020). An experiment in hiring discrimination via online social networks. *Management Science, 66*(3), 1005–1024.
21 Ghumman, S., Ryan, A. M., Barclay, L. A., & Markel, K. S. (2013). Religious discrimination in the workplace: A review and examination of current and future trends. *Journal of Business and Psychology, 28*(4), 439–454.
22 King, E. B., Shapiro, J. R., Hebl, M. R., Singletary, S. L., & Turner, S. (2006). The stigma of obesity in customer service: A mechanism for remediation and bottom-line consequences of interpersonal discrimination. *Journal of Applied Psychology, 91*(3), 579.
23 Bartels, L. K., & Nordstrom, C. R. (2013). Too big to hire: Factors impacting weight discrimination. *Management Research Review, 36*(9), 868–881.
24 Horvath, M., & Ryan, A. M. (2003). Antecedents and potential moderators of the relationship between attitudes and hiring discrimination on the basis of sexual orientation. *Sex Roles, 48*(3), 115–130. Hebl, M. R., Foster, J. B., Mannix, L. M., & Dovidio, J. F. (2002). Formal and interpersonal discrimination: A field study of bias toward homosexual applicants. *Personality and Social Psychology Bulletin, 28*(6), 815–825.
25 King, E. B., & Cortina, J. M. (2010). The social and economic imperative of lesbian, gay, bisexual, and transgendered supportive organizational policies. *Industrial and Organizational Psychology, 3*(1), 69–78.
26 Lindsey, A., King, E., McCausland, T., Jones, K., & Dunleavy, E. (2013). What we know and don't: Eradicating employment discrimination 50 years after the civil rights act. *Industrial and Organizational Psychology: Perspectives on Science and Practice, 6*(4), 391–413. http://dx.doi.org/10.1111/iops.12075
27 https://www.theatlantic.com/magazine/archive/2003/11/letters-to-the-editor/378568/
28 https://www.monster.com/career-advice/article/hr-googling-job-applicants

3 Job analysis

LEARNING OBJECTIVES

- Know the definitions of job analysis
- Appreciate the history of job analysis
- Know the purposes of conducting a job analysis
- Know methods of collecting job analysis information
- Understand the psychology underlying inaccuracies in job analysis information
- Know the difference between job analysis and competency modeling

Let's start this chapter with a riddle. What job is most similar to that of a homemaker (archaically known as "housewife")?

> **Position Analysis Questionnaire Job Dimensions of a Homemaker (Arvey & Begalla, 1975)[1]**
>
> Being aware of body movement and balance
>
> Being physically active/related environmental conditions
>
> Being aware of environmental conditions
>
> Engaging in personally demanding situations

In a study by Arvey and Begalla (1975),[2] researchers analyzed this job by administering a questionnaire and interview to 48 homemakers. The analysis indicated that the behaviors involved in the job dimensions listed above exceeded those found in other jobs. Furthermore, a comparison of all 32 job dimensions uncovered in the analysis to other jobs reveals the answer to our riddle. The profile similarity of a job closest to that of a homemaker is a *patrolman*! Also, annual salary predicted by the analysis for the job of a homemaker was about $58,000 (adjusted for inflation). Granted this analysis is quite dated, especially given the changing nature of jobs, this study nicely illustrates the utility of job analysis in helping us break a job into its smallest parts so that we can compare it to other jobs, determine salaries, and as you will see later in this chapter, help us make a host of other personnel decisions.

The foundation of personnel psychology

The number of definitions for job analysis is probably as long as its history. Broadly speaking, job analysis refers to the process of "discovering, understanding, and describing what people do at work."[3] Defined more technically, job analysis is the systematic process of gathering and analyzing information about worker activities, requirements, and the context in which the work is performed. Informally, you can think of job analysis as the who, what, where, why, and how of a particular job.

> **Job Analysis:** The process of studying a job to identify its necessary tasks, responsibilities, and work context.

Because organizations should not make any personnel decisions unless they know what the job entails, it should be of no surprise that job analysis is considered the foundation of all practices in personnel psychology. As asserted by Sanchez and Levine (2012), "job analysis constitutes the preceding step of every application of psychology to human resources (HR) management."[4] Although this sounds ambitious, we assure you that the importance of job analysis cannot be overstated. Through job analysis, organizations make use of systematic methods that allow them to identify the tasks entailed in a job as well as the knowledge, skills, and abilities that are required for a worker to effectively perform the identified tasks. Job analysis may also yield information regarding the physical context of a job, its scheduling demands, reporting relationships between the incumbent and others in the organization, and so forth. As you can imagine, this wealth of information is incredibly useful in the development of all the processes and practices within personnel psychology (e.g., recruitment, selection, training, and performance evaluation).[5] If this is not yet compelling, consider the *Uniform Guidelines* on selection[6]: "There should be a review of job information to determine measures of work behavior(s) or performance that are relevant to the job or group of jobs in question." Thus, job analyses are not only useful in supporting the many functions of personnel psychology but also necessary from a legal standpoint. Many adverse impact cases have been won or lost based on the quality of the job analysis.

A bit of history

Pioneering work on job analysis began as early as 1922. One of the first industrial psychologists, Morris Viteles, was hired by the Milwaukee Electric Railway and Light Company to help select employees for the job of streetcar motorman. In so doing, Viteles developed the job psychograph method, a job analysis method which assigns attribute levels to hiring qualifications. The results of Viteles' method are remarkably similar to modern job analysis methods, a testament to the enduring usefulness of job analysis in understanding jobs.[7]

Historically, the most well-known job analyses are the time-and-motion studies conducted by early industrial engineers and psychologists. One of these industrial engineers was Frederick Winslow Taylor, the father of scientific management, who studied how long it took for workers to complete specific tasks. By breaking tasks into their smallest components and timing how long it took workers to perform these discrete parts, Taylor surmised that work could be methodically analyzed so that workers could be trained to work more efficiently. The most important application of Taylors' principles was to the auto-manufacturing industry when Henry Ford, the founder of the Ford Motor Company, hired him to study auto workers. Using Taylor's methods, Ford streamlined his factories by having workers carry out very specialized tasks, reducing the time needed to perform various tasks, and ultimately setting up an assembly line that reduced the time it took to build a Model T to 2 hours and 30 minutes (from more than 12 hours).

Although time studies focus entirely on reducing the time it takes to complete tasks in order to increase worker efficiency, motion studies focus on the sequence of steps it takes to complete tasks. Developed by the husband-and-wife team of Frank and Lilian Gilbreth, the goal of motion studies was to not only increase efficiency but also reduce worker fatigue. Frank Gilbreth first realized the inefficiency of work on his first job as an apprentice bricklayer. He observed that not all workers carried out the same steps; moreover, there appeared to be many wasted motions, such as stooping to pick up bricks. As a solution, he invented a system to stack bricks as well as an adjustable scaffold so that workers could be at the most optimal level at all times. This not only increased efficiency by reducing the number of motions in laying bricks by more than half but also reduced worker fatigue as they did not have to stoop over to pick up bricks.

As a team, the Gilbreths conducted a number of motion studies by filming workers carrying out their tasks. Worker motions, broken into elemental parts called *therbilgs* ("Gilbreths" spelled backward, sort of), were analyzed so that steps could be re-sequenced or even removed. Serving as consultants, the Gilbreths helped numerous industries enhance the performance and experiences of workers.

The Gilbreths did not stop there, however; biographies by 2 of their 12 children revealed themselves as guinea pigs to their parents' experiments. Amusing details of this include Frank Gilbreth filming their children doing dishes to identify ways to wash faster, putting a vitrola in the bathroom so the children could learn a foreign language while attending to bodily functions, and teaching them to button their shirts from bottom-up as that was less time-consuming. Lillian Gilbreth designed their home for greatest efficiency, having invented a kitchen design she called "circular routing," which specifies the perimeters between the stove, sink, and refrigerator (currently called the "kitchen triangle"). Below is a humorous excerpt from the biography, *Cheaper by the Dozen*, by Frank Gilbreth Jr. and Ernestine Gilbreth about life with an industrial psychologist:

> Yes, at home or on the job, Dad was always the efficiency expert. He buttoned his vest from the bottom up; instead of from the top down, because the bottom-to-top process took him only three seconds, while the top to bottom took seven. He even used two shaving brushes to lather his face because he found that by so doing he could cut seventeen seconds of his shaving time. For a while he tried shaving with two razors, but he finally gave that up.
>
> "I can save forty-four seconds," he grumbled, "but I wasted two minutes this morning putting this bandage on my throat." [Page #]

Given the colorful history of job analysis, you may wonder where the field is currently. Today, job analysis entails much more than time-and-motion studies. Because of the changing nature of work within the last several decades, there have been questions over the term "job analysis," as some view the term as rather limiting. Among other changes, work today is more team-based and collaborative, involves more social and technological skills, often includes more changing activities, and is less bound by geography. In essence, modern work is more fluid and dynamic. Therefore, some suggest the term *work* analysis rather than *job* analysis.[8] However, because a job is defined as doing work for pay, until the new economy arrives when we can spend all our time on hobbies and leisure, it appears that this debate is just a matter of semantics.

The more substantive debate regarding job analysis centers around the idea of what job analysis should look like in the rapidly changing world of work. Traditionally, job analysis draws boundaries between a specific job and others in the organization by defining its activities and worker requirements. What if modern American workplaces resemble many of those in Japan, where employees have no job descriptions[9]? Also, the traditional job analysis describes work as it is at the point in time the information was gathered.[10] What if the job we are trying to understand changes frequently? Finally, within the confines of any particular job, each individual may enact their role in a rather specific way, possibly even tailoring their job responsibilities to their own strengths and weaknesses. This is known as **job crafting**, and is especially likely to occur within a changing workplace.[11] For examples of job crafting, observe your professors and the way they teach and interact with students. While they all have similar job requirements, they go about those requirements in different ways based on their own personal style.

> **Job Crafting:** The process by which employees customize their job tasks and processes, usually based on their strengths and weaknesses.

Although such concerns definitely shed light on the continual need to hone our tools, they do not render job analysis obsolete. Consider the earliest time-and-motion studies described earlier. Analyzing the time it takes to complete discrete tasks or boiling motions down to 18 basic elements was appropriate for physical labor jobs such as bricklayer or factory production worker, but it appears archaic in the current service sector. Yet, job analysis did not die with this shift in the economy. Rather, numerous methods have been developed within the last century to allow us to understand and describe the tasks and competencies associated with jobs that are social in nature or those that are cognitively demanding. As long as there is paid work regarding which organizational and personnel decisions are made, there is a need for job analysis. It is just a matter of ensuring that we continually re-craft our current tools and methods, or even invent new ones, to enable us to understand and describe what people do at work. Before we outline the different stages and processes of job analysis, let's first consider the various purposes for conducting a job analysis.

Purposes of job analysis

As described in the above brief history of job analysis, you can see that this process serves multiple purposes for an organization. Henry Ford was able to use the information to redesign work and achieve greater efficiency and productivity. Viteles used the results of a job analysis to validate and develop a selection instrument. Table 3.1 lists these and the many other purposes for which job analysis may be used by an organization, from writing job descriptions and recruitment ads to helping with organizational restructuring and labor relations.

Table 3.1 Purposes of job analysis information

Recruitment
Selection
Classification
Compensation
Performance appraisal
Training
Organizational structure and design
Orientation, training, and development
Labor relations
Engineering design and methods improvement
Job design
Safety
Vocational guidance and rehabilitation counseling
Career path planning

To provide you with more contemporary examples, let us describe some of the job analyses we had conducted when we worked in private industry and the public sector. At a utility company, I (Alexandra) conducted a job analysis for the purpose of assessing applicants for the job of utility lineman. A job analysis allowed us to discover the physical abilities that would be required of the men (and the few women who do this job) who brave often tumultuous weather so that the rest of us can turn on the lights, watch television, and surf the internet. Our analysis revealed several work activities that were integral to the job, including the ability to coordinate various limbs to scale heights, to reach with arms and legs while maintaining arm-hand steadiness, and to withstand blistering heat or subzero temperatures. These abilities – among many others – then served as the basis for devising an actual physical ability test to be used as part of the selection process.

The next example reminds us of a scene straight out of crime television shows such as *CSI* or *Law* and Order. Imagine a high-rise apartment building in a large metropolitan city. A tenant smells a certain stench wafting from a neighboring unit and calls the building superintendent to complain. Upon entering the unit, the building superintendent discovers a dead tenant! What we see in the crime shows is the investigation of the death and possible foul play, but we never see what happens to all the belongings of the deceased. In comes the estate investigator! This job is responsible for the investigation and inventory of the assets of a deceased who may not have an identified executor. The purpose of this job analysis was to develop tools to select applicants for the job of estate investigator. By uncovering the essential tasks and necessary qualifications of the job, we were able to develop a job knowledge test, interview questions, and a work sample to fill positions.

As noted by the examples above, job analyses provide useful information for the selection process, particularly with regard to selection tools. However, a proper job analysis will often serve multiple functions for the organization. Below, we outline the various purposes for which job analyses are conducted. By the end of this section, it should be clear to you why job analysis serves as the foundation for all HR-related functions within an organization.

Job description

A primary purpose of job analysis is to develop a thorough job description for the job in question. A **job description** provides a detailed explanation of the tasks, responsibilities, expectations, and qualifications necessary for a specific job. Though this is often taken for granted, a solid job description ensures that the organization has a complete understanding of what a job entails. This information is crucial in that it serves as the basis for subsequent decisions related to recruitment, selection, performance evaluation, and training. It also becomes especially important in demonstrating the legality of the decisions made surrounding the job in question. Therefore, all of the additional purposes of job analysis hinge on the development of an adequate job description.

> **Job Description:** A detailed explanation of job requirements and the attributes necessary to accomplish those requirements.

Job evaluation and classification

After job descriptions are formed for individual jobs, the process of **job evaluation** can be used to determine the monetary value of each job to the organization. This process allows for fair and equitable decisions with regard to compensation and pay structure within the organization. **Job classification**, however, may be used to organize jobs in a hierarchical structure, often by establishing groups of jobs that are similar in their content and training requirements (i.e., job families). Organizing jobs based on their similarities and value to the company allows businesses to develop plausible career paths for employees who want to work their way up the company ladder. For example, an organization may have a finance job family which includes jobs related to accounting, budgeting, payroll, and invoicing. If an employee has maxed out their promotion opportunities in the budgeting role, they may want to shift to a different job within the finance job family (perhaps in the accounting realm) to continue their career progression.

> **Job Evaluation:** The process of determining the monetary value of a job.

> **Job Classification:** The process of organizing and ranking jobs that are similar in duties, responsibilities, and scope.

Recruitment and selection

Job analysis information also plays a crucial role in the recruitment process. A job posting will often represent a mini version of the job description, providing the essentials of the position in a concise format. This allows applicants to self-select in or out of the application process. Furthermore, based on the job description, recruiting efforts can be tailored to attract and encourage a pool of qualified candidates to apply for jobs within the organization. If, for instance, a college degree in a specified field is required for the job, recent college graduates from a reputable program may be targeted for recruitment efforts.

In addition to recruiting a competent applicant pool, job analysis is vital for decisions related to the development and use of selection tests. Because a job analysis provides data regarding the knowledge, skills, and abilities necessary to perform essential job duties, personnel psychologists use this information to choose assessment tools (e.g., personality tests, cognitive ability tests, and interview questions) to be used as part of the selection process. These job-related assessments will help to screen and place applicants in the job(s) that are best suited for their skills.

Criterion development and performance appraisal

Just as pre-hire selection tests should be based on a thorough job analysis, so should post-hire performance criteria and employee evaluation methods. Indeed, the components of the job description (e.g., required tasks, responsibilities, and expectations) should serve as a guide for employees to determine whether or not they are meeting the expectations of the job. If a job analysis suggests that the most frequent and important tasks revolve around customer service interactions, the performance appraisal process should reflect this emphasis. Not only is establishing clear criteria beneficial for managers who are conducting the performance appraisal, but having well-defined and job-related evaluation methods can go a long way toward ensuring perceptions of fairness among employees being evaluated.

Training

Employees are obviously hired based on their qualifications and presumed competence for the job in question, but inevitably, there will be tasks that are difficult and potentially challenging for new hires to accomplish. Job analysis can identify these tasks. For example, incumbents in an administrative role may indicate that the computer software was especially difficult to learn. With this knowledge, training programs for new employees may be designed to provide greater exposure and mastery of the software they will be encountering on the job.

Job design

Sometimes, job analysis will reveal inefficiencies or problems related to job design and work processes. In these situations, job analysis information can be used to adjust and/or reconfigure work processes to better suit employee needs. Related to the software training issue presented above, a job analysis may reveal that the incumbents deem the current software as ineffective and out of date, thereby reducing their ability to accomplish essential work tasks. Based on this information, the organization may decide to overhaul their current software system in order to ensure a more up-to-date, user-friendly interface.

Litigation and validity evidence

Finally, job analysis provides the necessary base of information for demonstrating the legality of personnel decisions. In order for personnel decisions to be legal, there should be evidence to demonstrate that the decisions were based on job-related information. Given that a job analysis provides detailed information about work tasks required by a job – and the attributes necessary to accomplish those tasks – the job analysis process is the primary means for establishing evidence of job-related decisions within the organization. Accordingly, the (in)adequacy of the job analysis may mean the difference between winning and losing a court case related to alleged discriminatory work practices.

Now that you understand the many purposes for which job analyses are conducted, let's take a closer look at the process.

Job analysis as "art" and "science"

Below are the basic steps to conducting a job analysis:

1. Clarify or determine the purpose for the job analysis
2. Determine what type of information should be gathered
3. Use appropriate information gathering methods
4. Gather information from appropriate sources
5. Analyze information
6. Present results in a written report

If the above steps sound straightforward, let us warn you that conducting a job analysis is more difficult than it appears, involving as much art as science. The "science" part of job analysis involves using the appropriate information gathering methods, gathering accurate information, and then appropriately analyzing the results. The "art" part of conducting a job analysis involves clarifying the purpose for which the job analysis is conducted, and more importantly, being able to make various decision calls along the entire process which are not necessarily formula-based. In essence, conducting a job analysis involves a fair amount of agility required on the part of the job analyst, as s/he must be attuned to the purpose of the analysis, sensitive to the climate in which information is being gathered, and skilled in presenting the results of analysis so that they are clear and meet the needs of the organization.

To further clarify, let me provide an example of one of the first job analyses I (Alexandra) had conducted in my career as an I-O practitioner. The client was a manufacturing plant that planned to automate the work of its factory employees; hence, they wanted an assessment that would help determine the readiness of current employees to work on the new machines. Our team was contacted to help the client achieve this goal. Bear in mind that clients rarely ask for a job analysis as the end goal; clients contact I-O psychologists with particular problems they would like us to solve. It just so happens that because job analysis is the foundation of most practices in personnel psychology, this is where we usually start.

After first clarifying the purpose, we identified appropriate methods of gathering job information. Like many client-driven projects, we were asked to deliver the assessment on a short time-frame. Hence, we decided that a questionnaire was the most appropriate method for collecting information. Lo and behold, the results we received were disappointing. Few of the employees turned in their questionnaires; those that were completed yielded very inconsistent results that did not make sense. After further conversations with management, we learned that the reading levels of employees were at a very low level, which explained the inadequate completion of our written questionnaires. Hence, we switched to more in-depth face-to-face interviews with small groups of employees. Here, we were able to obtain rich amounts of information to understand the jobs.

The science in the above anecdote lies in our understanding of various information gathering methods. However, we were faced with an unanticipated barrier and had to adjust, which is where the "art" of conducting job analysis lies. Had we merely reported the information obtained via the questionnaire, our analyses would have been completely misleading. Furthermore, we had to be attuned to the needs and climate of the organization when altering our methods. Would face-to-face interviews be disruptive to the workday of employees? Would they be able to cogently talk to us about their jobs?

We would be remiss to not point out that one of the most difficult parts of carrying out a job analysis is not in gathering or analyzing the information, but rather in reporting the results. Much, much writing is involved. The writing has to be clear, specific, and concise. The report that is produced by a job analyst will be used by others in the organization to make a host of personnel decisions, from writing job descriptions to developing training programs. The report must speak for itself as clarification of any ambiguity may not be possible. If the analyst is an internal consultant, the individual may have left his/her position and would not even be available to contact. If the job analysis was conducted by an external consultant, if much time has lapsed, any clarification provided may not even be accurate.

What information is gathered?

Once we have determined the purpose for conducting a job analysis, we have set the tone for the subsequent steps. A general rule of thumb is that the type of information collected depends upon the purpose for which the job analysis was conducted.[12] For example, if a job analysis is conducted to develop a selection instrument, we would surely collect information on the qualifications we expect of employees at the time they are hired. However, if a job analysis is conducted to aid in the negotiation of labor contracts, we may collect information on how much time employees spend on particular tasks. Or, if the purpose is to assess and potentially redesign a physical workspace for better ergonomics and safety, we would gather information regarding the physical environment. Having said that, job analysis information typically includes (1) **tasks** performed by the worker; (2) **knowledge, skills, abilities, and other characteristics (KSAOs)** required to perform these tasks; and (3) the **context** in which work is performed. Let's explain each of these in turn.

Also referred to as duties or activities, tasks are basically what it is that the worker does in the course of his/her job. As an example, a cook "seasons and cooks food according to recipes or personal judgment and experience" and "portions, arranges, and garnishes food, and serves food to waiters or patrons."[13] For another example, see Table 3.2 which lists the tasks performed by an I-O psychologist who works for an external consulting firm.

> **Tasks:** Duties and activities performed by the worker in the course of his/her job.

Additional information regarding tasks are necessary, though the type and level of detail are dependent upon the purpose of the job analysis. Typically, information regarding **how frequently** the tasks are performed and **how important** they are to the job are obtained. If, say, the job analysis was conducted to write a recruitment ad, these details will allow us to include only those that are most critical to the job. In other words, we would not want a recruitment ad that is too lengthy. Not only would this cost too much, it would not be effective in conveying to potential applicants the primary gist of the job. Similarly, if we are conducting the job analysis to develop tools to select applicants for the job, we would use

Table 3.2 Example of tasks for the job of an I-O psychologist

• Conducting job analysis for a multitude of different organizations across multiple markets with a diverse client base
• Using evidence-based psychological theories and applications to ensure best practices and legal defensibility for clients
• Assessing executive training and selection models and implementing evidence-based solutions to update or create a new model
• Improving feedback through applying 360° feedback models to organizations
• Writing job analysis reports, validation reports, record keeping (project status update reports), generating invoices, and writing work documents
• Writing and responding to emails professionally and legibly within 24 hours of contact
• Writing contract agreements in specific terms so as to communicate a realistic project budget and timeline to the client
• Arranging travel plans that are based on different assignments
This job analysis was submitted for a class assignment by one of my students. Used with permission.

this information to delineate **essential functions** of the job. As a third example, if we were conducting a job analysis with the purpose of developing a tool to evaluate the performance of employees, we could use this information to identify behavioral anchors for the most important tasks of the job.

> **Essential Functions:** Most important and frequently performed tasks in a job.

The decision of which tasks to include as a job's essential functions is somewhat of an "art" as there are not cut-and-dry rules. Indeed, the determination of essential functions is based upon numerical ratings provided by those from whom we gather information (discussed later in this chapter). However, it is sometimes a judgment call on the part of the job analyst to determine appropriate cut-off scores at which a task's frequency or importance rating warrants that it be kept as one of the essential functions. Furthermore, it is not always the case that tasks are both frequently performed *and* important to the job. Take, for example, firing a gun in the course of a police officer's line of work. Fortunately, this is not a frequent occurrence; however, it is very important to the job as doing so usually means a life-and-death situation. In this example, the frequency rating of this task would be below any predetermined cut-off score, but its high importance should mean that the task be considered an essential function. Failing to keep an important but otherwise infrequently performed task may result in negative consequences for the employee and organization. For example, if firing a gun is not included as an essential function, it will not be included in a recruitment ad. Potential applicants may then not realize that this is part of the job, which could lead to poor fit between the person and job, and which may lead to lower job satisfaction, lower performance, and ultimately, turnover. Not including this as an essential function may also mean that the organization will not assess applicants with the knowledge, skills, or ability to fire a gun. Needless to say, the consequences of this are more than negative; they can be tragic.

KSAOs are collectively also called *worker requirements* or *competencies*. Knowledge refers to declarative facts and information within a particular area. For example, a chef must have the "knowledge of techniques and equipment for planting, growing, and harvesting food products (both plant and animal) for consumption, including storage/handling techniques."[14] Skills, however, refer to a level of acquired capacity to perform tasks. For a chef, two skills include critical thinking and time management.[15] In contrast to skills which may be acquired, abilities tend to be more enduring mental and physical characteristics. A chef, for instance, needs to have near vision and deductive/inductive reasoning abilities. Finally, other characteristics are requirements not captured by the first three categories. These could be personality traits, interests, or relevant experience. For additional examples of KSAOs, see Table 3.3.

> **Knowledge, Skills, Abilities, and Other Characteristics (KSAOs):** Worker requirements or competencies required by a worker to perform tasks in a job.

Table 3.3 Example of knowledge, skills, abilities, and other characteristics (KSAOs) for the job of an I-O psychologist

- Industrial/Organizational Psychology – Knowledge of fundamental principles including but not limited to recruitment, selection, job analysis, feedback systems, behaviorally anchored rating scales, organizational behavior, validation techniques, and empirical applications and ramifications
- Litigation – Knowing the impact of major EEO Laws and Executive Orders including but not limited to Title VII Civil Rights Act of 1964, Civil Rights Act of 1991, Americans with Disabilities Act of 1990, ADA Amendments Act of 2008, Age Discrimination in Employment Act of 1967
- Computers and Electronics – Intermediate or above knowledge of computer software including but not limited to Microsoft Office Suite, SPSS, ePrime, and Oracle; Basic knowledge of computers, components, and associated presentation devices
- Sociology – Knowledge of group behavior and dynamics, social trends and influences, ethnicity, and cultural heritages with the intention of fostering a mutually respectful work environment
- Interpersonal – Skill in building productive relationships between clients and other teammates on projects to ensure repeat business and quality of work; interpreting feelings and ideas from the viewpoint of clients and internal partners
- Statistical – Skill in using statistical analysis software to process data without error in a timely manner to comply with project deadlines
- Communication – Skills in conveying ideas and theories effectively in both verbal and written mediums
- Project Management – Ability to balance workload of up to 20 different projects while overseeing project group members' work in a timely manner
- Communication Adjustment – Ability to adjust communication styles between power levels such as you can communicate successfully with a factory worker and the CFO of the same organization
- Independence – Ability to structure work independently in order to complete exemplary work within project deadlines
- Persuasion – Ability to persuade or help clients understand what work is necessary to be done and how it will be delivered

This job analysis was submitted for a class assignment by one of my students. Used with permission.

In addition to KSAOs, **work context** refers to aspects of the physical and social environment surrounding the job. For example, the physical environment for a chef would include information regarding the often high temperatures and cramped spaces of restaurant kitchens. Social relations would include information regarding the fact that chefs work closely with others whom they supervise. Information about the work context could also include information regarding the work schedule, amount of travel required, and so forth.

Work Context: Aspects of the work setting that would be relevant to performing tasks and required KSAOs.

As you may have noticed from the examples presented earlier, tasks, KSAOs, and the work context tend to be quite detailed. However, this level of detail is not always the case. Like the type of information gathered, the level of detail needed in the job analysis depends upon the purpose for which the job analysis was conducted.[16] For example, if used to develop the content of selection instruments, a great level of detail is likely needed to ensure not only that we have representatively captured the contents of the job in our instrument but also that we may legally defend our practices.[17] However, a detailed level of analysis may not be needed if we are analyzing jobs to identify broader level competencies for talent management. This is an example again of the "art" of job analysis as these rules of thumb are not cut-and-dry; the job analyst must be able to make these judgment calls.

Methods of gathering job analysis information

Once we know what information needs to be gathered, the next step is to determine the method for collecting that information. Below, we review five of the most commonly used methods.

1. **Existing job information**: Information is gathered from previous job analyses that have been conducted or databases that contain job data. A previous job analysis may be one that was conducted within the same organization for which the current job analysis is needed, or it may be from another organization with the same type of job. An example of a database is the Occupational Information Network (O*NET) website,[18] which was created to provide public access to a vast database of job analysis information gathered for the U.S. Department of Labor.
2. **Questionnaire**: A questionnaire may be specifically developed by the job analyst for the job being analyzed, or it may be an "off-the-shelf" pre-developed inventory. In either case, the questionnaire should be carefully structured so that the data gathered are accurate. The questionnaire usually comprises task and KSAO statements, which are rated based on their frequency and importance for performing the job.
3. **Interview**: This is often face-to-face, but may be technologically mediated (i.e., tele- or video-conferencing), and may be individual- or group-based. This is an ideal method for gathering detailed information about the job as the analyst has an opportunity to ask for elaboration of described events.
4. **Observation**: This may be direct or indirect. In a direct observation, the analyst is physically present at the workplace, observing what the worker does. For an indirect observation, a worker may be video-taped doing his/her job, and then the recording is later viewed by the job analyst.
5. **Participation/job performance**: The job analyst actually performs the work.

Although the above list is not exhaustive, it captures the major methods used in job analysis. One question we often get from students is, "Which method is best?" You are probably not surprised to hear that the answer is, "It depends." It depends on the kind of job being analyzed. If a job involved is very cognitive in nature, observation may not yield much information. However, if a job involves minute physical tasks, observation may yield richer information than description via an interview. Determining which method is best also depends on logistical issues. If an interview is too time-consuming, then a questionnaire may be the better method. If a job involves a level of danger that may deem it too unsafe for job analyst participation or even in-person observation, the job analyst may want to only video-record or use other methods that keep him/her at a safe distance.

Finally, choosing a method depends on the purpose of the job analysis. This is most important because the purpose dictates how detailed the information needs to be, which, in turn, guides us toward the correct method. Ultimately, job analysis information must be accurate. Key questions for a job analyst include the following: Does the job analysis information truly capture the job? Does it actually identify the tasks, KSAOs, and context of the job? To answer these questions, the job analyst should be versed in the various data collection methods and be aware of their corresponding advantages and disadvantages. Table 3.4 displays the major methods listed above and the pros and cons of each. When resources are available, it is wise for a job analyst to utilize multiple methods. Courts, which rely heavily on job analyses in determining the validity of a test, seem to prefer that questionnaire data be supplemented with observation and/or interview data. Again, if possible, multiple methods are preferred.

Table 3.4 Methods of collecting job analysis information: Advantages and disadvantages

Information collection method	Advantages	Disadvantages
Existing Job Information		
Previous job analyses	Analyst does not have to start from scratch	Information may be outdated
Databases (e.g., O*NET)	Information is from a vast database of many jobs and SMEs	Information may be too generic
Questionnaires	Easy to administer Large sample of SMEs	Less rapport between job analyst and SMEs Limited by literacy level of SMEs SMEs can distort information
Interview	Provides information on jobs that require mental work	Time-consuming for analyst and SMEs
Observation	Provides rich picture Some jobs cannot be observed (e.g., jobs that require mental/cognitive ability)	SMEs may behave different under observation
Participation/Job Performance	Allows job analyst to fully experience the work	Some jobs cannot be observed by an untrained individual (unsafe)

Two general approaches

In addition to the data collection methods presented above, job analysts must decide on the type of job analysis they wish to conduct. Given that a job analysis may be completed for multiple purposes, the data collected by any given analysis may differ in its focus and description style. A **task-oriented approach** to job analysis, as the name implies, focuses on the specific tasks and duties to be carried out on the job. The end goal is to produce a list of essential tasks involved in a given job. The **worker-oriented approach**, however, emphasizes characteristics of the worker that are necessary to complete work tasks. This approach will yield a list of human capabilities needed for success in a given job. For example, below are two statements (one task-oriented, one worker-oriented) relating to the job of a waiter/waitress.

Task-oriented: Obtain customer food orders and relay to kitchen workers
Worker-oriented: Politely interact with customers to foster a pleasant dining experience

> **Task-oriented Approach:** Job analysis approach which focuses on the specific tasks and duties to be carried out on the job.

> **Worker-oriented Approach:** Job analysis approach which focuses on characteristics of the worker that are necessary to complete work task.

In reality, whether the task-oriented or worker-oriented approach is used, both serve the purpose of understanding the job in question through the creation of statements pertaining to that job. Thus, these two techniques are simply different ways of achieving the same overarching goal. It is quite common for job analysts to take a hybrid approach, in which they generate task-oriented and worker-oriented statements. Generally speaking, the more types of information you collect, the better understanding of the job you can obtain.

Job analysis tools

Now that you have some background on the different strategies for collecting data within a job analysis, let's take a look at a few of the specific job analysis instruments used by practitioners. There are many tools available to assist with job analysis. Because each tool varies with regard to its general purpose and focus, there are pros and cons associated with each method.

The **Task Inventory** method is a task-oriented approach in which those familiar with the job in question – incumbents, supervisors, or job analysts – generate a list of task statements relevant to the specified job. After a list of task statements has been made, incumbents rate each task on how frequent and important the task is to their work. This process provides a simple and straightforward overview of the duties to be accomplished in any given job. An extension of the task inventory method, representing a more worker-oriented approach, is **cognitive task analysis**. Rather than focusing on the concrete tasks of the job, this method focuses on the cognitive operations – such as thought processes and mental strategies – underlying task performance.[19] The benefit of cognitive task analysis, above a traditional task inventory, is that it is well-suited for the changing nature of the work setting, allowing for in-depth exploration of how employees navigate more complex and technologically based work environments. The downside is that this method is time-consuming and more difficult to conduct, as cognitive behavior is not directly observable. Although cognitive task analysis may be beneficial for jobs involving complex reasoning and judgment, it may not be as feasible or necessary for jobs with relatively straightforward and unchanging tasks/duties.

> **Task Inventory:** A list of task statements generated by people familiar with the job in question and rated by incumbents based on the frequency and importance to their job.

> **Cognitive Task Analysis:** A process used to gain insight into the mental processes underlying work performance.

The **critical incident technique**, another task-oriented approach, seeks to discover actual instances that represent successful or unsuccessful job performance. In this method, incumbents are asked to think of and describe instances when they were very effective and ineffective in their job. They are then asked to discuss what they did, or did not do, in those situations.[20] Using the critical incident technique may help discover tasks that are very important to the job even if they are not frequently performed. Because we tend to think more about tasks we perform most frequently, critical incidents may sometimes be overlooked with other data collection methods. The critical incident technique is also useful in helping to identify behaviors for performance rating forms and generating training-related activities. For your reading pleasure, below is a critical incident of poor performance generated by one of your book authors (Justin) from his time working in a large home improvement store:

> One time a customer came in to pick up a window they had ordered a month earlier. It was a large window (roughly 10-foot long and 5-foot tall) and was stored on the top shelf in our storage area, so a lift was needed to get the window down. Normally, we need two people on the lift to bring down a window of that size. However, we were really busy that day and my coworkers were helping other

customers. So, I decided I could handle the window myself. I went up on the lift, and as I started to move the window from the shelf onto the lift, I lost control of the window and it fell and shattered on the ground… the customer watched the whole scenario play out. I then had to inform the customer we would need to re-order the window and it would be a month or so before they could pick it up. Needless to say, the customer was not happy!

> **Critical Incidents Technique:** Method used in job analysis to uncover specific examples of good and poor employee behavior.

The **Functional Job Analysis** (FJA) method provides a more thorough exploration of the tasks associated with a particular job. Originally designed as a method to be used by the federal government to analyze and compare thousands of jobs, FJA focuses on the fact that all work incorporates three basic functions: people, data, and things. Of course, the degree to which workers interact with people, data, and things varies greatly between jobs. FJA incorporates this into the job analysis process. The practice of FJA begins by using focus groups to generate a list of task statements. Each task is broken down into a behavior (what a worker does) and a result (what gets done).[21] Each task statement addresses the following questions: Who? Does what? To what end (i.e., what result is accomplished)? Using what tools or equipment? With what instructions?

After tasks are carefully determined, participants in the FJA then rate (1) the overall percentage of time incumbents spend in each function (data, people, things), and (2) the complexity of each individual task to determine the level/intensity of interaction with data, people, or things. The FJA method provides great detail about the job and the tasks involved. The primary downside to this method is that it requires a large amount of time and effort on the part of the job analyst.

> **Functional Job Analysis:** A task-oriented job analysis approach that determines the extent to which an incumbent is involved with data, people, and things.

One of the most well-known job analysis tools is the **Position Analysis Questionnaire** (PAQ). The PAQ is a structured, pre-developed survey designed to be used for a broad range of jobs. This instrument would fall under the worker-oriented approach to job analysis and contains 195 items assessing general work behaviors. These behaviors are broken down into six work-related dimensions: information input, mental processes, work output, relationships with other persons, job context, and other job characteristics (e.g., work schedule and pay).[22,23] Those taking the survey are asked whether each item is relevant to the job in question, and also asked about the frequency and importance of each item as it relates to their job. Once completed, the survey is then scored online and a profile of the job can be generated. The major benefits of the PAQ are that it is readily available, inexpensive, easier than creating task statements from scratch, and has been shown to be a reliable instrument. Because it has been used for several decades, current responses can be added to a large database of previously collected information. The downside, however, is that the PAQ uses rather broad items and therefore does not provide much fine detail about particular jobs. Another criticism is that the PAQ requires a relatively high (college level) reading capacity, which may limit those who can take and/or administer the survey. An alternative approach to the PAQ is the Job Elements Inventory (JEI), which only requires a 10th-grade reading level.[24]

> **Position Analysis Questionnaire:** A structured job analysis instrument focusing on general work behaviors.

Another off-the-shelf inventory, similar to the PAQ, is the **Job Components Inventory** (JCI). Using the worker-oriented approach, this instrument breaks worker requirements into five categories: tools and equipment, physical and perceptual requirements, mathematical requirements, communication requirements, and decision-making and responsibility requirements.[25] Although the PAQ has respondents rate each item based on frequency and importance, the JCI employs a simple yes/no response to each item. As such, this inventory may not provide as much detail with regard to essential functions of a particular job. Though there is less published research on this inventory than the PAQ, it advances on the PAQ by including a specific dimension focusing on tools and equipment used within the job.

> **Job Components Inventory:** A structured job analysis instrument focusing on worker requirements for performing a job.

In terms of simplicity and ease of use, the **Fleishman Job Analysis Survey** represents one of the more user-friendly instruments for job analysis. Designed to be completed by incumbents and/or job analysts, this survey incorporates several different types of knowledge, skill, and ability scales – including cognitive, psychomotor, sensory-perceptual, and social categories. Respondents are asked to rate the extent to which each ability/knowledge category is needed to perform job duties. This method is backed by over 30 years of research and represents an easy to use method for both incumbents and job analysts.[26]

> **Fleishman Job Analysis Survey:** A structured job analysis instrument focusing on the abilities necessary for performing a job successfully.

A few job analysis methods have focused more on traits than on actual tasks, skills, and abilities. For example, the **Threshold Trait Analysis** uses 33 items to assess five trait-based categories (physical, mental, learned, motivation, and social) relevant to the work setting. The benefits of this method are that it is relatively short and has shown to be a reliable indicator of job-relevant traits.[27] Although this provides another viable worker-oriented approach, the downside to this inventory is that it is not commercially available. The **Personality-Related Position Requirements Form** (PPRF), however, represents a commercially available trait-based approach. This procedure is unique in that it was designed to indicate the personality types required to perform work tasks.[28] Based on the Big 5 personality traits, the PPRF outlines 12 personality dimensions that may differ between jobs. Although trait-based approaches provide an alternative to traditional task and ability-based methods, they may not provide as much job-specific information as the previously discussed approaches.

> **Threshold Trait Analysis:** A job analysis questionnaire designed to assess the traits relevant for successful job performance.

> **Personality-Related Position Requirements Form:** A job analysis questionnaire developed to determine job-related personality requirements.

Finally, as mentioned above, many job analyses these days use a hybrid approach, combining both task- and worker-oriented techniques. The **Combination Job Analysis Method** (C-JAM) generates both tasks and KSAOs in order to understand both what gets done on the job and the human attributes necessary to perform job tasks. First, tasks statements are developed and rated based on frequency and importance (similar to FJA). Then, a list of KSAOs are developed and rated on their importance for job performance (similar to several of the worker-oriented procedures listed earlier). After this is completed, the ratings for items and KSAOs are interpreted and used for developing selection methods and training programs.[29] By using both description techniques, this technique provides a fuller understanding of the job in question.

> **Combination Job Analysis Method:** A job analysis technique employing both task- and worker-oriented approaches.

O*NET is another great example of the hybrid approach, as the database provides both task-oriented and worker-oriented statements for a variety of jobs. This database assumes that jobs can be understood at four levels of analysis: economic, organizational, occupational, and individual. The O*NET website provides a wealth of information that can be useful for many applications. Because O*NET data is publicly available and easily accessible, it serves as a valuable resource to those completing job analyses or to those who simply want to find out more about what a job entails.

As can be seen, there are many tools at the disposal of personnel psychologists tasked with performing a job analysis. The purpose of the job analysis will dictate which method is most appropriate in any given situation.

Competency modeling

Conceptually similar to job analysis, competency modeling represents an alternative method of identifying what it takes to be successful on the job. As discussed earlier in this chapter, there is a trend toward the term *work analysis*, rather than job analysis, with the broader concept of "work" being the fundamental unit of analysis (rather than a specific job). Corresponding to this shift is a movement toward discussing competencies (broader combinations of KSAOs relevant for work performance) rather than individual KSAOs relevant for a particular job task. As a result, there is a large industry related to **competency modeling**, which identifies the capabilities needed to perform successfully in a particular industry and/or work setting.

Although there are many similarities between competency modeling and traditional job analysis, Campion et al. (2011)[30] point out some key differences (presented in Table 3.5). A primary difference is that competency models are often aligned with business priorities, strategies, and organizational mission statements. Traditional job analysis is a bottom-up process (i.e., we start with studying workers and the nature of work), whereas competency modeling starts top-down, asking corporate leaders about business priorities and then linking aspects of the job to those priorities. Campion et al. note that executives pay more attention to competency models, suggesting that these models may serve as a strategy to increase

Table 3.5 Differences between job analysis and competency modeling

1. Executives typically pay more attention to competency modeling.
2. Competency models often attempt to distinguish top performers from average performers.
3. Competency models frequently include descriptions of how the competencies change or progress with employee level.
4. Competency models are usually directly linked to business objectives and strategies.
5. Competency models are typically developed top-down (start with executives) rather than bottom-up (start with line employees).
6. Competency models may consider future job requirements either directly or indirectly.
7. Competency models may be presented in a manner that facilitates ease of use (e.g., organization-specific language, pictures, or schematics that facilitate memorableness).
8. Usually, a finite number of competencies are identified and applied across multiple functions or job families.
9. Competency models are frequently used actively to align the HR systems.
10. Competency models are often an organizational development intervention that seeks broad organizational change as opposed to a simple data collection effort.

the likelihood the organization will use job analysis information in employee management decisions. Competency models also have a more future-oriented focus, exploring how competencies may change and develop over time, what distinguishes top-level performers from average performers, and how job requirements may change over time. Finally, although job analysis is typically viewed as a data collection effort to understand a job (often tailored to a specific purpose), competency modeling is often viewed as an organizational development intervention that leads to broader organizational change across multiple HR functions.

Although competency modeling and job analysis are often completed for similar purposes (i.e., selection, performance appraisal, training, and compensation), the methods used and the end product often look quite a bit different. Competency modeling has a broader focus and is typically more worker-oriented compared to job analysis. Even with their differences, the basic approach of job analysis and competency modeling remains the same: study the job in great detail and document the findings.

> **Competency Modeling:** The process of establishing the competencies necessary for success within a work setting.

Sources of job analysis information

Having just learned about the methods of collecting information, you may be wondering where we would get the information? To whom do we administer questionnaires or interview? The source of information we gather should come from people who are most familiar with the job. These are referred to as **subject matter experts (SMEs)**. Typically, SMEs are employees who currently perform the job, also referred to as job incumbents, as they know best the tasks and requirements of their job. Sometimes, supervisors may also serve as SMEs in a job analysis. It is important to be selective of the job incumbents we include to make sure that they have enough knowledge about the job so that our information is accurate. Again, more as a guideline than a hard-and-fast rule, job incumbents who serve as experts should have at least six months of experience on the job. In most jobs, the first three months are spent learning about the job and the organization. Hence, six months of experience on the job allows us to include employees who not only had time to move past the learning curve but also another three months for when they probably made meaningful contributions.

In addition to tenure on the job, it is important to consider other characteristics of job incumbents who should serve as SMEs. It is important that our sample is representative of the population. Think about job incumbents here as the sample, and the population to include all possible other people who could be in the job. If we are hoping to generalize our findings beyond our sample, we have to ensure that there are no meaningful differences between the sample and the population. Let's go back to the example of the utility lineman presented earlier and the intended purpose of that job analysis, which was to develop a physical ability assessment. What would the problem be if our sample of SMEs comprised only male incumbents?

In case you have not answered the above question, here are some hints: open-water or marathon swimming, very long-distance running, gymnastics, and horseracing. Still stumped? These are sports in which women outperform their gender counterparts. The point here is that there are differences between men and women in their physical abilities; although men have overall higher physical abilities, there are some areas in which women outperform their male counterparts. Therefore, it may be possible that men and women may harness their different physical strengths to accomplish the same tasks. What if utility linewomen use, say, more of their lower-body strength in climbing power poles, whereas utility linemen rely upon their upper-body strength? If we included only male job incumbents in our SME sample, we may be capturing only a subset of required physical abilities. This would render the job analysis incomplete or even inaccurate. Furthermore, if the physical ability assessment we have developed on the basis of this job analysis was used to select both male and female applicants, we may be led to incorrect decisions. That is, in assessing upper-body strength only and not including an assessment of lower-body strength at all, we could end up hiring a disproportionately lower number of females. Not only does this limit our human capital, but also poses a possible legal concern if female applicants challenge the fairness of the selection process.

Along with job incumbents, supervisors or managers often serve as SMEs in job analysis. Although they may not be able to describe the technical aspects of the job as well as incumbents who actually perform the work, they may have insight into the KSAOs required by the tasks and the organization and not just the tasks themselves. Furthermore, supervisors or managers may be able to anticipate changes in the job that would enable a more forward-looking analysis.

Although job incumbents and managers or supervisors have traditionally been the sources of job analysis information, contemporary analysts are also including customers, team members, and technical experts as SMEs.[31] This broadened lens is exemplary of re-crafting the tool of job analysis for a changing workplace.

Sources of inaccuracy in job analysis information

Although job analysis involves systematic methods, it ultimately involves *people*, and when anything involves people, things are not as clear-cut as they may appear. When we gather information for a job analysis, we have to rely primarily on the employees and what they have to tell us about their work. Because of the important uses of job analysis results, it is crucial that the data reflects the truth about what the job entails; otherwise, we will be making wrong decisions about what to assess applicants for, how to allocate pay for different positions, what kind of training programs to design, and so forth. Hence, psychological research on job analysis has been focused on understanding the sources of inaccuracy and how to make this process as objective as possible. In their article "A Framework of Sources of Inaccuracy in Job Analysis," Frederick Morgeson and Michael Campion[32] draw upon social and cognitive psychology research to identify 16 potential sources of inaccuracy in job analysis (see Table 3.6).

Table 3.6 Social and cognitive sources of potential inaccuracy and their hypothesized effects on job analysis data

Source of inaccuracy	Interrater reliability	Interrater agreement	Discriminability between jobs	Dimensionality of factor structures	Mean ratings	Completeness of job information
Social sources						
Conformity pressures	√	√				
Extremity shifts		√		√	√	√
Motivation loss			√	√		
Impression management					√	
Cognitive sources						
Social desirability					√	√
Demand effects					√	
Information overload	√		√	√	√	√
Heuristics			√	√		√
Categorization			√	√		√
Carelessness	√		√	√		
Extraneous information					√	
Inadequate information	√					√
Contrast and order effects						√
Halo				√	√	
Leniency and severity				√	√	
Method effects	√			√		

Truth be told, some employees may consciously inflate the information they provide about their work. If you have seen the movie *Office Space*, you may understand how a fear of losing one's job can motivate an employee to exaggerate the tasks and requirements of his/her job. In a 2004 study, Morgeson and colleagues determined that, indeed, ability statements were subject to inflation as job incumbents engaged in self-presentation processes.[33]

Once I (Alexandra) had conducted a job analysis to determine the appropriate typing skill level for typists. The hiring manager had a difficult time filling positions as applicants were passing all the other selection tests but seemed to fail short of the current 70-word-per-minute requirement. Like many I-O psychologists who work as internal consultants, I was part of a team in the HR department of this organization. The HR generalist called on us to express the problem described above and asked for a solution. As you may guess, our first step was to conduct a job analysis. During the first meeting with job incumbents who served as SMEs, they insisted that 70 words per minute was an essential minimum qualification. However, after additional gathering of data via observing current employees at work, actually performing the work myself, and most importantly, ensuring the incumbents that their jobs would not be threatened by any personnel decisions arising from the job analysis, I determined that the typing requirement was really just 45 words per minute for an employee to effectively perform! It turned out the 70-word-per-minute requirement was based on a very outdated job analysis conducted when typists were using a typewriter, without the luxury of being able to copy and paste text in programs such as Microsoft Word. More interesting, I also learned that the SMEs were all employees who had been in their positions for more than ten years, who all had less than a college degree, and who, frankly, would not have many options if they were terminated. Understandably, they felt threatened by the job analysis as they thought that lowering the minimum requirement would mean that they were more replaceable.

Given the potential biases and inflated responses that can occur, what could a job analyst do? Below are the guidelines:

1. Establish rapport with SMEs so they do not feel threatened by the job analysis process. Let them know this is about gathering data about the *job*, and that they are not being evaluated. Reassurance from their immediate supervisors would help because consultants, such as Bob and Bob from *Office Space*, are likely to be mistrusted.
2. Write task and KSAO statements as specifically as possible as vague and holistic statements are more vulnerable to inaccurate responding.
3. Choose the data collection method that best suits the climate or situation. For example, if it appears that job incumbents mistrust the purposes of the job analysis, a face-to-face interview would better allow for developing rapport than an anonymous questionnaire.

Summary

As previously stated, job analysis is truly the foundation of almost everything that we write about in subsequent chapters. Often, the outcome of court cases depends on the quality of a job analysis. If the job analysis was done sloppily, it may be difficult to establish the validity of a test, especially if the I-O psychologist relies on content validity as a method (see Chapter 5 for more discussion on this). Although there has been a recent shift toward the term work analysis to address the rapid changes in the world of work, the basic framework of job analysis has remained similar over the past 75 years. This is a testament to the lasting importance of the job analysis process. Simply put, understanding what a job entails represents the first step in completing every other HR function. As you read through the remaining chapters of this book, we encourage you to reflect back on how/why job analysis is fundamental to the topics covered within each chapter.

According to the Pew Research Institute, the percentage of men who are stay-at-home dads is 3.5%, double the percentage of what we saw in the 1970s. Although significantly lower than the percentage of women who are homemakers, this increase signals a rise in changing gender roles.

REVIEW QUESTIONS

1. What is a job analysis and what information is uncovered?
2. What are the primary purposes of conducting a job analysis?
3. Compare and contrast tasks and KSAOs.
4. Compare job analysis and competency modeling. What are similarities and differences between the two?
5. Compare and contrast the task-oriented and the worker-oriented job analysis approaches.
6. What are the major job analysis tools and how do they differ from one another?

DISCUSSION QUESTIONS

1. How would you feel about job crafting? Would you like to be able to do in your own job?
2. If you were asked to provide information about your job for a job analysis your employer is conducting, what might motivate you to not provide the most accurate information?
3. What do you think are the most common reasons for inaccuracy in job analysis among those listed?
4. Considering the job description provided for an I-O psychologist, would you be interested in becoming one?

Notes

1. Arvey, R. D., & Begalla, M. E. (1975). Analyzing the homemaker job using the Position Analysis Questionnaire (PAQ). *Journal of Applied Psychology, 60,* 513–517.
2. Arvey, R. D., & Begalla, M. E. (1975). Analyzing the homemaker job using the Position Analysis Questionnaire (PAQ). *Journal of Applied Psychology, 60,* 513–517.
3. Morgeson, F. P., Brannick, M. T., & Levine, E. L. (2020). *Job and work analysis: Methods, research, and applications for human resource management.* Sage.
4. Sanchez, J. I., & Levine, E. L. (2012). The rise and fall of job analysis and the future of work analysis. *Annual Review of Psychology, 63,* 397–425.
5. Morgeson, F. P., Brannick, M. T., & Levine, E. L. (2020). *Job and work analysis: Methods, research, and applications for human resource management.* Sage.
6. Equal Employment Opportunity Commission. (1978). *Uniform Guidelines on Employee Selection Procedures.* Uniform Guidelines. https://www.uniformguidelines.com/uniform-guidelines.html
7. Meloun, J. M. (2008). Job analysis: The basis for all things HR. In D. V. Tesone (Ed.), *Handbook of hospitality human resources management* (pp. 23–42). Routledge: London.
8. Sanchez, J. I., & Levine, E. L. (2012). The rise and fall of job analysis and the future of work analysis. *Annual Review of Psychology, 63,* 397–425.
9. Yamada, H. (1997). *Different games, different rules: Why Americans and Japanese misunderstood each other.* Oxford University Press.
10. May, K. (1996). Work in the 21st century: Implications for job analysis. *The Industrial Organizational Psychologist, 33*(4), 98–100.
11. Wrzesniewski, A., & Dutton, J. E. (2001). Crafting a job: Revisioning employees as active crafters of their work. *Academy of Management Review, 26,* 179–201.
12. Morgeson, F. P., Brannick, M. T., & Levine, E. L. (2020). *Job and work analysis: Methods, research, and applications for human resource management.* Sage.
13. O*NET Online. https://www.onetonline.org/
14. O*NET Online. https://www.onetonline.org/
15. O*NET Online. https://www.onetonline.org/
16. Society for Industrial and Organizational Psychology. (2018). *Principles for the Validation and Use of Personnel Selection Procedures.* https://www.apa.org/ed/accreditation/about/policies/personnel-selection-procedures.pdf
17. Equal Employment Opportunity Commission. (1978). *Uniform Guidelines on Employee Selection Procedures.* Uniform Guidelines. https://www.uniformguidelines.com/uniform-guidelines.html
18. https://www.onetonline.org/
19. Vicente, K. J. (1995). Task, analysis, cognitive task analysis, cognitive work analysis: What's the difference? *Proceedings of the Human Factors and Ergonomics Society Annual Meeting, 39,* 534–537.
20. Flanagan, J. C. (1954). The critical incident technique. *Psychological Bulletin, 51,* 327–358.
21. Fine, S. A. (1988). Functional job analysis. In *Symposium proceedings: Occupational research and the Navy-prospectus 1980* (pp. 64–75).
22. McCormick, E. J., Jeanneret, P. R., & Gael, S. (1988). Position Analysis Questionnaire (PAQ). In *Symposium proceedings: Occupational research and the Navy-prospectus 1980* (pp. 78–86).
23. McCormick, E. J., Jeanneret, P. R., & Mecham, R. C. (1972). A study of job characteristics and job dimensions as based on the Position Analysis Questionnaire (PAQ). *Journal of Applied Psychology, 56,* 347–368.
24. Cornelius III, E. T., Hakel, M. D., & Sackett, P. R. (1979). A methodological approach to job classification for performance appraisal purposes. *Personnel Psychology, 32,* 283–297.

25. Banks, M. E., Jackson, P. R., Stafford, E. M., & Warr, P. B. (1983). The Job Components Inventory and the analysis of jobs requiring limited skill. *Personnel Psychology, 36*, 57–66.
26. Fleishman, E. A., & Reilly, M. E. (1992). *Handbook of human abilities: Definitions, measurements, and job task requirements.* Consulting Psychologists Press.
27. Lopez, F. M., Kesselman, G. A., & Lopez, F. E. (1981). An empirical test of a trait-oriented job analysis technique. *Personnel Psychology, 34*, 479–502.
28. Raymark, P. H., Schmit, M. J., & Guion, R. M. (1997). Identifying potentially useful personality constructs for employee selection. *Personnel Psychology, 50*, 723–736.
29. Morgeson, F. P., Brannick, M. T., & Levine, E. L. (2020). *Job and work analysis: Methods, research, and applications for human resource management.* Sage.
30. Campion, M. A., Fink, A. A., Ruggeberg, B. J., Carr, L., Phillips, G. M., & Odman, R. B. (2011). Doing competencies well: Best practices in competency modeling. *Personnel Psychology, 64*, 225–262.
31. May. K. (1996). Work in the 21st century: Implications for job analysis. *The Industrial Organizational Psychologist, 33*(4), 98–100.
32. Morgeson, F. P., & Campion, M. A. (1997). Social and cognitive sources of potential inaccuracy in job analysis. *Journal of Applied Psychology, 82*, 627–655.
33. Morgeson, F. P., Delaney-Klinger, K., Mayfield, M. S., Ferrara, P., & Campion, M. A. (2004). Self-presentation processes in job analysis: A field experiment investigating inflation in abilities, tasks, and competencies. *Journal of Applied Psychology, 89*, 674–686.

4 Recruitment

LEARNING OBJECTIVES

- Define recruitment
- Distinguish recruitment from selection
- Compare and contrast prospecting versus mating theories of recruitment
- Compare and contrast applicant and employer perspectives on recruitment
- Know the goals of recruitment for organizations
- List commonly used recruitment tactics and provide examples of each
- Know research findings regarding each recruitment tactic
- Understand extrinsic and intrinsic factors in organizational attraction
- Understand social identity theory in relation to recruitment
- Define realistic job information and explain why it is important
- Know ways effectiveness of recruitment strategies may be evaluated

Recruitment

Consider the following job ads and recruitment website:

> **Ad 1:**
>
> We want a few first-class men who have had a SUCCESSFUL experience in the Life Insurance business to sell a policy just issued by one of the best Old Line Companies. This policy has new and attractive features. Liberal inducements will be offered to a few good men. In reply, state experience.
>
> Address, Manager, P.O. Box, 787, New York City.

> **Ad 2:**
>
> INSURANCE CONTRACT ANALYST Excellent opportunity with a leading diversified financial organization USLIFE CORPORATION seeks a college graduate with a minimum of 1–2 years experience in life insurance contract drafting, policy fillings, product development and readability compliance. The ideal candidate will have exposure to interest sensitive and indeterminate premium products. Salary commensurate with experience. We offer excellent benefits including 100% tuition reimbursement, major medical coverage, salary and investment program and a company subsidized cafeteria. For immediate consideration, send resume or apply in person to the Personnel Dept., Tues.–Fri. 9:00AM–4:30PM. USLIFE CORPORATION 125 Maiden Lane New York, NY 10038 Equal Opportunity Employer M/F

> Online company recruitment website:
> https://jobs.metlife.com/

If you were an applicant, which ad would you find most appealing? If you were an employer, which ad would you use? Job ads 1 and 2 were published in *The New York Times* classifieds, in 1900 and 1984, respectively. The third example is a link to MetLife's current corporate careers website. Obviously, recruitment has come a long way, so let's first point out some major differences across these three examples which span 114 years:

- As you know from Chapter 2 (Discrimination and Employment Law), ad 1 illegally excludes female applicants.
- Ad 2 notes that the organization is an equal opportunity employer, while the third example goes further to visually and verbally embrace diversity.
- Example 3 leverages the current technology that wasn't available just 20 years ago.

Despite these pointed differences, the primary goal of recruitment remains the same: to attract applicants. All three examples try to do so by advertising the benefits of working for their respective company. However, the goal is not merely to attract any applicant; rather, employers want to attract *quality* applicants. Hence, all three examples specify the desired qualities they are seeking in their ideal candidate. The question, then, is which ad does it best? In this chapter, we will attempt to answer this question as we "unpack" the psychology behind personnel recruitment. First, let's clarify some definitions.

What is recruitment?

Compared to selection

As will be covered in later chapters, personnel selection is the process used to hire applicants. In the interest of drawing boundaries, we can say that recruitment precedes selection. Recruitment brings people to the door, whereas selection allows employers to invite in only the most desirable candidates. However, the two processes overlap and are highly related. Consider an employer who has successfully recruited a pool of applicants. As the few most suitable candidates are invited to an interview and other selection processes, the employer needs to continue to make a positive impression to not lose any of these final candidates during any of these stages. Furthermore, when the employer is finally able to make an offer, the recruitment process continues as the employer must influence that final candidate to accept the job offer. Finally, consider an employer who does a poor job of recruitment. If there are very few qualified applicants, even the best selection tool will fail to identify high-quality applicants if there were none recruited to apply.

Defined simply as the practices and process used by employers to find and attract job applicants, **recruitment** may be viewed from two perspectives. The first approach is the **prospecting theory** of recruitment, which views recruitment as a one-way process, in which organizations search for and try to influence applicants. In reality, however, job seekers also search for and evaluate potential employers as they decide which positions to pursue and ultimately accept. Applicants themselves also engage in impression management strategies to influence how employers perceive them. This **mating strategy** perspective more aptly captures the reality that recruitment is a *two-way* process. Likened to the dance that occurs between individuals seeking romantic partners, recruitment is sort of a tango between employer and applicant. Each party sends out signals and gestures to hopefully attract, rather than repel, the other. Should a "marriage" occur, how everlasting and happy that union is depends partly on what has transpired during this process. Hence, to increase the probability of a successful union, we need to understand recruitment from both the employer's and the applicant's perspectives. As a student, you have probably had more experiences as an applicant than as an employer or recruiter, so let's start there.

> **Recruitment:** Practices and process used by employers to find and attract job applicants.

> **Prospecting Theory:** A view of recruitment as a one-way process, in which organizations search for and try to influence applicants.

> **Mating Strategy:** A view of recruitment as a two-way process, in which organizations search for and try to influence applicants, and applicants enhance their attractiveness to employers.

The applicant's perspective

For the applicant, recruitment may fulfill several purposes:

1. It enables the applicant to know what job openings exist and allows the opportunity to apply for any interested positions.
2. It provides information for the applicant to determine if the position and organization offer what s/he is looking for in a job.
3. It provides the applicant some insight into what it would be like to work for the organization.
4. It allows the applicant a chance to assess whether there would be a "fit" with the organization.
5. It provides the applicant an early opportunity, even before selection, to make an impression on the employer.

Knowing where to search for existing openings is key for job seekers. In the opening of this chapter, we presented three classified ads. However, newspaper ads are least likely used nowadays, and are one of the least effective.[1] So, where should applicants look for job openings? First of all, beware that many job openings, especially higher-level positions, are not publicly advertised. Rather, employers frequently use employee referrals, which entails having current employees refer people they know to the organization. Or they may rely on headhunter firms that court applicants for particular positions. Hence, individuals looking for a job should take a more proactive approach. To take advantage of the employee referral strategy used by many employers, the applicant could reach out to his/her informal networks (e.g., friends, family members, and associates) to spread the word about his/her employment interests. In addition, if they have specialized skills, they might reach out to headhunting firms to let them know of particular interest in types of jobs. As the Department Chair, Mike often gets contacted by headhunting firms looking to recruit people to apply for Academic Dean positions. If Mike actually wanted to be a Dean (he doesn't!), he should return those phone calls and emails and let the headhunters know what type of jobs he is looking for.

Job seekers should also leverage the current technology as employers are veering away from print ads toward internet-based job boards (e.g., Monster.com, Indeed.com, and ZipRecruiter.com), social networking sites (e.g., LinkedIn and Facebook), and their own corporate websites. Applicants may also be more proactive by posting their own situation-wanted ads online. Finally, employers themselves are using even more proactive recruiting strategies to seek out "passive job seekers." One way this is done is by hiring recruiters to scout social media profiles in order to identify high-potential employees. Hence, individuals who are not actively looking for a job but may be open to other opportunities would benefit from creating and maintaining professional profiles on social media networking sites.

Employers always advertise that working for their organization will provide the applicant with an array of benefits. Job Ad 1, for example, announces that "liberal inducements will be provided to a few good men." In Job Ad 2, these inducements are specified to include tuition reimbursement, major medical coverage, and an investment program. Before applying for a job, it would help job seekers to reflect on what they are looking for in a job or employer. Ask yourself what is most important: pay, benefits, location, and/or opportunities for advancement? Weighing what one values at the beginning of the job search process will help the applicant from committing a number of errors that can occur in decision-making.[2]

In attempting to attract applicants, employers emphasize the positive aspects of their organization and of the job. Hence, applicants should be discerning recipients of such information. If possible, seek out multiple, credible sources to verify employer's claims regarding their organization. Such other sources include business magazines, HR publications, and entities dedicated to evaluating workplaces. For example, the American Psychological Association sponsors a Psychologically Healthy Workplace Award (PHWA) program that "shines the spotlight on exemplary organizations" excelling in the following areas: employee involvement, work-life balance, employee growth and development, health and safety, and employee recognition. In addition, there are now websites such as Glassdoor.com that compile information about what it is like to work for particular companies, so applicants should seek out that information. Finally, some of the most credible information may come from past and current employees, so applicants should also consider reaching out through their own networks to find these connections.

Person-organization fit

As an applicant, it is important to determine how well one would fit with the job or organization. Research suggests that when there is greater person-organization (P-O) fit, employees are more likely to experience outcomes such as higher job satisfaction and better performance.[3] You may be wondering what contributes to P-O fit beyond one's intuitive "gut feeling" when evaluating employment opportunities. Applicants may consider two key dimensions of P-O fit: complementary fit and supplementary fit.[4,5] *Complementary fit* occurs when the wants or limitations of the employer are addressed by the characteristics of the applicant, or vice versa. For example, an applicant may provide the knowledge, skills, and abilities that the organization desires for an open position, whereas the organization can provide an appealing salary and benefits to the applicant. In this scenario, the applicant and employer fill each other's voids, so to speak. *Supplementary fit*, however, occurs when there is a shared similarity between the person and the organization, often in the form of value congruence. For example, if both the person and the organization believe that flexible work schedules are important to ensure a productive and pleasant work setting, this would be an example of supplementary fit.

> **Person-Organization Fit:** The compatibility between an individual and an organization.

While most of the P-O fit research has focused on the employee, Cable and Judge[6] examined P-O fit from a distinctively job seeker's perspective. They concluded that perceived fit is primarily determined by the match between the applicant's and organization's values (i.e., supplementary fit), and predicts job choice intentions and future work attitudes. A recent meta-analysis by Uggerslev and colleagues[7] reported that perceived fit was indeed the strongest predictor of applicant attraction to an organization. Hence, job seekers would benefit by finding out as much as possible about an organization in order to evaluate whether their own values "fit" those of the organization. A quick and easy way for applicants to get a sense of their potential fit with an employer is by taking a look at company websites.[8] Many businesses now have websites highlighting their mission, goals, and values. Of course, much more goes into P-O fit than a quick perusal of a company website, but this provides a great starting point and may help applicants refine their job search.

Social networking

As noted above, social networking sites (SNS) have become a widely used recruiting tool, with a 2013 survey by the Society for Human Resource Management reporting that 77% of employers use SNS to attract applicants. In the same survey, 20% admit to using SNS and online search engines to screen job candidates in order to make hiring decisions.[9] Although a very limited number of studies suggest a model level of accuracy in judging character and personality attributes based upon an individual's online profiles, research shows biases and potential discrimination of protected classes when using SNS to screen job applicants.[10] For example, Acquisti and Fong[11] found discrimination against job applicants based upon religious affiliation. Using dummy resumes and social media profiles, the researchers found that candidates whose public profiles indicated they were Muslim were less likely to be invited for interviews than applicants whose public profiles suggested they were Christian. Hence, job seekers need not only ensure that their social media profiles and internet reputations are professionally desirable, but also that any information which could result in negative biases be omitted or not be viewable by the public.

Now, let's shift perspective here and consider what employers are hoping to achieve via their recruitment practices and processes.

The employer's perspective

For the employer, recruitment may serve five primary goals:

1. To generate not just more but more qualified applicants
2. To influence the job choice decisions of final candidates
3. To abide by legal requirements regarding the demographic composition of its workforce
4. To fulfill the organization's goals and values regarding the demographic composition of its workforce
5. To help increase the success rate of the selection process

The first two goals capture the primary reason employers recruit, which is to fill vacancies in their organization with employees who have the requisite knowledge, skills, and abilities to be effective performers. In terms of the third goal, recruitment may enable an organization to abide by legal employment requirements in several ways. First, via recruitment, the organization can demonstrate that it is an equal opportunity employer. This can be accomplished simply by including such a statement on its job ad, as seen in Ad 2. An organization may also target specific demographic groups via its recruitment efforts. For example, recruiters could be sent to job fairs at historically Black colleges and universities. Employers may be interested in not just merely meeting legal obligations, but may be motivated to recruit as widely as possible or even target specific groups in order to meet the organization's values. Diversity, for example, serves as a core value for many current organizations. By targeting recruitment efforts toward specific demographic groups, the organization is able to increase the probability of having a more diverse applicant pool and subsequently, greater diversity among employees.

As discussed above, although recruitment and selection are two different processes, the two are highly related and overlap. Hence, the fifth purpose that recruitment may serve for the employer is to increase the success of its selection rate. If the employer successfully attracts and maintains the interest of highly qualified applicants, then come time for selection, the organization has the luxury of being able to choose from the cream of the crop.

As can be seen, recruitment serves several purposes for both the applicant and the employer. Ultimately, it fulfills the same need for both parties, by helping each find its match. In so doing, the foremost goals of both parties are congruent with one another: recruitment allows the applicant to know what position openings exist and enables the employer to generate interest from as many qualified applicants as possible. An inherent conflict exists, however, between the two parties. The applicant is hoping to find out accurate information about the job and organization in order to decide if s/he wants to apply and ultimately accept should an offer be made. At the same time, the employer is trying to attract employees and in trying to do so, may inflate the attractive features of the organization or downplay (or even conceal) its negative aspects. Another conflict that exists involves the overlap between recruitment and selection. As a mating strategy, it serves the applicant's best interest to put his/her best foot forward even before formal selection begins. During job fairs, for example, the applicant could dress professionally and express enthusiasm when interacting with recruiters, even for jobs in which s/he is ambivalent. In telephone or email inquiries about open positions or the application process, expressing courtesy and respect would send positive signals to the employer. Although such behaviors are recommended and could very well accurately reflect the applicant's character, to the extent that people can *fake* their personalities and the employer relies too heavily on such initial impressions to make hiring decisions, these efforts could muddle the selection process.

The question, then, is how recruitment can concurrently serve the interests of both the applicant and the employer. Essentially, both parties should clearly understand and bear in mind the perspectives of the other party while pursuing their own objectives. This is especially important for the employer because they are the primary drivers of the process, after all. In this next section, we outline recruitment strategies or tactics that may be used by employers. For each recruitment strategy, we discuss psychological research used to evaluate the recruitment strategy, explain psychological theories or concepts related to the strategy, and provide examples so you get a sense of how recruitment occurs in the real world.

Recruitment strategies

Advertise inducements

Inducements refer to those offerings, such as salary, challenging assignments, and flexible work arrangements that an employer can convey to applicants during the recruitment process. This can be done as early in the process as within the job ad, or as late as during the interview (remember, recruitment and selection highly overlap). These inducements can be categorized as either *extrinsic* or *intrinsic*. Extrinsic inducements are those that are external to the job, such as pay or benefits. Intrinsic inducements are those that are integral to the job, such as challenging tasks or opportunities for growth or development. Put another way, intrinsic offerings are intrapsychic, whereas extrinsic offerings tend to be more materialistic.

Research suggests that individual differences and demographic characteristics may moderate the effects of inducements on applicants. For example, one study found that applicants higher in cognitive ability and achievement value interesting and challenging work more than those lower on these characteristics.[12] Gender[13] and ethnic identity[14] have also been found to be related to the types of inducements that applicants find to be attractive. In the interest of attracting a diverse applicant pool, employers should bear these demographic differences in mind; however, care must be taken not to discriminate against any protected classes in the process.

Organizational examples

- Deemed the "King of Perks" by CNN Money, *Google* is well known for its efforts to attract the best and brightest. Extrinsic offerings include on-site laundry and childcare, flex hours, health benefits that include on-site physician and dental care, free massage and yoga, outdoor recreation, stock options, free drinks, and meals.
- Google, Genentech, and 3M all offer "20% work," which means employees are allowed one day during each week to pursue their own projects.
- Recreational Equipment, Inc. (REI) offers discounts on adventure travel and adoption assistance.

Use employee referrals

A review[15] showed that employees recruited through internal sources, as compared to those recruited externally, had more positive organizational outcomes such as staying longer with the organization and higher performance. One explanation for this is that employees referred receive more accurate information about the job and organization, since they are receiving such information from job incumbents who are most likely friends or family members. Another explanation for this has to do with similarity in interpersonal relationships: people tend to have friends who are similar to themselves. So, for example, someone who gets along with his/her supervisor and coworkers and is satisfied with the organization as a whole is more likely to be friends with others who would have the same disposition (i.e., is just an agreeable, easy-to-get-along-with, and easy-to-please person) or preferences (e.g., for a certain type of organizational culture). Finally, the employee making the referral is serving as a sort of "filter" for the potential applicant, in the way that self-selection occurs on the behalf of the organization by the applicant.

Employers should heed caution in using employee referrals. Since "like attracts like," the organization may find itself staffed by a rather homogenous group of employees. Research does suggest that this similarity in attraction effect extends beyond race and other salient characteristics, to also include deep-level characteristics such as skills and knowledge.[16] Hence, organizations that rely on creativity may suffer from the lack of diversity that follows employee referrals. Not only that, homogenous hiring may also put the company at risk for legal concerns such as discrimination (as outlined in Chapter 2). The positive benefits of employee referral systems suggest that they can be a powerful component to recruiting, although the concern about reduced diversity suggests that these systems should be used with caution and be supplemented by other techniques as well.

Convey organizational values

Being a member of an organization is an important part of one's social identity. As noted by Highhouse and colleagues,[17] job seekers pay attention to particular parts of an organization in deciding whether they are interested in applying. Drawing from the marketing literature, the researchers have delineated these organizational characteristics as instrumental or symbolic. The instrumental features of an organization are those that are more functional in nature (e.g., pay, benefits, and opportunities for advancement). In contrast, the symbolic features of an organization are those that provide meaning to the employee in terms of his/her social identity. Furthermore, social identity concerns included two dimensions: social adjustment and value expression. Social adjustment refers to an applicant's desire to impress others by his/her affiliation with high-status or high-prestige organization, while concern for value expression represents the job seeker's desire to express socially approved values.

When pay, type of work, and other instrumental values are equivalent, research suggests that symbolic values are what would attract an applicant to one's organization versus a competitor's. More importantly, conveying organizational values would lead to P-O fit as the applicant can assess whether these values match with his/her own. As noted above, P-O fit has positive outcomes for both the employee and the employer.

Provide realistic job information

Realistic job information, also called **realistic job previews** (RJPs), is as the name implies: information provided by the employer to realistically let the applicant know what it is like to work in the organization. Below are examples of RJPs from various organizations:

- Easyjet has an online quiz for prospective applicants to take to determine if the company and job are the right fit.
- Applicants to the Idaho State Police Department ride with real troopers during their shifts to talk about the job and observe.
- Sheetz, a convenience store group with 15,000 employees in 400 locations, presents detailed job profiles in an online audiovisual format by a beverage host or hostess, sales associate, shift supervisor, assistant manager, and associate manager.
- The Home Depot has a kiosk in its stores at which applicants may view videos of current employees at work.

> **Realistic Job Preview:** A recruitment tool used to inform applicants of the good and undesirable aspects of a job.

As can be seen in the examples listed above, there are many different methods of providing RJPs. Applicants may be exposed to realistic job information via booklets or brochures, multimedia presentations, testimonials on company websites, office tours, meetings with current employees, structured observations, or actually performing job duties as part of an informal audition. Research has indicated that the utility of an RJP may depend on the medium used to provide the information. In a meta-analysis on RJP effectiveness, Phillips (1998)[18] found that RJP methods incorporating a verbal, two-way communication process demonstrated more positive effects for later job satisfaction, commitment, and turnover than methods using a one-way communication channel (e.g., videos and brochures). Phillips concluded that RJP methods fostering more active processing of information will lead to more enduring attitude change among applicants. Although the type and complexity of the job may influence which method is most appropriate, the purpose of the RJP remains the same: to provide the applicant with a realistic understanding of what it would be like to work at the organization.

As the employer is trying to attract the applicant, it may seem counterintuitive to provide any information that may paint the organization or job in a negative light. Research suggests, however, that providing both positive and negative information leads to small though positive outcomes, such as increased credibility, reduced turnover, and higher job satisfaction.[19]

So, how do RJPs work to enhance positive outcomes? Several explanations exist. The first is that RJPs enhance self-selection. By being aware of undesirable information about the job or organization, the applicant may decide to not apply at all, withdraw from the hiring process, or not accept the job offer. Hence, only those who "fit" with the organization will remain through the whole process and if hired, will be more satisfied and more likely to remain with the organization. The second explanation for how RJPs work is based on expectations theory. As applicants may have high expectations based on the attractive features that organizations tend to emphasize in their recruitment efforts, RJPs may lower any unrealistic expectations.[20] A third possible explanation is that by providing RJPs, the applicant is led to believe that the organization is more honest and trustworthy.

In a 2011 meta-analysis,[21] researchers examined a number of mediator variables to unravel the relationship between RJPs and turnover. Similar to previous research, they found the overall effect to be modestly small corrected $r = -.07$). This study, however, did shed light on the mechanisms underlying the effects of RJPs. The researchers found that providing realistic job information led to applicant perceptions of honesty on the part of the organization, which then led to reduced voluntary turnover. The researchers also examined the design and timing of RJPs. To reduce turnover, the authors suggest orally providing realistic job information in the post-hire stage.

Internet-based recruiting

Like applicants, many employers have turned to the internet to recruit. A survey by CareerBuilder showed that 85% of 5,518 job candidates reported using the internet, with growing usage in social media platforms such as Facebook. As discussed above, applicants should be aware of employer biases when using these sources, and wary in how they maintain their internet profiles. For the employer, using the internet to merely attract applicants has numerous benefits in reaching more people. However, the advice is to not use social media profiles to screen or select applicants, due to the biases that can occur. In a recent study,[22] researchers found that recruiter ratings of applicants' Facebook information were unrelated to supervisor ratings of job performance, turnover intentions, and actual turnover. Furthermore, the researchers found evidence of subgroup difference in ratings that tended to favor female and White applicants. On a positive note, the internet may help organizations recruit candidates with specialized skills that are hard to find in their locale. For example, health care organizations in more rural areas often are faced with local talent shortages and may find that targeted recruitment using sites like LinkedIn may be effective in finding applicants to fill needed positions.

Although there are still many questions surrounding the use of social media, company websites serve as a valuable internet-based recruiting tool. Organizations can, and often do, tailor their websites toward recruitment by providing job-seekers with information about open positions, job descriptions, the organization's mission, goals, and values, and even employee and/or customer testimonials. Several studies have shown that recruiting websites can go a long way toward influencing applicants' perceptions of fit and attraction to the organization.[7,23] These websites may serve as a valuable self-screening tool for applicants, particularly when the website provides objective P-O fit feedback to prospective applicants.[24] This has led some to encourage companies to offer a "fit check," whereby applicants complete an online survey about their values and receive feedback as to how well they would likely fit within the organization based on their responses.[25] Regardless of whether formal P-O feedback is provided, recruiting websites have helped tremendously in streamlining the application process for both individuals and organizations.

Evaluating effectiveness of recruitment strategies

There are two general approaches organizations may use to assess the effectiveness of their recruitment strategy. The focus can be centered around characteristics of the recruitment process itself, or on the attitudes and outcomes of new hires. Each of these methods will be discussed below.

Evaluating the recruitment process

In evaluating a recruitment program, organizations are typically focused on numbers. How many applicants were generated? How many positions were filled? How long did the recruitment process take? How many dollars were spent? Two important criteria to consider include cost per new hire and yield ratio.[26]

Cost per new hire simply refers to the amount of money it takes to make a new hire. This can be calculated by taking the sum of all recruiting costs divided by the number of new hires

Recruitment

in a given time period. Research shows that recruiting is not cheap. In fact, a recent report from SHRM indicates that the average cost per new hire is around $4,700![27] This represents the *hard cost* associated with recruitment. When you factor in the *soft cost* – including the time and effort managers spend assisting in HR-specific functions of the hiring process – recruiting can consume a lot of resources beyond those that are strictly financial. Of course, the cost of hiring an employee will vary for different recruiting methods and different types of jobs. For example, posting a formal advertisement on an online job board will be more expensive than an informal employee referral. Accordingly, organizations must be diligent in determining when higher recruitment costs are justified and when they are not.

> **Cost Per New Hire:** A recruiting metric that measures the amount of money it takes to hire a new employee.

A second metric for evaluating the recruitment process is **yield ratio**, which is calculated by taking the number of new hires divided by the total number of applicants produced by a recruiting method. For example, if an online job posting generates 60 applicants, of which three are hired, the yield ratio would be 5%. A *recruiting yield pyramid* may also be used to track and evaluate the proportion of applicants that move from the initial stages of recruitment to later stages of the hiring process (see Figure 4.1). Companies may use this

Yield Ratio – 0.8%

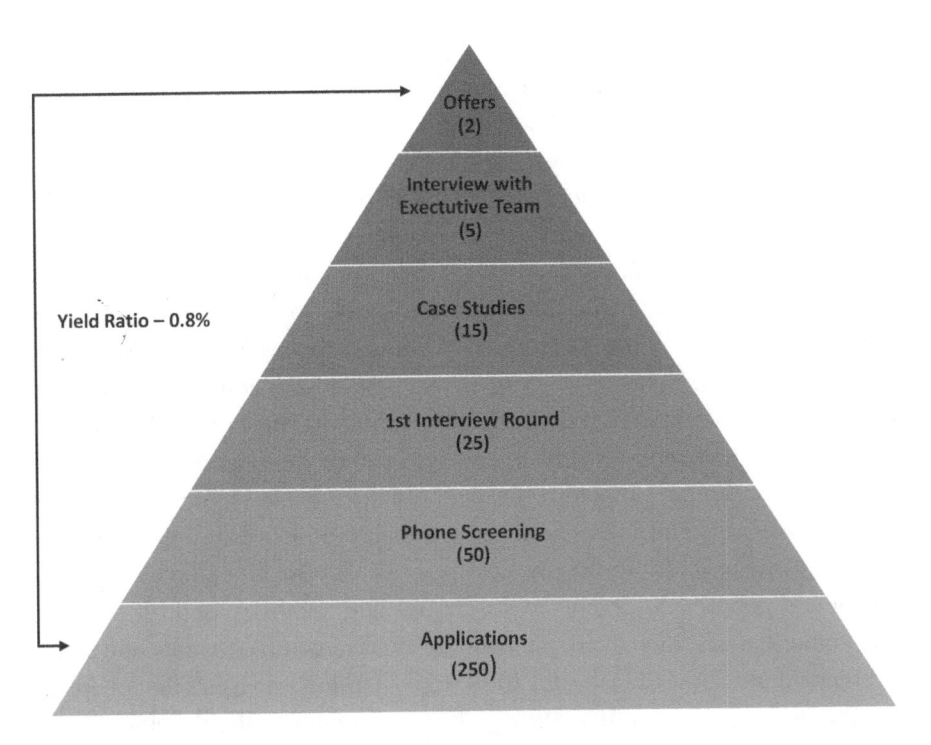

- Offers (2)
- Interview with Exectutive Team (5)
- Case Studies (15)
- 1st Interview Round (25)
- Phone Screening (50)
- Applications (250)

Figure 4.1 Recruiting yield pyramid

information to evaluate the effectiveness of a particular recruiting method, and/or to determine the number of applicants they must generate for future positions (provided they are using a similar recruiting method). Let's say an organization wants to hire four new managers for their company, and the yield ratio for their last round of manager recruitment was 2%. In this scenario, the company may estimate that they need 200 applicants in order to hire four new managers. Given that different recruitment methods may generate varying yield ratios, examining this information can be very helpful in the recruitment planning process.

Evaluating new hires

In addition to evaluating the aggregate numbers and ratios generated by the recruitment process, companies may also evaluate the newly hired employees. Of course, before applicants are hired, each candidate is assessed based on the KSAOs they possess. One way to examine the effectiveness of a recruitment strategy is by simply evaluating the quality of the applicant pool with regard to required KSAOs. A recruitment strategy that generates an unqualified applicant pool would obviously be deemed ineffective. Beyond this simple pre-hire evaluation, organizations are often interested in several post-hire outcomes as well.

Over and above a qualified applicant pool, organizations prefer that their recruitment methods result in high levels of job performance and job satisfaction, commitment to the organization, and low levels of turnover among hired applicants.[28] If the majority of new hires turn out to be mediocre performers with low satisfaction and high turnover, this should raise a red flag and the current recruiting methods should be re-evaluated. Companies may also want to know whether applicants' pre-hire expectations surrounding the job are met once they are hired. For example, if there is a trend among new hires indicating that the information presented during an RJP is not congruent with their actual work experiences, the organization may want to modify their RJP approach.

Finally, P-O fit represents a crucial part of the recruitment process for both individuals and organizations. Companies want to attract and hire applicants who are not only qualified, but also those who genuinely fit and want to stay at the organization. P-O fit is a large contributor to on-the-job outcomes and has been shown to be related to subsequent job satisfaction, commitment, and actual turnover.[29] Moreover, the effects of P-O fit do not stop at the individual level. Schneider's (1987)[30] Attraction-Selection-Attrition (ASA) model demonstrates the importance of P-O fit as a contributing factor to **organizational culture**. The first step of the ASA model asserts that people will be more attracted to organizations they perceive to be similar to themselves (e.g., the organization's goals and environment match their personality and values). The second step proposes that organizations will be more likely to recruit and hire people who possess KSAOs the company desires. These steps imply that people and organizations choose one another based on how well they meet each other's needs, directly in line with the ideas of complementary and supplementary fit discussed previously. Finally, the third step – attrition – suggests that people who do not fit within the organization will leave. A key contributor to the development of value congruence (i.e., P-O fit) is organizational goals.

> **Organizational Culture:** The shared values and beliefs that guide and inform member behavior within a workplace.

Taken as a whole, Schneider's ASA model indicates that an organization's culture will be shaped by the people who are recruited, selected, and stay at the organization. Moreover, organizational culture, in turn, can directly influence the types of applicants who become attracted to the organization.[31,32] Therefore, post-hire assessments of P-O fit may help organizations evaluate whether their recruitment methods are providing the right information about their organizational culture. To the extent that organizations can establish accurate applicant perceptions of P-O fit *during* the recruitment process, this will lead to more positive outcomes for both the employee and the organization. At the same time, however, the notion of P-O fit demonstrates the unpredictability associated with the recruitment process, as applicants may not develop a full comprehension of their P-O fit until after they are hired and gain some on-the-job experience.

Strategic workforce planning

Strategic workforce planning is a broad topic that includes a large recruitment component, but extends far beyond the recruitment process. Generally, you can think of **strategic workforce planning** as an HR initiative to plan for future staffing needs. This process typically involves many stakeholders and should be based on job analysis information, the current composition of the workforce, and anticipation of future needs. SHRM[33] outlines four key analyses integral to the strategic workforce planning process:

1. Supply analysis: examination of the organization's current labor supply and demographics
2. Demand analysis: review of future business plans and objectives
3. Gap analysis: comparison of supply and demand analyses to identify skill surpluses and deficiencies
4. Solution analysis: developing strategies to address the gaps between current staffing and future needs (e.g., recruiting, training and development programs, and outsourcing)

> **Strategic Workforce Planning:** Analyzing the workforce and preparing for future staffing needs.

This four steps entail many processes relating to the organization's overall mission, strategic plan, and future goals. An example of an intervention resulting from strategic workforce planning is **succession planning**. This involves identifying critical positions within the company and developing an action plan for filling those positions once they are vacated.

Succession planning is usually accomplished by (1) identifying current qualified employees who would be good candidates to fill a leadership role and (2) preparing them to assume the specified position. For example, if a top-level manager has expressed their plans to retire at the end of the year, the organization may not wait until the manager retires to fill the position. Rather, they may select a suitable predecessor and begin the transition process months in advance. The goal is to provide a seamless transition for the organization and its members. Thus, succession planning can be thought of as a specialized form of recruitment directed at identifying talent within the company.

> **Succession Planning:** The process of identifying and preparing employees to fill key roles within the company after current employees leave their position.

Summary

In this chapter, we discussed recruitment from the viewpoint of the applicant and the employer. From the applicant's perspective, the goal is in obtaining a job with a high degree of P-O fit based on value congruence. The goal for the employer is to attract the most qualified applicants who will likely stay at the organization once hired. To meet these goals, applicants should put forth due diligence in evaluating the position for which they applied and reflecting on what they desire in a work setting, and organizations should be transparent as to what the day-to-day working conditions entail. If each does their part, the recruitment process will end in a mutually satisfactory relationship between the hired applicant and their employer.

REVIEW QUESTIONS

1. What is the definition of recruitment?
2. Compare and contrast recruitment and selection.
3. Compare and contrast prospecting versus mating theories of recruitment.
4. Compare and contrast applicant and employer perspectives on recruitment.
5. What are the goals of recruitment for organizations?
6. What are some commonly used recruitment tactics, and the research regarding each?
7. What is the difference between extrinsic and intrinsic factors in organizational attraction?
8. What is social identity theory and how is this theory related to recruitment?
9. What realistic job information and why it is important?
10. What are ways organizations evaluating their recruitment strategies to determine if they are successful?

DISCUSSION QUESTIONS

1. Consider the goals of recruitment for the employer and the applicant. Where is there the greatest conflict? What can each party do to align their interests?
2. Personally, are you more attracted by intrinsic or extrinsic offers?
3. When do you think realistic job information should be presented to applicants? In what format (video-based, in-person, written) do you think realistic job information would be most effective?
4. Do you think it is unethical for an employer to exaggerate the positive aspects of a job, or to hide the negative aspects from applicants?
5. Think of a job for which you have recently applied. What attracted you to apply? Did you use any information to determine if you would be a good fit with the organization?

Activities

1. Think of one or two organizations for which you would love to work. Why are you attracted to these employers? Do any of the theories of attraction support your feelings?
2. Visit the hiring websites of two different organizations. Then using theories of recruitment presented in this chapter, evaluate these websites in terms of how effective they are in attracting applicants. What tactics are effective? What would you recommend to improve the website?

Notes

1. Zottoli, M. A., & Wanous, J. P. (2000). Recruitment source research: Current status and future directions. *Human Resource Management Review, 10,* 353–382.
2. Slaughter, J. E., & Highhouse, S. (2003). Does matching up features mess up job choice? Boundary conditions on attribute-salience effects. *Journal of Behavioral Decision Making, 16*(1), 1–15.
3. Kristof-Brown, A., Zimmerman, R. D., & Johnson, E. C. (2005). Consequences of individual's fit at work: A meta-analysis of person-job, person-organization, person-group, and person-supervisor fit. *Personnel Psychology, 58*(2), 281–342.
4. Kristof, A. L. (1996). Person-organization fit: An integrative review of its conceptualizations, measurement, and implications. *Personnel Psychology, 49*(1), 1–49.
5. Cable, D. M., & Edwards, J. R. (2004). Complementary fit and supplementary fit: A theoretical and empirical integration. *Journal of Applied Psychology, 89*(5), 822–834.
6. Cable, D. M., & Judge, T. A. (1996). Person–organization fit, job choice decisions, and organizational entry. *Organizational Behavior and Human Decision Processes, 67*(3), 294–311.
7. Uggerslev, K. L., Fassina, N. E., & Kraichy, D. (2012). Recruiting through the stages: A meta-analytic test of predictors of applicant attraction at different stages of the recruiting process. *Personnel Psychology, 65*(3), 597–660.

8. Braddy, P. W., Meade, A. W., & Kroustalis, C. M. (2006). Organizational recruitment effects on viewers' perceptions of organizational culture. *Journal of Business and Psychology, 20,* 525–543.
9. Society for Human Resource Management. (2013, April, 11). Social networking websites and recruiting/selection. https://www.shrm.org/hr-today/trends-and-forecasting/research-and-surveys/pages/shrm-social-networking-websites-recruiting-job-candidates.aspx
10. Brown, V. R. & Vaughn, E. D. (2011). The writing on the (Facebook) wall: The use of social networking sites in hiring decisions. *Journal of Business Psychology, 26*(2), 219–225.
11. Acquisti, A. & Fong, C.M. (2015). An experiment in hiring discrimination via online social networks. http://ssrn.com/abstract=2031979 or http://dx.doi.org/10.2139/ssrn.2031979
12. Christine, Q. T., Rynes, S. L., & Bretz, Robert D., Jr. (2002). Attracting applicants in the war for talent: Differences in work preferences among high achievers. *Journal of Business and Psychology, 16*(3), 331.
13. Konrad, A. M., Corrigall, E., Lieb, P., & Ritchie, J. E. (2000). Sex differences in job attribute preferences among managers and business students. *Group & Organization Management, 25*(2), 108–131.
14. Combs, G. M., Milosevic, I., Jeung, W., & Griffith, J. (2012). Ethnic identity and job attribute preferences: The role of collectivism and psychological capital. *Journal of Leadership & Organizational Studies, 19*(1), 5–16.
15. Zottoli, M. A., & Wanous, J. P. (2000). Recruitment source research: Current status and future directions. *Human Resource Management Review, 10*(4), 353–382.
16. Schlachter, S. D., & Pieper, J. R. (2019). Employee referral hiring in organizations: An integrative conceptual review, model, and agenda for future research. *Journal of Applied Psychology, 104,* 1325–1346.
17. Highhouse, S., Lievens, F., & Sinar, E. F. (2003). Measuring attraction to organizations. *Educational and Psychological Measurement, 63*(6), 986–1001. Highhouse, S., Thornbury, E. E., & Little, I. S. (2007). Social-identity functions of attraction to organizations. *Organizational Behavior and Human Decision Processes, 103*(1), 134–146.
18. Phillips, J. M. (1998). Effects of realistic job previews on multiple organizational outcomes: A meta-analysis. *Academy of Management Journal, 41*(6), 673–690.
19. Breaugh, J. A. (2013). Employee recruitment. *Annual Review of Psychology, 64,* 389–416.
20. Breaugh, J. A., & Starke, M. (2000). Research on employee recruitment: So many studies, so many remaining questions. *Journal of Management, 26*(3), 405–434.
21. Earnest, D. R., Allen, D. G., & Landis, R. S. (2011). Mechanisms linking realistic job previews with turnover: A meta-analytic path analysis. *Personnel Psychology, 64*(4), 865–897. http://dx.doi.org/10.1111/j.1744-6570.2011.01230.x
22. Van Iddekinge, C. H., Lanivich, S. E., Roth, P. L., & Junco, E. (2016). Social media for selection? Validity and adverse impact potential of a Facebook-based assessment. *Journal of Management, 42*(7), 1811–1835.
23. Cober, R. T., Brown, D. J., Keeping, L. M., & Levy, P. E. (2004). Recruitment on the net: How do organizational website characteristics influence applicant attraction? *Journal of Management, 30*(5), 623–646.
24. Dineen, B. R., Ash, S. R., & Noe, R. A. (2002). A web of applicant attraction: Person-organization fit in the context of web-based recruitment. *Journal of Applied Psychology, 87*(4), 723–734.
25. Barrick, M. R., & Parks-Leduc, L. (2019). Selection for fit. *Annual Review of Organizational Psychology and Organizational Behavior, 6,* 171–193.
26. Rafaeli, A., Hadomi, O., & Simons, T. (2005). Recruitment though advertising or employee referrals: Costs, yields, and the effects of geographic focus. *European Journal of Work and Organizational Psychology, 14*(4), 355–366.

27. Navarra, K. (2022, June 23). *The real costs of recruitment*. Society for Human Resource Management. https://www.shrm.org/resourcesandtools/hr-topics/talent-acquisition/pages/the-real-costs-of-recruitment.aspx
28. Breaugh, J. A. (2008). Employee recruitment: Current knowledge and important areas for future research. *Human Resource Management Review, 18*(3), 103–118.
29. O'Reilly, C. A., Chatman, J., & Caldwell, D. F. (1991). People and organizational culture: A profile comparison approach to assessing person-organization fit. *Academy of Management Journal, 34*(3), 487–516.
30. Schneider, B. (1987). The people make the place. *Personnel Psychology, 40,* 437–454.
31. Catanzaro, D., Moore, H., & Marshall, T. R. (2010). The impact of organizational culture on attraction and recruitment of job applicants. *Journal of Business and Psychology, 25,* 649–662.
32. Judge, T. A., & Cable, D. M. (1997). Applicant personality, organizational culture, and organization attraction. *Personnel Psychology, 50*(2), 359–394.
33. Society for Human Resource Management. (2022, June 23). *Practicing the Discipline of Workforce Planning*. https://www.shrm.org/resourcesandtools/tools-and-samples/toolkits/pages/practicingworkforceplanning.aspx

5 Validity

LEARNING OBJECTIVES

- Understand the concept of validity
- Know the meanings of predictor and criterion terms
- Understand the inferential linkages made between constructs and measures
- Be able to compare and contrast criterion-related and content-related validation studies
- Be able to compare and contrast predictive and concurrent studies
- Know the major steps in the various validation studies
- Know the approaches to content validation
- Know the difference between a local validity study and validity generalization

Personnel selection is ultimately about being able to make predictions regarding how applicants will behave after they have been hired. We cannot fully trust human judgment and decision-making to make such predictions. This chapter is about the types of evidence I-O psychologists rely upon to make more accurate predictions. Specifically, we will cover how validation studies are conducted to establish inferences between what we can find out about applicants before they are hired and what we are hoping to assess in terms of their behaviors on the job.

The concept of validity

The decisions that are made based on psychological measures can have a significant impact on people's lives. For example, somebody may get the job they have always desired because they scored well on a particular test, or they may be denied an important promotion because they performed poorly on a promotional examination. To justify using a test, we need to make sure that it is valid for our intended purpose. **Construct validity**, often referred to simply as validity, is the extent to which we are able to draw inferences from any measure we use to assess a human trait, behavior, or condition.[1] Establishing construct validity is a process. There are several types of evidence, as well as multiple types of data collections that can be used to demonstrate validity. The first step in the validation process is verifying the reliability of the measure(s) being used.

> **Construct Validity:** The extent to which we are able to draw inferences from any measure used to assess a human trait, behavior, or condition.

Reliability as a necessary precondition

Reliability refers to *consistency* in measurement. For example, if we measure a person's eye color at one time and then again at another time, we would get the same results. With the exception of a minority of people whose eye color changes, the majority of us would have blue, brown, hazel, or green eyes at both points in time. This test can be said to be perfectly reliable. To use a more psychological example, let's say we administered a cognitive ability test to someone and then gave this person the same test again six months later. To the extent that a person's intelligence does not change within such a timeframe and they have not memorized the contents of the test, we would expect the two test scores to be highly correlated. Consistency across the two test scores would demonstrate *test-retest reliability*. Unlike eye color, however, there will always be a certain amount of measurement error involved when assessing psychological constructs. Accordingly, although we strive for a high degree of consistency in our measures, we cannot expect to obtain perfect reliability when measuring psychological constructs.

> **Reliability:** The consistency of a measure.

Another method of demonstrating reliability involves gauging whether different observers provide similar ratings in their evaluation of others (i.e., *inter-rater reliability*). This method of assessment may be useful for determining the reliability of employment interviews. If two people observe the same interview and come up with similar ratings of the interviewee's likelihood of success on the job, this would demonstrate high inter-rater reliability. If raters differ widely in their assessments, then we would say that the inter-rater reliability was low.

Finally, many psychological constructs (e.g., personality, intelligence, and ability) are measured by using multiple items on a standardized psychological assessment. *Internal consistency reliability* examines whether individuals tend to respond consistently across all of the items within a particular measure. For example, if we used a five-item measure to assess your level of sociability, we would expect you to respond similarly to each of the five items on that measure. Given that each item is presumed to be measuring the same construct, the items should yield similar responses. If there is a lot of within-person variability across the five sociability items, this measure would have low internal consistency reliability. A general standard that is often used to indicate acceptable reliability is an inter-item correlation of .8 or above.

In summary, reliability refers to the extent to which a measure is consistent across time (test-retest), between raters (inter-rater), or across items (internal consistency). A measure with low reliability has substantial error influencing individual scores. In other words, the measure is untrustworthy. Just as you would not trust an unreliable person to show up on time, psychologists cannot trust an unreliable measure when making personnel decisions. Although establishing reliability is an important part of the validation process, this does not ensure validity. Imagine we use eye color to assess an individual's intelligence. Although our measure is sure to be reliable (i.e., a person's eye color will not change), we cannot make accurate inferences about a person's intelligence based on a measure of eye color. This demonstrates the distinction between reliability (i.e., consistency) and validity (i.e., ability to draw inferences). Reliability is simply concerned with consistency in measurement whereas validity is concerned with the operational definition of the measure itself. Therefore, reliability is necessary, but not sufficient, for establishing construct validity. Once reliability has been established, we can move on to explore additional pieces of validity evidence.

Sources of validity evidence

After establishing reliability, we want to ensure that the measure(s) we use actually represents the construct(s) we hoped to measure in the first place. In other words, does our chosen assessment measure what it purports to measure? This question directly addresses the adequacy of the operational definition for a given variable. Let's say we are giving a cognitive ability test to job applicants. Surely, we want to make sure that this test is actually assessing levels of intelligence, and not some other construct (especially if it's not related to the job!). As part of this process, one may simply look at the items on the assessment and reflect on whether the instrument *seems* like a good measure. This is known as **face validity**, and represents a shallow and informal source of validity evidence. However, it may serve as a useful starting point when selecting assessments. If, for some reason, a researcher did use a measure of eye color to represent the construct of intelligence, this would fail to pass the face validity test. When an operational definition is this blatantly off base, it is obviously not useful for our intended purpose of measuring intelligence.

> **Face Validity:** A subjective assessment of whether a test appears (at face value) to cover the concept it purports to measure.

A more formal approach for evaluating whether a test measures what it purports to measure is by examining convergent and discriminant validities. Both of these sources of validity evidence rely on calculating a correlation coefficient. **Convergent validity** refers to the extent to which a measure is correlated with other similar measures. If a test is developed to measure one's spatial ability, for example, this test should be positively correlated with other tests of spatial ability. At the same time, a test of spatial ability should not be related to constructs that are theoretically unrelated to spatial ability, such as the personality trait of agreeableness. These two constructs have no relation to one another and there is no theoretical rationale for why they should be related. Therefore, to demonstrate **discriminant validity**, a measure should provide scores that differentiate the measured construct from dissimilar constructs. Taken together, convergent and discriminant validities provide formal evidence that your measure is assessing what you expect it to measure.

> **Convergent Validity:** The extent to which a measure is correlated with other theoretically similar constructs.

> **Discriminant Validity:** The extent to which a measure is uncorrelated with other theoretically dissimilar constructs.

In addition to demonstrating convergent and discriminant validities, we also want to be sure that a measure provides a complete picture of the construct we are measuring. **Content validity** is concerned with whether a measurement instrument fully captures the entirety of the construct of interest. You can think of content validity as *coverage*. For example, if a test purports to measure a person's mathematical ability, but only contains questions involving addition and subtraction, this measure would be lacking content validity as it neglects to include two important mathematical components: multiplication and division. A test including questions related to addition, subtraction, multiplication, and division would demonstrate adequate content validity (i.e., coverage) of the mathematical ability construct.

> **Content Validity:** The extent to which a measure adequately covers the entirety of the construct of interest.

Finally, tests/measures are typically not used in a vacuum, but for a given purpose. In the personnel context, we are interested in inferring future work behavior[3] from test scores because selection is ultimately about prediction. In other words, we are interested in **criterion-related validity**, which provides evidence of an empirical relationship between scores on a specific measure and work-related behaviors and outcomes. For example, we may use a test of spatial ability to try to predict future performance on jobs requiring spatial tasks (e.g., architects and engineers). To ensure the adequacy of our predictions, we would collect data – before and/or after using the test – to ensure that scores on the spatial ability test are, indeed, related to performance on tasks completed within the job of interest.

> **Criterion-related Validity:** The extent to which scores on a measure are empirically related to work behaviors and outcomes.

To summarize, construct validity is a complex process involving multiple sources of evidence. Later in this chapter, we will describe studies that are conducted to obtain these different kinds of validity evidence. Regardless of the type of validity study being conducted, it is important to keep in mind that these different strategies to validation all attempt to accomplish the same goal of assessing a test's ability to make particular inferences of interest. Validity itself is a unitary concept.[4,5] We may rely on various types of evidence to support our ability to make inferences, but this is all subsumed under a single definition of validity.

What are we validating?

Now that you understand the concept of validity, you may be wondering what it is we are validating. Simply put, we are validating the inferences we make from the use of a selection measure. For example, if we administer a physical ability test to individuals applying for the job of a firefighter, we are hoping to infer from their scores how well they will perform during rescues which require carrying heavy loads of equipment and possibly victims. Although it is often claimed that a particular test is valid, that is an inaccurate usage of the concept of validity. Tests are not by themselves valid. They are only valid for particular inferences or purposes. A physical ability test may very well be valid for predicting how well the firefighter will meet the physical demands of the job, but not whether s/he will steal from the scenes of fires.

We are using the term "measure" quite broadly to mean whatever we are using to assess any human trait, behavior, or condition. These selection measures may take the form of paper-and-pencil or computer-administered tests such as cognitive and personality tests, screening tools such as the resume or application, or hands-on assessments such as physical ability or simulated performance tests. There are many other terms used to refer to selection measures, including (but not limited to) "tools," "devices," "methods," "procedures," "assessments," "tests," and "predictors." Although most of these terms are often used interchangeably and without much confusion, the latter two terms need further clarification. First, the term "test" is not simply referring to tests of facts or knowledge. Rather, the term is used in a much broader sense within the I-O psychology literature to include assessments of personality and interests, and even selection procedures such as the interview, references, or background checks.

Within this list, the term *predictor* (or selection predictor) is most commonly used in the technical and scientific literature to refer to a measure used in selection. It is important, however, to distinguish between the construct being measured and the method or procedure used to measure the construct. The **predictor construct** is "a specific behavioral domain" that can arise from theories of psychological constructs or job demands.[6] In the personnel context, these are the knowledge, skills, abilities, and other attributes (KSAOs) uncovered via a job analysis. For example, cognitive ability, conscientiousness, and physical ability are all predictor constructs relevant to the job of a firefighter. The **predictor measure** refers to the specific method used to elicit specific behavioral domain information or KSAOs.[7] To measure cognitive ability, we could use a predictor measure such as a computer-administered test of cognitive ability or even a job interview.[8] Thus, the predictor construct is abstract, whereas the predictor measure is directly observable.

> **Predictor Construct:** A specific behavioral domain that can arise from theories of psychological constructs or demands of the job.

> **Predictor Measure:** The specific method used to elicit specific behavioral domain information or KSAOs.

What are we inferring?

Because selection is ultimately about prediction, we are trying to infer subsequent work behavior based upon predictor measure data. For example, will firefighter applicants who score higher on a cognitive ability test have fewer accidents than those with lower scores?

Will those who score higher on a test of conscientiousness be less absent or tardy from work? Will they help co-workers out even if this is not part of their formal job description? We are trying to infer what their job behaviors or outcomes will be in the future. These job behaviors or outcomes are referred to as the **job performance domain**,[9] which may be uncovered by conducting a job analysis, or may be set by the standards, expectations, or values of the organization. For instance, safety behaviors may be part of the job performance domain for a firefighter.

> **Job Performance Domain:** Job behaviors or outcomes as defined by job analysis, organizational standards, expectations, and values.

> **Criterion Measure:** A measure of the job performance domain.

Similar to the predictor construct, the job performance domain is an underlying construct not to be confused with the method used to assess the construct. The **criterion measure** is the method used to assess the job behaviors or outcomes. For example, safety behaviors as a job performance domain may be measured by gathering data regarding the number of accidents a firefighter has within a certain time period. This safety report is the criterion measure of the job performance domain of safety. Other commonly used criterion measures include (but are not limited to) supervisor ratings, training program scores, sales, error rates, productivity indices, absenteeism, and length of time on the job (job tenure).

See Figure 5.1 for a visual summary of what we have covered thus far. Linkage 1 refers to whether the underlying construct being measured by a test is related to the job performance domain. Inferential linkage 2 refers to the content validity of the predictor measure

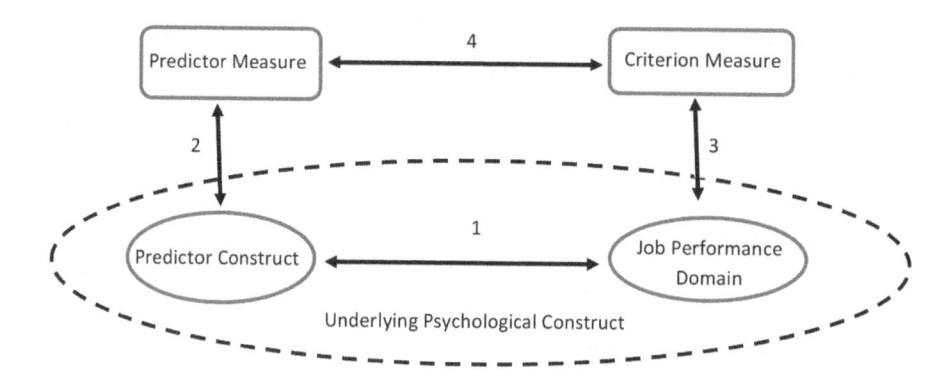

Figure 5.1 A framework for conceptualizing the inferences for personnel selection
Adapted from Arthur and Villado (2008)[2]

in terms of how well it captures the predictor construct. Inferential linkage 3 refers to the content validity of the criterion measure in terms of how well it captures the job performance domain.

When inferring subsequent work behavior from predictor measures, we are interested in linkage 4 or the relationship between the predictor and criterion measures. To put this in perspective, recall the definition of a hypothesis as a predictive statement regarding the relationship between variables or differences between groups. Validation is ultimately hypothesis testing[10] as we are seeing if there is a relationship between scores on a predictor measure and a criterion measure. Below, we will cover the specific types of validation studies that are conducted to establish this relationship.

Validation studies

As noted above, various types of evidence may be gathered to examine the validity of inferences we are trying to make from using a predictor measure. There are various types of validation studies that may be conducted to gather evidence of validity. Regardless of the study used, the goal of a predictor measure is to determine whether scores on those measures will predict effectiveness on the job.[11] Below, we cover the various types, beginning with criterion-related validation studies.

Criterion-related validation studies

Criterion-related studies help us assess how effective a predictor measure is in predicting job effectiveness by examining the empirical relationship between scores on the predictor measure and scores on the criterion measure. There are two types of criterion-related validation studies. The first is the **concurrent validity study**. In this type of study, participants are current employees (job incumbents) to whom we would administer the predictor and criterion measures. Once we obtain these scores, we would statistically analyze them to see if there is a possible relationship.

The second type of criterion-related validity study is equally empirical and also involves examining the relationship between scores on the predictor measure and scores on the criterion measure. Rather than using job incumbents as participants, we would collect predictor and criterion measure scores from job applicants. This type of criterion-related study is called a **predictive validity study**. Let's say, for example, we are interested in using a personality test to assess job applicants for the job of a customer service representative. We would assess the applicants using what predictor measure has already been in place; in addition, we would give them the personality test. Then at some point later when we have data on the criterion measure, we would analyze the data to see if there is a statistically significant relationship. If there is, this would provide evidence of criterion-related validity by showing that the personality test is related to work outcomes. It is important to

Validity

note here that the predictor measure being studied in the predictive validity study not be used to make hiring decisions until there is demonstrated evidence of validity.

> **Concurrent Validity Study:** A type of criterion-related validation study, which involves collecting predictor and criterion scores from job incumbents, then analyzing the data to examine the relationship between predictor and criterion measures.

> **Predictive Validity Study:** A type of criterion-related validation study which involves collecting predictor and criterion scores from job applicants, then analyzing the data to examine the relationship between predictor and criterion measures.

Table 5.1 outlines the major steps in the concurrent validation and the predictive validation studies. Note that both involve conducting a job analysis to identify KSAOs (or predictor constructs). Thereafter, the steps continue to be similar, with the major difference being whom we collect scores from (job incumbents versus applicants). Also, a practical difference exists between the two. The predictive study takes more time because we have to wait until our applicants have worked on the jobs long enough in order to collect criterion data. In contrast, scores on a criterion measure would be currently available if participants are job incumbents. Although concurrent validity studies can be completed more quickly, a challenge is **range restriction** on the job performance measures. Presumably, individuals who are incumbents over a period of time remain in their job because they are successful performers. Therefore, the criterion measure may have less variance for incumbents than for a sample of newer employees, some who may eventually be dismissed because

Table 5.1 Steps in concurrent validation versus predictive validation studies

Concurrent validation	Predictive validation
1. Conduct a job analysis to identify KSAOs	1. Conduct a job analysis to identify KSAOs
2. Choose predictor measures	2. Choose predictor measures
3. Administer predictor measures to job incumbents	3. Administer predictor measures to job applicants
4. Gather appropriate criterion data	4. Wait for an appropriate amount of time to gather criterion data
5. Statistically analyze data to examine relationship between predictor measure scores and criterion measure scores	5. Gather appropriate criterion data
	6. Statistically analyze data to examine relationship between predictor measure scores and criterion measure scores

of low performance. Range restriction is a problem because it can result in lower correlations. There are statistical techniques for correcting range restriction but they require knowing what the variance for a measure is in an unrestricted sample, a challenge for many employers.

When is a predictor measure considered to be "valid" in criterion-related validation studies?

Because of the empirical nature of criterion-related validation studies, statistical analyses are conducted to determine the relationship between predictor measure and criterion measure scores. Most commonly, correlational analysis is used to analyze the data. A correlation coefficient tells us the strength and direction of the relationship between variables. In validating predictor measures, the correlation coefficient is referred to as a **validity coefficient**. The conventional *p*-value of .05 is typically used as the standard level to determine statistical significance. Therefore, at $p < .05$, the validity coefficient is considered to be statistically significant. It is important to note that factors such as the sample size of the study can affect the observed *p*-values. Therefore, when conducting criterion-related validation studies, the researcher needs to be aware of this issue when interpreting results. Failing to do so may result in concluding that a predictor measure is not valid when in fact it really is (i.e., a Type II error in statistical language), or concluding a predictor measure is valid when it in fact is not (i.e., a Type I error).

> **Validity Coefficient:** A term used in personnel selection to refer to the correlation coefficient (Pearson's *r*), which tells us the strength and direction of the relationship between predictor measure and criterion measure scores.

Another way to statistically determine validity is to obtain effect sizes, such as **the coefficient of determination**. Statistically denoted as r^2, the coefficient of determination is obtained by simply squaring the validity coefficient. It tells us the amount of variance in scores on the criterion measure that is accounted for by the variance of scores on the predictor measure. Let's say we have conducted a concurrent validity study and have administered a cognitive ability test (predictor measure) and gathered productivity rates (criterion measure) of employees at a computer factory. It is to be expected that we will obtain many different scores on the predictor measure as well as on the criterion measure. In other words, we will observe variability in scores. The extent to which this variability is shared between the predictor measure and the criterion measure is r^2. If we analyze the data and find that the validity coefficient of a cognitive ability test in predicting productivity rates is $r = .50$, r^2 would then be .25. This means that 25% of the variance in productivity rates is accounted for by the variance in scores on the cognitive ability test. This may not sound like much, but performance – like all human behavior – is difficult to predict, and any amount of variance that we *can* explain is important and valuable in the personnel selection process. Thinking about the validity coefficient in terms of how much variance is accounted for by the predictor measure puts a bit more meaning into r and also addresses the possibility that a small validity coefficient may still obtain statistical significance due to a large sample size.

> **Coefficient of Determination:** The amount of variance in scores on the criterion measure that is accounted for by the variance of scores on the predictor measure.

Another way to decide whether the inferences we are making from a predictor measure are valid is to compare the validity of a single predictor to other potential predictor measures. One way to do this is to examine **incremental validity**. A predictor measure is said to have incremental validity if it explains additional variance in the criterion measure beyond existing predictor measures. In other words, incremental validity is concerned with whether a measure adds additional predictive power after all the other predictor measures have been taken into account. Let's say, for example, that a fire department is currently using a physical ability test, a cognitive ability test, and a job interview to assess job applicants. Would adding a personality test allow us to predict any more of the variance in job effectiveness, above and beyond what is already accounted for by the existing measures? Considering the incremental validity of predictor measures is important because the results of a validity study may show that a measure alone does not yield a high validity coefficient. However, it may still add to the overall predictive power of the entire selection process because it contributes prediction above and beyond existing measures.

> **Incremental Validity:** The increase in predictive ability provided by an additional predictor measure.

When incremental validity can be established, it is common for selection systems to include multiple predictor measures (often referred to as a test battery) for a single criterion. In such situations, the validity coefficient would be presented as R, signifying the *multiple correlation* between several predictor measures and the criterion measure. Similarly, the coefficient of determination would be designated as R^2, representing the proportion of variance in the criterion that can be accounted for by the *multiple* predictor measures. Thus, although they are conceptually similar, r and r^2 are based on bivariate correlations (i.e., a single predictor), whereas R and R^2 are based on multiple correlations (i.e., two or more predictors).

Another type of comparison can be made by examining norms that are published by academic researchers and test publishers. Let's say we find in our own validity study that the validity coefficient of a cognitive ability test in predicting job performance is .30. Knowing that cognitive ability tests generally have higher validity coefficients should lead us to consider reasons why the validity coefficient obtained in our own study is lower, besides prematurely dismissing the predictor measure as being useless. For example, we could have chosen an inappropriate criterion, or one or both of the measures demonstrate low reliability, or we had an inadequate sample. Research has shown that much of the variation in obtained validity coefficients in different studies may be attributed to statistical artifacts and sampling error.[12] Failure to detect a relationship that in truth exists (i.e., Type II error) could cause us to miss using an effective selection tool. By knowing what norms are, and comparing them, we are really gaining further evidence of validity.

What is needed to conduct a criterion-related validation study?

In order to carry out a criterion-related validation study, a number of requirements need to be met. The first two conditions are the same ones that need to be met in any good research study. First, we need to have an adequate sample size in order to conduct a meaningful statistical analysis. Second, we need to have a representative sample from the population of interest. As you may recall from previous courses, the sample is the group of people we actually study, whereas the population is the group of people whom we really want to study. In the case of criterion-validation studies, the population is all job applicants because those are the individuals who we really want to know about, in terms of whether their scores on predictor measures relate to scores on criterion measures. The sample, or the group we actually study, may only consist of current employees or, if they are job applicants, the sample may consist of applicants only at a specific time period. The sample of job applicants included in a particular predictive validation study may be meaningfully different from the entire pool of potential applicants. For example, if our sample includes only female participants, we would not be able to generalize the findings to the entire population which includes both female and male applicants.

After obtaining a sample, we need a construct-valid measure of the job performance domain (i.e., criterion measure). Current reports suggest that performance data in many organizations is severely lacking or flawed.[13] Therefore, any criterion measure data should be as carefully gathered and considered as predictor measure data. For concurrent validation studies which involve job incumbents, participants should be employees whose performance has stabilized (typically six months to a year, depending on the complexity of the job).

Finally, communication is critical to carrying out a good validity study. For the concurrent study, it is highly important to clearly communicate to employees from whom we are administering predictor and criterion measures the intent of the study (i.e., to validate a predictor measure, and not to make any firing decisions). As discussed in Chapter 3, job incumbents who fear for their job security may inflate tasks and/or KSAOs when providing data for a job analysis. Similarly, job incumbents in concurrent validity studies may not perform at their "true" level, thereby compromising the integrity of any gathered data.

Thus far, we have discussed criterion-related validation studies as if they are conducted for a specific job within a specific organization. Such studies are referred to as **local validity studies.** As discussed earlier, sampling represents a key issue. One of the reasons sampling is so important is the fact that the validity coefficients resulting from a local validity study are optimized for the specific sample that was used. Given that there is error associated with any particular sample (i.e., sampling error), the prediction equation generated in one sample will usually not perform quite as well in another new sample. As a result, the coefficient of determination may be smaller (i.e., shrink) when applying original test data from a local validation study to a new sample of applicants. This phenomenon is known as **validity shrinkage** and represents a potential problem for the organization when seeking to maximize predictive accuracy.

> **Local Validity Study:** Validity study conducted for a specific job within a specific organization.

> **Validity Shrinkage:** Reduction in the coefficient of determination when applying a predictive equation to new data.

One potential way to gather information on validity shrinkage is to perform **cross-validation**, in which a researcher splits the original sample into two subsets. One subset of participants is used for generating a validity coefficient and subsequent prediction equation, and the second subset is then used to apply the prediction equation to produce predicted scores for participants on the criterion measure. The predicted scores for members of the second sample can then be correlated with their actual, observed scores on the criterion measure to generate a *cross-validity coefficient*. The difference between the original validity coefficient and the cross-validity coefficient would represent validity shrinkage. To the extent that shrinkage is smaller, we can be more confident in the generalizability of our original sample data.

> **Cross-Validation:** A validation method that uses multiple subsets of data to examine the predictive accuracy of a test/model.

Validity generalization

There are a number of requirements that need to be met in order to carry out a local validity study. Many small businesses, however, would not have an adequate sample for meaningful statistical analyses inherent to criterion-related validation studies. For example, a popular coffee shop in Bowling Green, Ohio, Grounds for Thought, has about 15 employees, a sample too small to accurately estimate correlations. Fortunately, **validity generalization** allows us to "generalize" evidence of validity from other studies to the current job for which a local validity study is not possible.

Validity generalization is essentially based upon the use of **meta-analysis** to provide accumulated evidence of validity for a specific predictor measure, across many different jobs, organizations, and samples. Meta-analytic evidence of validity is more useful than validity provided by a single local study[14] given the limitations of any individual study (e.g., small sample, sampling biases, and low reliability of measures). However, great care must be taken to ensure the quality of the meta-analysis, and appropriateness of inferring the evidence of validity to a different situation. For instance, it would not be appropriate to use evidence of validity for studies of a managerial job to an entry-level job.[15]

> **Validity Generalization:** Based upon evidence of validity accumulated from many studies using meta-analysis, validity is generalized to a specific job for which a local validity may not have been possible.

> **Meta-Analysis:** A research design that combines the results of multiple studies on the same topic to compute an overall effect size.

When empirical validation is not possible, either through a local validity study or validity generalization, organizations may use the synthetic validation approach. **Synthetic validity** is defined as the logical process of inferring the validity of a test battery based on the relationships between job components and tests of the attributes needed to perform those components.[16,17] The general premise of synthetic validity is that if we know the basic components of a job, we can then synthesize a combination of valid predictors based on a review of previous research on those predictors and their association with job components. Mossholder and Arvey (1984) present the following example to demonstrate the general process of synthetic validity:

> Assume that for four tests (A, B, C, D) and four job components (1, 2, 3, 4), it has been shown that the tests predict component performance in the following fashion: A with 1, B with 2, C with 3, and D with 4. If it has been determined through job analysis that particular components (e.g., 1 and 4) comprise the essence of a given job, it would be possible to assemble a valid test battery by including the appropriate tests (i.e., A and D) and weighting them properly. The validity of the battery is inferred from preexisting information about job component and test relationships. (p. 323)

> **Synthetic Validity:** The logical process of inferring validity based on the relationships between job components and tests of the attributes needed to perform those components.

The synthetic validation process involves three steps.[15,16] First, a job analysis is conducted to identify key job components. Second, predictor tests are selected based on a review of prior research demonstrating the relationships between relevant job components and predictor tests. A general assumption of this step is that the validity of a predictor for a particular job component is relatively constant across jobs. The third and final step involves developing a test battery based on the validity evidence collected in step 2. In other words, the validity of the chosen predictor(s) is estimated and inferred based on previous research.

Synthetic validity represents a creative validation method and can be particularly useful when traditional criterion-related validation is not possible (e.g., for newly created jobs and jobs with small sample sizes). Although there is not much legal precedent when it comes to synthetic validity, there is evidence to suggest that synthetic validity coefficients are very similar to validity coefficients calculated in traditional local validation studies.[18]

Content-related validation studies

As outlined above, there are certain requirements that have to be met in order for criterion-related validation studies to be conducted. What should an organization do when any or all of these requirements are not met? For example, what if the sample size is too small for meaningful statistical analyses? What if there is not a good criterion measure? The Uniform Guidelines specifies the use of content validation to establish the validity of a predictor measure. Compared to the criterion-related studies, content-related validity studies do not require data from a criterion measure. Instead, content validity is demonstrated by showing that the predictor measures constitute a representative sample of the work domain.[19] Table 5.2 outlines the differences between the criterion-related validation study and the content-related validation study.

Table 5.2 Criterion-related versus content-related validation

Criterion-related validation	Content-related validation
Demonstration of relationship between scores on predictor and criterion measures	Demonstration of a linkage between the content of the predictor measures and important work behaviors, activities, worker requirements, or outcomes on the job
Empirically based, using predictor and criterion measure data	Based upon the qualitative judgment of subject matter experts (SMEs)
Success is closely related to quality of the data and a well-designed research process	Success is closely related to the qualifications of SMEs

There are several approaches to conducting a content-related validation study: (1) domain representativeness; (2) performance requirements approach; and (3) linkage methods.[20] The first approach is to show "the behavior(s) demonstrated in the selection procedure are a representative sample of the behavior(s) of the job in question or that the selection procedure provides a representative sample of the work product of the job."[21] For example, a prep cook in a restaurant would be required to prepare sauces, chop and slice vegetables, and tenderize meats. Let's say applicants for a prep cook position are asked to carry out these tasks at the time they come in for an interview. Domain representativeness would be established here because the behaviors demonstrated in the selection procedure are representative of those in the actual job. In the second approach, the predictor measure is considered to be content valid if it measures the KSAOs required for successful job performance. An example here is a job knowledge test or structured interview questions. Subject matter experts (SMEs) may review these selection tools to determine the KSAOs assessed are required for the job. The third approach involves having SMEs assess whether KSAOs required to do well on a predictor measure actually overlap with those KSAOs required to perform well on the job. In the first step of this approach, SMEs link required KSAOs to the essential functions of the job. Then, linkages are made between KSAOs assessed by the predictor measure and those required by the job. To the extent that there are significant commonalities, the predictor measure can be considered to have content validity.

Regardless of the approach used, the *judgment* of SMEs – rather than empirical evidence – is relied upon to determine content validity. Hence, content validity approaches have been criticized for this reason. Although considered by the *Uniform Guidelines* and other authorities in validation to be an appropriate method to gathering evidence of validity, there is some debate among I-O psychologists regarding whether content validity is actually "validity" because evidence from content validity studies does not directly show that scores on predictor measures are predictors of job performance.[22] If content validity is used as the validation strategy, it is very important to have a thorough job analysis that is used as the foundation of the efforts.

Summary

The concept of validity is one that is quite often been misunderstood by test developers and test users. It is irresponsible to label a test as valid, without any qualifying statement about what the test is valid for. A test may be valid for predicting success for some types of jobs, but not others. Also, the process of demonstrating a test's validity is often an ongoing series of data collections. For example, early stages of test development may evaluate a test's convergent validity by correlating the test with measures of similar constructs. Later, validity evidence may include criterion-related validity using a variety of different jobs and criteria. Also, as noted in the discussion on validity generalization, individual samples may be problematic due to small samples and so the accumulation of samples and the aggregation via meta-analysis are key. In short, the process of test validation should be ongoing.

REVIEW QUESTIONS

1. What does it mean to say a predictor measure is "valid?"
2. What type of evidence is needed to establish evidence of empirical validity?
3. What is needed to conduct a criterion-related validation study?
4. When is it appropriate to conduct a content-related validity study instead of a criterion-related study?
5. What are the major differences between concurrent and predictive validation studies?
6. What are the three approaches to content validation?
7. What is the role of job analysis in the various types of validation studies?
8. What is the role of SMEs in content validation studies?
9. What is the difference between a local validity study and validity generalization?

DISCUSSION QUESTIONS

1. If you were an employer in need of a validity study, which one would you most prefer? Why?
2. Is it possible for a selection predictor to have high criterion-related validity but not be content-valid? Explain your answer.
3. Do you think validity generalization offers sufficient evidence of validity?

Notes

1. American Educational Research Association, American Psychological Association, & National Council on Measurement in Education. (1999). *Standards for educational and psychological testing*. American Educational Research Association.
2. Arthur, W., Jr., & Villado, A. J. (2008). The importance of distinguishing between constructs and methods when comparing predictors in personnel selection research and practice. *Journal of Applied Psychology, 93*(2), 435–442.
3. Society for Industrial and Organizational Psychology, Inc. (2003). *Principles for the validation and use of personnel selection procedures* (4th ed.). Uniform Guidelines on Employee Selection Procedures, 1978.
4. American Educational Research Association, American Psychological Association, & American Council on Measurement in Education. (1999). *Standards for educational and psychological tests*. American Psychological Association.
5. Binning, J. F., & Barrett, G. V. (1989). Validity of personnel decisions: A conceptual analysis of the inferential and evidential bases. *Journal of Applied Psychology, 74*, 478–494.
6. Arthur, W., Jr., & Villado, A. J. (2008). The importance of distinguishing between constructs and methods when comparing predictors in personnel selection research and practice. *Journal of Applied Psychology, 93*(2), 435–442.

7. Arthur, W., Jr., & Villado, A. J. (2008). The importance of distinguishing between constructs and methods when comparing predictors in personnel selection research and practice. *Journal of Applied Psychology, 93*(2), 435–442.
8. Huffcutt, A. I., Conway, J. M., Roth, P. L., & Stone, N. J. (2001). Identification and meta-analytic assessment of psychological constructs measured in employment interviews. *Journal of Applied Psychology, 86,* 897–913.
9. Arthur, W., Jr., & Villado, A. J. (2008). The importance of distinguishing between constructs and methods when comparing predictors in personnel selection research and practice. *Journal of Applied Psychology, 93*(2), 435–442.
10. Binning, J. F., & Barrett, G. V. (1989). Validity of personnel decisions: A conceptual analysis of the inferential and evidential bases. *Journal of Applied Psychology, 74,* 478–494.
11. Murphy, K. R. (2009). Content validation is useful for many things, but validity isn't one of them. *Industrial and Organizational Psychology: Perspectives on Science and Practice, 2*(4), 453–464.
12. Callender, J. C., & Osburn, H. G. (1980). Development and testing of a new model of validity generalization. *Journal of Applied Psychology, 65,* 543–558; Hunter, J. E., & Hunter, R. F. (1984). Validity and utility of alternative predictors of job performance. *Psychological Bulletin, 96,* 72–88.
13. https://hbr.org/2015/02/most-hr-data-is-bad-data
14. Society for Industrial and Organizational Psychology, Inc. (2003). *Principles for the validation and use of personnel selection procedures* (4th ed.). Uniform Guidelines on Employee Selection Procedures, 1978.
15. Society for Industrial and Organizational Psychology, Inc. (2003). *Principles for the validation and use of personnel selection procedures* (4th ed.). Uniform Guidelines on Employee Selection Procedures, 1978.
16. Scherbaum, C. A. (2005). Synthetic validity: Past, present, and future. *Personnel Psychology, 58*(2), 481–515.
17. Mossholder, K. W., & Arvey, R. D. (1984). Synthetic validity: A conceptual and comparative review. *Journal of Applied Psychology, 69*(2), 322–333.
18. Johnson, J. W., & Carter, G. W. (2010). Validating synthetic validation: Comparing traditional and synthetic validity coefficients. *Personnel Psychology, 63,* 755–795.
19. Society for Industrial and Organizational Psychology, Inc. (2003). *Principles for the validation and use of personnel selection procedures* (4th ed.). Uniform Guidelines on Employee Selection Procedures, 1978.
20. Murphy, K. R. (2009). Is content-related evidence useful in validating selection tests? *Industrial and Organizational Psychology: Perspectives on Science and Practice, 2*(4), 517–526.
21. Uniform Guidelines on Employee Selection Procedures. (1978). 29 C.F.R. 1607.
22. Murphy, K. R. (2009). Content validation is useful for many things, but validity isn't one of them. *Industrial and Organizational Psychology: Perspectives on Science and Practice, 2*(4), 453–464.

6 Criterion terms, concepts, and measures

LEARNING OBJECTIVES

- Understand what the "criterion problem" means
- Know how the criterion and predictor are conceptually different
- Understand why it is important to be aware of the criterion problem
- Know the multiple dimensions of performance (task, citizenship, and counterproductive)
- Compare and contrast the conceptual and actual criterion
- Compare and contrast contamination and deficiency
- Compare and contrast objective and judgmental criterion measures
- Know how various criterion measures are contaminated and deficient

Let us start this chapter with a quick quiz:

Choose the word below which goes best with "selection":

a. Prediction
b. Decision-making
c. Assessment

You are correct if you chose any of the above options, although you get a bonus point if you picked "prediction." Let's follow up with another question: "What are we predicting?" Give yourself another point if your answer is "criterion," "performance," "future work behaviors," or something along these lines. As noted in the chapter on validity (Chapter 5), selection is ultimately about prediction as we are trying to infer subsequent work behavior based upon predictor measure data. Simple? Actually, not so fast! What do we mean by "criterion" or "performance?" How would we measure performance of work behaviors? And which behaviors should we measure? These are just a few questions to illustrate what has been referred to as **the criterion problem**, an issue that has vexed industrial-organizational psychologists during almost 100 years of scientific research on criteria.[1]

The criterion problem

Although complex, the **criterion problem** may be simply referred to as the difficulties in conceptualizing and measuring performance constructs. Compared to predictor constructs, performance constructs are conceptually different. As noted by Binning and Barrett,[2] "construct domains on the predictor side are conceived by the research psychologist with reference to some theoretical framework developed to explain general regularities in human behavior."[3] In contrast, construct domains on the criterion side are largely determined by organizational decision-makers, as they translate the objectives of the organization into performance expectations. Recall the chapter on validity (Chapter 5), in which the term *job performance domain* was noted as being *defined by organizational standards, expectations, and values*. The job performance domain is the same as what is being discussed here as "performance domains" or "construct domains on the criterion side."

> **The Criterion Problem:** Difficulties in conceptualizing and measuring performance constructs.

As an example, consider a cognitive ability test as the predictor measure. The predictor construct of cognitive ability is theoretically conceptualized and most measurement considerations surround ensuring that the test measures what it purports to measure (i.e., construct validity). However, the construct domain on the criterion side is more complicated. What we hope to predict from the use of any predictor measure is ultimately success or effectiveness on the job. But what does it mean to be successful or effective? Are we simply concerned with worker behaviors? The outcomes that result from those behaviors? A combination of both? Such determinations are based upon what the organization's objectives are, what it values, who is doing the determining, and so forth. In other words, there are external determinants that make conceptualizing the criterion more complex than the predictor.

Consider the Wonderlic, a cognitive ability test used widely by organizations such as the NFL, Subway Restaurants, as well as a variety of employers in the banking, health, manufacturing, and public sectors. All these organizations use the Wonderlic as a selection predictor to assess overall intellectual functioning.[4] Although the predictor is the same for all who use it, the criterion that employers are looking to predict with this test varies. Success at playing football differs from success at making sandwiches. Even within the same industry, the definition of effective performance varies. Success at a large Fortune 500 bank is different from success at a financial cooperative because such organizations are likely to have different objectives and values, which are then translated into different performance expectations for their employees.

The multiple dimensions of performance

Even within a single organization, effective performance is not simple to conceptualize because job performance itself is a multidimensional construct. Decades of research indicate that job performance consists of three broad components: (a) task performance; (b) citizenship performance; and (c) counterproductive performance.[5]

Task performance

Task performance has garnered several definitions from various researchers: the accomplishment of duties and responsibilities of the job,[6] activities that are formally recognized as part of the job and which contribute to the organization's technical core,[7] and "behaviors that contribute to the production of a good or provision of a service."[8] Scoring a touchdown for an NFL player and producing sandwiches to the satisfaction of customers for a Subway Restaurant employee represent examples of task performance. Essentially, task performance can be thought of as the requirements outlined in a job description.

> **Task Performance:** Behaviors which result in a product or service and accomplishment of duties and responsibilities that are formally recognized as part of the job and which contribute to the organization's technical core.

Citizenship performance

Citizenship performance, also referred to as "organizational citizenship behavior," "extrarole behavior," and "prosocial behavior," encompasses behaviors that are not task-related and are not required by the organization, yet contribute positively to the organizational environment.[9] These behaviors are commonly known as "going above and beyond" at work. For example, former NFL quarterback Peyton Manning was well known not only for his play on the field but also for mentoring younger players. An employee at Subway could demonstrate citizenship behaviors by gathering coworkers together to celebrate someone's birthday. Such behaviors result in positive individual-level outcomes, such as higher managerial ratings,[10] greater end-of-the-workday feelings of energy,[11] and a higher sense of meaningfulness at work[12] and organizational-level outcomes,[13] including decreased turnover and absenteeism, and increased productivity and customer satisfaction.

> **Citizenship Performance:** Discretionary behaviors that are not task-related but contribute to the positive functioning of the organization.

Counterproductive performance

Counterproductive performance is those behaviors that are voluntary and which bring harm to the organization.[14] Such behaviors include theft, property damage, substance abuse, and time theft. As an example, imagine a football player that regularly shows up to team meetings, or even games, under the influence of drugs or alcohol. Suppose this same player constantly finds himself in altercations with teammates, coaches, and/or officials, possibly even getting ejected from games as a result of his conduct. Whether the player's conduct is a result of drug use, this player shows a pattern of counterproductive performance that harms the organization and the people within it. However, a worker at Subway may encourage his/her friends to visit the restaurant during their shift, allowing the friends to order meals without paying for them. Although this behavior may not seem as egregious as stealing large amounts of money from the cash register, both would represent counterproductive performance.

> **Counterproductive Performance:** Behaviors that are voluntary and which bring harm to the organization.

Criterion terms

Having covered the complexity of conceptualizing the criterion, let's discuss next the measurement difficulties that underlie the criterion problem (see Figure 6.1). In doing so, let's introduce you to basic criterion terms:

Conceptual criterion: The abstract idea of performance. This can be thought of as the ultimate "truth" of what we are trying to capture.
Actual criterion: What we actually use to measure the conceptual criterion.
Relevance: The extent to which the actual criterion captures the conceptual criterion.

Criterion terms, concepts, and measures

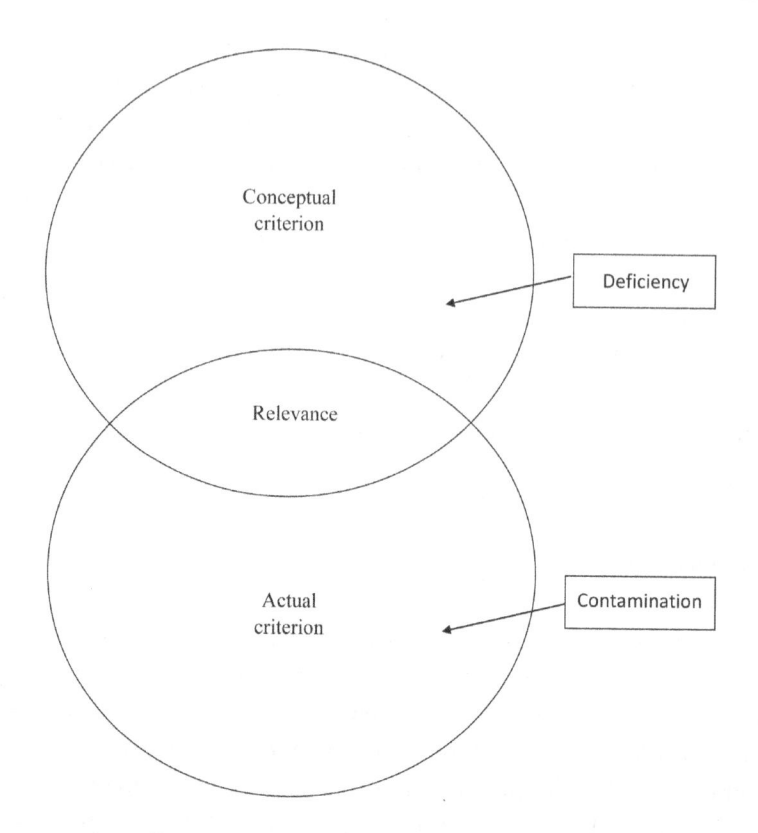

Figure 6.1 A Venn diagram of criterion terms

Deficiency: The part of the conceptual criterion that we fail to measure with the actual criterion.
Contamination: Factors that affect the actual criterion and which do not have to do with the conceptual criterion.

For example, let us use a job with which we are all familiar – a college instructor. For the conceptual criterion, let's say it is "teaching." And let the actual criterion be the student evaluations of the instructor (i.e., the form most of you are asked to fill out at the end of each quarter or semester). If you have ever completed one of these evaluation forms, take a moment to reflect upon the content of the form. To what extent do the questions really get at how effective the instructor was? To the extent that there is concurrence between what is on the form and your idea of adequate teacher performance, this would represent *relevance*. In contrast, is there something about the criterion of teaching performance that you just don't think the form asks? We would say, for example, that an important part of teaching entails challenging students to think about issues from different perspectives, and helping them think especially from perspectives other than what their existing schemas have allowed. On the evaluation form our students complete, however, there are no such questions. Hence, the actual criterion of the student evaluation can be said to be *deficient* in capturing the entire conceptual criterion of teaching. Finally, think about the last time you completed one of these evaluation forms. What factors affected how you rated your instructor other than how well or poorly s/he taught? Did the subject matter affect your ratings? How about your mood that day? Or, how well or poorly you were doing in the class? Did the instructor try to bribe you by providing donuts on evaluation day? These could all be *contamination* factors in the sense they affected the actual criterion but really do not have anything to do with the conceptual criterion. Good criterion measures will minimize contamination and eliminate deficiency by capturing all relevant aspects of performance.

Criterion measures

Criterion measures (i.e., the actual criterion) may be broadly categorized as objective or judgmental. Objective measures are those which measure performance that can be counted without any subjective judgment, whereas judgmental measures are those that require a person to make a subjective evaluation regarding the employee's performance.

> **Objective Measures:** Measures of the criterion that are countable, without any subjective judgment.

> **Judgmental Measures:** Measures of the criterion that require subjective evaluation.

Objective measures

Although the term "objective" connotes a flawless measure, it is by no means invulnerable from deficiency and contamination. To illustrate, let's consider several specific types of objective measures that are used to assess production data and withdrawal measures.

Production data

The number of touchdowns a football player scores, the number of sandwiches a Subway employee makes, the number of students who pass a class – these are all examples of production data; in other words, production data are the results of an employee's work. Such task performance data contribute to the organization's technical core, are countable, and seemingly easy to gather. So, what is the problem? (We're sure you knew this was coming!)

Let us start with contamination. Besides individual strength, speed, and knowledge of the playbook, other factors that could be contributing to the number of touchdowns a football player scores include how well the rest of the team is playing, how good or bad the other team is, or even the weather. Before we exhaust our knowledge of sports, let's move on to a more familiar territory. For college instructors such as ourselves, the number of students who pass our classes could reflect how well or poorly we teach. But what other factors could come into play? Perhaps the subject matter contributes to student performance ("Zombies in Popular Media" or "The Joy of Garbage," anyone?). The prior knowledge of students, their cognitive ability,[15] and/or how much time they spend studying can also affect passing rates. As a check to see if we are explaining things clearly, answer the below question regarding the scenario in which Subway counts the number of sandwiches their employees make as an actual measure of performance:

Which of the following is *not* a possible contamination factor?

a. The time of day (hence, the number of customers ordering).
b. The availability of ingredients.
c. The speed of other workers in the typical Subway sandwich assembly-line.
d. Whether customer orders are correctly filled.

All of the above are possible contamination factors except for *d*, which is deficiency. As in the earlier examples, contamination factors affect production data (the actual criterion) which are often beyond the control of the employee, and which do not reflect his/her true performance (the conceptual criterion).

To illustrate the possibility of deficiency, answer this question: Do you think the number of touchdowns, number of sandwiches, or number of students passing a class fully captures the performance of each of these employees? If you answer "no," you would be in good company with John Campbell,[16] Kevin Murphy,[17] and other researchers who argue that performance should be defined as the actions and behaviors of the employee rather than the results of their actions. A wide receiver may be great but if he isn't matched with a quality quarterback, his touchdowns will suffer even though he has run his routes perfectly and caught everything that was within reach. In another example, sales data are often used as production outcomes and they are highly susceptible to seasonal trends as well as the economy of the nearby market. It would not be wise to judge the production of two insurance salespeople based solely on sales metrics if one had a prosperous home turf and the other a relatively impoverished sales area.

Although the main concern underlying this definition is that employees do not have full control over the results of their work, we could turn this point on its side by arguing that production data are deficient because they do not capture the behaviors or actions of employees. Pass rates do not tell us anything about how clearly the instructor explains difficult concepts or whether s/he gives students timely and specific feedback. A Subway worker could produce many, many sandwiches but while doing so, could be unfriendly to customers. Herein lies the essence of the criterion problem – it is very difficult to fully and accurately measure performance.

In summary, production data are useful metrics that do align with the organization's technical core and, to some extent, reflect whether bottom-line goals are being met. However, using these data as measures of employee *performance* poses problems which reveal that such "objective" measures may not be so objective after all.

Withdrawal data: Tardiness, absenteeism, and turnover

Showing up late for work, not showing up at all, quitting, or being let go – these are all within a class of withdrawal behaviors, defined as the "physical withdrawal from a particular workplace, either for part of a day, an entire day, or permanently."[18] Withdrawal data are frequently used as actual criteria because these behaviors represent actions that organizations would like to be able to predict (and therefore, avoid). While individual differences are related to withdrawal, there are also situational factors, some of which are beyond the employee's control, that cause him/her to be late or absent.[19] An employee may be late to work because his/her car did not start on a frigid winter morning; in contrast, another employee may be late because s/he partied all night and chose to sleep the next morning. An employee may be absent because s/he was sick, whereas another employee skipped work for the day to go to the movies. In each of the above examples, involuntary withdrawal has occurred due to factors beyond the employee's control; in other words, the measure is contaminated. It is not always easy to distinguish between each type of withdrawal behavior. An employee who's skipped work to go to the movies most likely did not state this as the reason when s/he called in "sick!"

Voluntary versus involuntary turnover poses even greater complexity. When an employee quits his/her job, this is obviously voluntary, whereas being fired or let go would be involuntary turnover. An employee may quit his/her job because s/he found a better opportunity elsewhere, or may be leaving because s/he has been performing poorly at the current position and is quitting to preempt a disciplinary action. Because of the imprecise nature of withdrawal behaviors, these should not be the sole criteria of interest when examining employee performance.

> **Withdrawal Behaviors:** Physical withdrawal from the workplace, including tardiness, absenteeism, and turnover.

Judgmental measures

In contrast to objective ratings, judgmental measures are based on evaluations of employee performance based on different constituent groups, such as supervisors, coworkers, customers, and subordinates. Ratings of performance are the most commonly used criteria used by I-O psychologists. Asking supervisors to evaluate an employee's performance on a series of items is the most commonly used measure in criterion-related validity. Some of the popularity of supervisory ratings is due to their ease in data collection. It might be a lot easier to ask a supervisor to fill out a five-minute survey than to track down objective performance data. In addition, as part of an employee's regular evaluation, some degree of supervisor evaluation might tend to happen anyway. Those evaluations might be used not only for test evaluation purposes but for determining pay raises and promotions, as well as identifying areas for training and development. Given the popularity of judgmental measures, thankfully there is also a large body of research evaluating these ratings. First, it should be noted that the same concepts used to evaluate objective criteria can be used to evaluate judgmental measures. Concerns for contamination and deficiency are relevant. In Chapter 13, we will cover judgmental measures in greater depth when we discuss performance evaluation.

So what *is* the problem?

Having read about these issues regarding the criterion problem, you may be thinking, "What exactly *is* the problem?" You may be further thinking, "Aren't issues of contamination and deficiency also potential problems in capturing the predictor construct, or any psychological construct, for that matter?" Remember, though, the criterion problem is not just about measurement but also about conceptualization. Moreover, it is a problem because the criterion is the standard with which all personnel decision-making is tied.[20] For example, criterion-related validation studies require a criterion to assess whether the predictor is of any value and should be used for selection purposes. However, a criterion may be inadequately conceptualized, for example, by not being aligned with the organization's objectives. If the ultimate goal of selection is to predict future work-related performance, the failure to conceptualize performance which is most relevant to the organization really makes the whole process no longer worthwhile. There could also be measurement issues whereby we have little variance in the criterion scores. When this occurs, the observed validity coefficient is suppressed. A researcher may erroneously conclude that a predictor has no value when, in fact, it is the criterion that is flawed.

So what can we do about the problem?

The goal of this chapter is neither to be depressing nor frustrating, so let's conclude with some ways to address the criterion problem. Stated broadly, we should pay as much attention to the criterion as to the predictor. Stated specifically, we should:

1. Expand the criterion space
2. Consider using various measures
3. Think beyond the present state of the organization

First, it is quite common practice for researchers conducting a validation study to use whatever criterion data happens to be conveniently available. When this happens to be production data or supervisory ratings, we fail to regard the multidimensionality of performance. Hence, the first suggestion in addressing the criterion problem is to expand the criterion space, by considering not just task performance but also citizenship performance.[21]

Summary

As we know, actual criteria all have their advantages and disadvantages. It is important to bear in mind the possible contamination and deficiency of any measure. A multitrait-multimethod approach, when possible, should be taken. For example, using both objective and judgmental measures to fully capture the conceptual criterion will enhance the relevance of the actual criterion. Finally, organizations change and so do the jobs within them.

As such, the criteria of what successful performance entails may also change. In order to ensure that the performance criteria being used are relevant and current, they should be created based on the information generated from a job analysis.

REVIEW QUESTIONS

1. What is meant by the "criterion problem?"
2. Compare and contrast the terms "criterion" and "predictor."
3. Explain the multiple dimensions of performance (task, citizenship, and counterproductive).
4. Compare and contrast the conceptual and actual criterion.
5. Compare and contrast contamination and deficiency.
6. Compare and contrast objective and judgmental criterion measures.
7. Explain the difference between criterion contamination and deficiency.

DISCUSSION QUESTIONS

1. What do you think is worse – a contaminated or deficient criterion measure? Why?
2. What are some examples of citizenship performance that you have exhibited or observed in a job you've held? How did such performance benefit employees and the organization?
3. What do you think about the idea of rewarding or punishing employees on the basis of citizenship performance? Would this be fair?
4. Think of some jobs you've had. What are some examples of production data in these jobs? If this data was gathered to determine whether you would get a raise or promotion, would you be in favor? Why or why not?

Notes

1. Austin, J. T., & Villanova, P. (1992). The criterion problem: 1917–1992. *Journal of Applied Psychology, 77*(6), 836–874. http://dx.doi.org/10.1037/0021-9010.77.6.836
2. Binning, J. F., & Barrett, G. V. (1989). Validity of personnel decisions: A conceptual analysis of the inferential and evidential bases. *Journal of Applied Psychology, 74*(3), 478–494. http://dx.doi.org/10.1037/0021-9010.74.3.478
3. Binning, J. F., & Barrett, G. V. (1989). Validity of personnel decisions: A conceptual analysis of the inferential and evidential bases. *Journal of Applied Psychology, 74*(3), 478–494. http://dx.doi.org/10.1037/0021-9010.74.3.478
4. Matthews, T. D., & Lassiter, K. S. (2007). What does the Wonderlic personnel test measure? *Psychological Reports, 100*(3), 707–712.
5. Rotundo, M., & Sackett, P. R. (2002). The relative importance of task, citizenship, and counterproductive performance to global ratings of job performance: A policy-capturing approach. *Journal of Applied Psychology, 87*(1), 66–80.

6 Murphy, K. R. (1989). Dimensions of job performance. In R.F. Dillon & J.W. Pellegrino (Eds.), *Testing: Theoretical and applied perspectives* (pp. 218–247). Praeger Publishers.
7 Borman, W. C., & Motowidlo, S. J. (1993). Expanding the criterion domain to include elements of contextual performance. In N. Schmitt & W. C. Borman (Eds.), *Personnel selection in organizations* (pp. 71–98). Jossey Bass.
8 Rotundo, M., & Sackett, P. R. (2002). The relative importance of task, citizenship, and counterproductive performance to global ratings of job performance: A policy-capturing approach. *Journal of Applied Psychology, 87*(1), 66–80.
9 Dekas, K., Bauer, T., Welle, B., Kurkoski, J., & Sullivan, S. (2013). Organizational Citizenship Behavior, Version 2.0: A review and qualitative investigation of OCBs for knowledge workers at Google. *The Academy of Management Perspectives, 27*, 219–237.
10 Podsakoff, N. P., Whiting, S. W., Podsakoff, P. M., & Blume, B. D. (2009). Individual- and organizational-level consequences of organizational citizenship behaviors: A meta-analysis. *Journal of Applied Psychology, 94*(1), 122–141.
11 Lam, C. F., Wan, W. H., & Roussin, C. J. (2016). Going the extra mile and feeling energized: An enrichment perspective of organizational citizenship behaviors. *Journal of Applied Psychology, 101*(3), 379–391.
12 Lam, C. F., Wan, W. H., & Roussin, C. J. (2016). Going the extra mile and feeling energized: An enrichment perspective of organizational citizenship behaviors. *Journal of Applied Psychology, 101*(3), 379–391.
13 Podsakoff, N. P., Whiting, S. W., Podsakoff, P. M., & Blume, B. D. (2009). Individual- and organizational-level consequences of organizational citizenship behaviors: A meta-analysis. *Journal of Applied Psychology, 94*(1), 122–141.
14 Rotundo, M., & Sackett, P. R. (2002). The relative importance of task, citizenship, and counterproductive performance to global ratings of job performance: A policy-capturing approach. *Journal of Applied Psychology, 87*(1), 66–80.
15 Kuncel, N. R., & Hezlett, S. A. (2010). Fact and fiction in cognitive ability testing for admissions and hiring decisions. *Current Directions in Psychological Science, 19*(6), 339–345.
16 Campbell, J.P. (1990). Modeling the performance prediction problem in industrial and organizational psychology. In M.D. Dunnette and L.M. Hough (Eds.), *Handbook of industrial and organizational psychology* (Vol. 1, pp. 687–732). Consulting Psychologists Press.
17 Murphy, K. R. (1989). Dimensions of job performance. In R.F. Dillon & J.W. Pellegrino (Eds.), *Testing: Theoretical and applied perspectives* (pp. 218–247). Praeger Publishers.
18 p. 233 in Johns, G. (2002). The psychology of lateness, absenteeism, and turnover. In N. Anderson, D. Ones, & S. Deniz (Eds.), *Handbook of industrial, work and organizational psychology* (pp. 232–252). Sage.
19 Zimmerman, R. D., Swider, B. W., Woo, S. E., & Allen, D. G. (2015). Who withdraws? Psychological individual differences and employee withdrawal behaviors. *Journal of Applied Psychology.* http://dx.doi.org/10.1037/apl0000068
20 Gottfredson, L. S. (1991). The evaluation of alternative measures of job performance. In B.F. Green & A.K. Widgdor (Eds.), *Performance assessment for the workplace, vol. 2: Technical issues* (pp. 75–126). National Academy Press.
21 Austin, J. T., & Villanova, P. (1992). The criterion problem: 1917–1992. *Journal of Applied Psychology, 77*(6), 836–874. http://dx.doi.org/10.1037/0021-9010.77.6.836

7 Applicant reactions and fairness perceptions

LEARNING OBJECTIVES

- Understand the concept of organizational justice and its three dimensions
- Know how allocation rules and equity sensitivity contribute to justice perceptions
- Appreciate the individual differences that influence applicant reactions
- Understand how structural and social characteristics of the selection process impact applicant reactions
- Recognize the ten procedural justice rules proposed by Gilliland, and why they are important to the selection process
- Know the individual and organizational outcomes associated with applicant reactions

"That's not fair!" This is a common phrase wailed by young children after being taught some of life's harshest lessons. This phrase, however, is not only relevant to young children. Indeed, you've probably chatted with other students – or at least reflected to yourself – about your reactions to some of the exams administered in your college courses. Likely, a key issue was the perceived (un)fairness of the exams. Just as you react to the evaluation methods used in your college courses, it is not uncommon for job applicants to react – positively or negatively – to the selection practices used by hiring organizations. These reactions may consider events that happened before, during, or after the selection decision took place. In this chapter, we'll explore the implications that these reactions have for individuals and organizations, as well as the factors that contribute to applicant reactions with an emphasis on organizational justice.

Importance of applicant reactions

Think of a time when you had a horrible customer experience. When this happened, did you talk to your family, friends, or acquaintances about the experience? If so, this experience not only left a lasting impression on you but also had a second-hand influence on others' views of the organization. The same can be true for applicant reactions to the selection process. Whether the experience is positive or negative, candidates are likely to share their experiences with others. Accordingly, applicant reactions can have implications for both the individual applicant and the organization as a whole.

Individual outcomes

One of the most immediate outcomes associated with applicant reactions is subsequent performance on selection tests. Specifically, applicants' perceptions have been shown to be related to test-taking anxiety, motivation, self-evaluated performance, and actual performance on selection tests.[1,2,3,4] This demonstrates, from both the applicant's and the organization's perspectives, the importance of managing applicant expectations throughout the selection process. Ensuring fairness can not only impact applicants' perceptions but also ensure that candidates perform to the best of their ability during selection tests. This will, in turn, increase the likelihood that the best employee is hired for the job. As for on-the-job performance, although it was once believed that applicant reactions may impact one's job performance after being hired, the actual effect of applicant reactions on later job performance appears to be negligible.[5] Accordingly, when it comes to performance, applicant reactions seem to have a more substantial impact on selection tests than on-the-job performance.

If you've taken several college courses, you've probably developed a preference for certain types of tests and evaluation methods. This can happen in the context of selection as well. There is evidence to suggest that applicants may prefer certain selection procedures over others.[6] Specifically, work sample tests and interviews seem to be the most preferred selection tests among job applicants. Resumes, references, cognitive ability tests, personality tests, and biodata show a moderate degree of favorability, whereas honesty tests, personal contacts, and graphology tend to be the least preferred selection methods.[7,8] This relates back to our discussion of face validity in Chapter 5. Recall that face validity represents an informal evaluation of whether a test *seems* to measure what it is supposed to measure. In the selection context, a test would have face validity if applicants believe – at face value – that the test is useful for predicting their ability to perform the job for which they are applying. Selection methods that are viewed more favorably by applicants (i.e., having higher face validity) will likely be perceived as more appropriate, useful, and fair by job candidates.

Reactions to the selection process can also have a more personal impact. The perceived fairness of selection systems can potentially influence a variety of self-perceptions, including one's self-esteem (evaluation of self-worth), self-efficacy (belief in one's competence), and core self-evaluations (positive self-regard).[9,10,11] The specific way in which these self-perceptions are influenced may hinge upon applicants' **attributions** regarding the selection decision. Attributions refer to the causal explanations people assign to the events they encounter. *Dispositional attributions* presume an outcome to be the result of personal characteristics, whereas *situational attributions* assume an outcome is due to external circumstances. Applicants that assign a dispositional attribution to the selection decision (i.e., "I did not get the job because of my lack of ability") will be more likely to internalize the decision – in the form of positive or negative self-perceptions – than those who assign a situational cause to the selection decision ("I did not get the job because there was someone more qualified"). Although an organization has no control over an individual's attributions, providing feedback for hiring decisions in a diplomatic and respectful manner may help to reduce any negative effects that may arise as a result of the attributional process. Furthermore, striving to ensure the face validity and perceived fairness of the selection process can lead to more positive reactions, and, in turn, more positive outcomes related to applicants' self-perceptions. Strategies for ensuring perceived fairness will be reviewed later in this chapter.

> **Attributions:** Causal explanations (dispositional or situational) assigned to events.

Organizational outcomes

Applicant reactions are also related to views toward the organization as a whole. It is well established that perceived fairness in the selection system is related to applicants' satisfaction with the selection process. Not surprisingly, when applicants perceive fair and impartial treatment, they are generally more satisfied with the procedures used. Similarly, perceptions of fairness are positively related to organizational attractiveness.[12,13] Views regarding organizational attractiveness can be shaped by one's own experiences with an organization, or second-hand knowledge of the organizations' selection methods. Thus, applicant reactions often spill over to impact the organizations' recruiting efforts. To the extent that applicants have more positive reactions, they are more likely to recommend the organization to others as a potential employer.[14,15] Consequently, increasing fairness perceptions will not only lead to more positive individual reactions but can also benefit the organization indirectly by enhancing its reputation and attractiveness among prospective job seekers.

In addition to general attitudes toward the organization, applicant reactions have been shown to be related to subsequent behavioral intentions related to the job offer. Perceived fairness of the selection process is positively related to job offer acceptance intentions and actual job acceptance.[16,17] In the case where applicants have been rejected, fairness perceptions can impact whether an applicant intends to reapply to the organization.[24] This further demonstrates the importance of fostering positive applicant reactions, as the organization can benefit from having qualified candidates – who were rejected on their first attempt – reapply for positions in the future.

Another factor that has large implications for an organization's reputation and general image is litigation concerns.[18] Although no link has been shown between applicant reactions and actual litigation, multiple studies have shown a negative relationship between fairness perceptions and litigation intentions.[19,20,21] Given that litigation – or even the threat of legal action in and of itself – is problematic to an organization for a variety of reasons, this serves as yet another reason to ensure fair treatment and positive reactions of all job applicants throughout the entirety of the hiring process.

Finally, as for more general, post-hire job attitudes, more examination is needed to make firm conclusions. There is some speculation that fairness perceptions regarding the selection process may be related to organizational commitment, job satisfaction, and turnover intentions among current employees.[22] Although there is no firm empirical link between applicant reactions and these important job attitudes, it is safe to say that enhancing fairness and striving for more positive reactions to the selection process will certainly not hurt the culture and attitudes emitted within an organization.

Given the implications of applicant reactions reviewed above, an important question for organizations to answer is "how do we foster positive applicant reactions and perceived fairness in the selection process"? This question is usually addressed through the lens of organizational justice.

Organizational justice

For many applicants, exposure to an organization's recruiting and selection process represents their first formal experience with the organization. During this process, most applicants are not just passively "going through the motions." Rather, they are consciously evaluating the selection tests they are exposed to, paying close attention to the way they are treated and the outcomes resulting from the selection process. **Organizational justice** refers to the perceived fairness of organizational practices.[23] Within the context of selection, organizational justice focuses on whether applicants perceive a selection test, or a selection system to be fair.[24] In making this determination, applicants consider three specific dimensions of organizational justice: distributive, procedural, and interactional justice.

> **Organizational Justice:** The perceived fairness of organizational practices.

Distributive justice is defined as the fairness associated with the distribution of outcomes within an organization. Relevant outcomes pertaining to the selection process include the hiring decision itself (hired or not), starting pay, benefits, or feedback provided. If these outcomes are perceived to be allocated unfairly, distributive justice will be low. For example, let's pretend you and a seemingly less qualified friend of yours applied for the same job, and your friend received a job offer while you did not. You would likely perceive unfairness related to this undesirable result, particularly given the fact that you believed you were more qualified than your friend. In contrast, your friend may have no problem with the end result, thereby perceiving a high degree of distributive justice. Thus, the same outcome distribution may be interpreted differently by different people.

> **Distributive Justice:** Fairness associated with the allocation of outcomes within an organization.

Whereas distributive justice is concerned with outcomes, themselves, **procedural justice** refers to the perceived fairness of the procedures used to determine those outcomes. This dimension of justice focuses on the selection methods used to make the hiring decision. Here, applicants may consider the consistency and transparency of the selection process, the perceived accuracy of the information used to make selection decisions, and whether the decisions appear to be conducted in an unbiased and ethical manner. Regarding the scenario presented above, if you found out that your friend was hired simply because he was friends with the owner of the organization, you would probably view the hiring process as biased and unfair (i.e., low procedural justice). Alternatively, if you performed poorly on a job-related test, whereas your friend performed much better on the same test, you would be less likely to view the process as biased or unfair, thereby leading to a higher degree of procedural justice.

> **Procedural Justice:** Fairness associated with the procedures used to determine outcome distribution.

Finally, **interactional justice** is concerned with the treatment an individual receives as decisions are made and implemented within the organization. Colquitt (2001) notes that interactional justice can be broken into *informational* and *interpersonal* justice.[25] Informational justice refers to whether the individual is provided with adequate explanation and rationale for a decision in a timely manner. Interpersonal justice, on the other hand, refers to whether the individual was treated with dignity and respect. Thus, even if you are upset that you were not offered a job (lacking in distributive justice) and you do not see the value in the selection tests used to make the hiring decision (lacking in procedural justice), you may still perceive a high degree of interactional justice if you received respectful treatment and diplomatic communication throughout the selection process.

> **Interactional Justice:** Fairness associated with the interpersonal treatment throughout the decision-making process.

To summarize, below are three questions applicants may ask themselves while developing justice perceptions:

Distributive justice: "Did/do I *deserve* to get the job?"
Procedural justice: "Was/is the hiring *process* fair?"
Interactional justice: "Was/am I *treated* respectfully?"

Allocation rules and equity sensitivity

Just as you may differ from your peers with regard to the criteria you use to evaluate the fairness of an exam, applicants may differ from one another in the ways they evaluate the fairness of a selection system. Conceptually, the three dimensions of organizational justice are relatively straightforward. The way in which those fairness perceptions are developed, however, can be quite complex.

A key factor in the formation of justice perceptions, particularly with regard to distributive justice, is the "rule" by which one adheres to when determining what is considered to be fair. Applicants may evaluate outcomes based on three different **allocation rules**: equity, equality, or need.[26] To demonstrate each rule, imagine you were involved in a group project where you were the most competent group member. You completed 75% of the work for the project, and yet each group member received the same grade and the same amount of praise from the instructor. Below are three different ways of interpreting the fairness of this scenario:

Equity: Outcomes would be deemed equitable to the extent that they are *distributed proportionally to* each individual's contributions. Proportionality is determined by an individual comparing their inputs (e.g., time and effort) and outcomes (e.g., grade and praise) to another person's inputs and outcomes. The group scenario above is likely to lead to perceived unfairness on your part due to your disproportionate contribution to the project relative to the outcomes you received. In other words, the outcome/input ratio among group members was inequitable.

Equality: One would perceive fairness to the extent that outcomes are *distributed equally* to everyone, regardless of effort, contribution, or performance level. The scenario above would be deemed fair when viewed through the lens of equality, as each member received the same outcomes.

Need: When fairness is judged based on need, one would prefer outcomes be *distributed based on each individual's unique personal situation*. Need may consider factors such as ability level, health status, and additional commitments (academic, family, or social) in order to determine how much effort each group member should provide and how outcomes should be allocated. Thus, more information would be needed about each group member in order to determine whether the above situation would be deemed fair from the need perspective.

> **Allocation Rule:** Standard for judging the fairness of outcome distribution(s).

While equity is the most commonly employed rule for evaluating distributive justice, the importance of equality and need may vary depending on the situation. For example, when it comes to the ability to apply for a job, equality is the predominant rule given the legal standard of equal employment opportunity. In contrast, for decisions such as pay, equity may serve as the principal rule – when an individual provides greater contributions to a company's success, they will likely expect to be rewarded for those contributions. Regarding selection decisions, need may play a role in many peoples' reactions when it comes to providing reasonable accommodations for applicants with disabilities. Some applicants may need differential support upon entering the organization, whereas others will need less accommodations in order to be successful. Thus, the allocation rule applied may vary based on individual differences and environmental context.

In addition to employing different allocation rules, individuals may be differentially sensitive when it comes to perceived (in)equity. The concept of **equity sensitivity** refers to an individual's preferences regarding equity and is based on perceptions of outcome/input ratios. Previous research has proposed four categories of people: benevolent, equity-sensitive, entitled, and equity-indifferent.[27,28] Those who are *benevolent* prefer their outcome/input ratio to be less than that of others. In other words, they prefer their inputs to be disproportionately higher than their received outcomes. *Equity-sensitive* individuals would prefer a proportional outcome/input ratio, with equal emphasis placed on outcomes and inputs. Those classified as *entitled* prefer their outcome/input ratio to exceed that of others, thus seeking to be over-rewarded relative to their inputs. Finally, *equity-indifferent* people would be those who are relatively unaffected by outcome/input ratios. You may be able to think of some of your friends and acquaintances that fit into each of these categories, and how this may impact their fairness perceptions.

> **Equity Sensitivity:** Individual difference reflecting an individual's preferences regarding equity.

To summarize, the allocation rule(s) employed in any given situation, paired with applicants' equity sensitivity, combine to impact overall organizational justice perceptions. These perceptions represent a central factor in determining applicant reactions to the selection process. Now that you have some background information on organizational justice, let's explore some of the other ways in which applicant reactions develop.

Developing reactions: Individual differences

As scholarly interest in applicant reactions has grown, so too have the theoretical frameworks for evaluating these reactions. Although organizational justice is the primary lens through which applicant reactions are typically viewed, recent research has expanded upon the justice literature to examine *why* applicants react the way they do.[29] This research sheds additional light on the broader individual differences that contribute to justice perceptions, and applicant reactions more generally.

Test perceptions, expectations, and attributions

Have you ever dreaded the thought of taking an exam? If you're like most college students, you have. In fact, you may have developed such a strong attitude toward an upcoming exam that it created a substantial amount of anxiety and possibly hindered your performance. This can happen to job applicants as well. Indeed, **test perceptions** – an applicants' attitudes, beliefs, or opinions toward employment tests – can impact their performance on those tests and their general reactions toward the selection process.[30,31] It is important to note that test perceptions may not always be negative. Believe it or not, some people *like* taking tests. For these individuals, the thought of taking a selection test could lead to a surge of motivation, rather than anxiety. Thus, preconceived notions (positive or negative) regarding the testing process can influence the perceived fairness of any given selection test or selection system.

> **Test Perceptions:** Attitudes, beliefs, or opinions toward employment tests.

In addition to test perceptions, another factor that has been shown to directly influence applicant reactions is one's **expectations** (beliefs about the future) regarding the selection process. There is evidence to suggest that applicants with higher *justice expectations* – expectations of fair treatment in the selection process – are more likely to perceive fairness during the selection process. Conversely, those who anticipate unfair treatment are more likely to perceive injustice.[32] Accordingly, applicant reactions can arise not only from actual experiences but also from expectations going into the selection process. In fact, expectations may lead to confirmation bias, in which applicants seek evidence to confirm their initial assumptions related to the selection process.

> **Expectations:** Beliefs regarding the selection process as a whole.

Applicants may not only differ with regard to their test perceptions and expectations regarding the selection process but also in their attributional style. Recall from earlier in this chapter that attributions refer to the causal explanations people assign to the events they encounter, and can be dispositional or situational. Ployhart and Harold (2004) suggest that perceptions of fairness are a consequence of the attributions individuals make about how they were treated and the outcomes they obtain from the selection process.[33] For example, if an individual applied for a job and was rejected, he may attribute his rejection to the biased selection process (situational attribution) or to his poor performance on a selection test (dispositional attribution). The assigned attribution will lead to a variety of affective, behavioral, and cognitive reactions. A large amount of research indicates a self-serving bias among applicants, indicating that those who were hired are more likely to view the selection process as fair, whereas those who were rejected are more likely to view selection procedures as unfair.[34] Therefore, it may not necessarily be the outcome received from the selection process that drives justice perceptions, but rather, its associated attribution.

Personality traits

Although there has been less exploration within the realm of personality, previous research has demonstrated the potential importance of traits in understanding applicant reactions. Similar to the impact of expectations described above, certain personality traits may predispose applicants to react positively or negatively to the selection process, regardless of the procedures used and the way they were administered. Reflecting on your own experiences regarding fairness, you probably know of some people who rarely, if ever, perceive injustice due to their relatively easy-going and positive personality. Similarly, you may know others who are always on edge, constantly looking for ways in which the world, or other people, have wronged them. This demonstrates that people's general patterns in thinking, feeling, and behaving (i.e., their personality) can greatly impact the lens through which they view the selection process.

The Big Five personality traits – particularly neuroticism and agreeableness – have been shown to impact applicants' justice perceptions.[35,36] Agreeable individuals may be predisposed to react more positively to selection procedures, whereas those high in neuroticism may be prone to react negatively. Furthermore, conscientiousness has been shown to be related to test motivation in that more conscientious individuals demonstrate greater motivation for test-taking.[37] The potential impact of personality also extends beyond the Big Five. For example, applicants with a resilient personality have been suggested as having more favorable perceptions with regard to test fairness.[38] Similarly, positive and negative affectivity may moderate the extent to which perceived unfairness will lead to applicants' behavioral intentions following the selection decision.[39] Consequently, personality represents an important factor to consider when examining applicant reactions to the selection process.

Developing reactions: Characteristics of the selection process

Although there are many individual differences that impact how one develops fairness perceptions, the nature of the selection process – including the types of tests used and how they are administered – can go a long way toward fostering positive or negative applicant reactions. Several researchers have examined characteristics of the selection process in relation to applicant reactions. This body of research has highlighted the importance of "structural fairness" (characteristics of selection methods) and "social fairness" (how applicants are treated during the process) within the selection system.[40,41]

Structural components of the selection process

If you were to be evaluated and compared against other people (in any domain), what would you look for in order to ensure that the process is fair? Likely, at the top of your list is whether the evaluation methods used are relevant and appropriate for the task at hand. In the selection context, perhaps the most important characteristic of the selection process is that it be job-related.[42] As such, grounding selection tests and procedures on a thorough job analysis represents a key prerequisite to establishing a fair selection system.[43] To ensure the job-relatedness of a selection system, one must consider various forms of validity evidence.

Before, during, and after the administration of a selection test, applicants may consider whether the selection methods *seem* like a good measure of their ability to perform the job in question. As discussed earlier in this chapter, this subjective assessment represents **face validity**, or more broadly, applicants' informal "eye test" of the adequacy of selection procedures. Related to your college experience, if you've ever taken an exam and thought to yourself, "that test had nothing to do with the content covered in class or in the textbook," that test would lack face validity.

While face validity is certainly not the gold standard for determining the usefulness of selection tests, it is obviously not desirable for a large majority of applicants to be confused regarding the relevancy of a particular selection method. The concept of face validity demonstrates the importance of developing a selection system in which the purpose is explicitly clear and transparent. To the extent that face validity is enhanced among applicants, the more positive perception applicants will have toward the selection process.[44]

> **Face Validity:** A subjective assessment of whether a test appears (at face value) to cover the concept it purports to measure.

More sophisticated measures of validity – content and criterion-related validity – provide further objective evidence of a selection system's job-relatedness. **Content validity** refers to whether the content of a selection test is directly related to the job in question. Thus, the selection methods used should directly reflect job-related subject matter and/or assess psychological constructs relevant to the job in question. **Criterion-related validity**, on the other hand, ensures that performance on a particular selection test is related to performance on the job. Establishing these two forms of validity evidence is crucial to demonstrating the job-relatedness of selection procedures. Refer to Chapter 5 for a detailed explanation of the methods used to establish content and criterion-related validity.

> **Content Validity:** The extent to which contents of a measure capture or match the content of the job.
> **Criterion-related Validity:** The extent to which scores on a measure are empirically related to work-related behaviors.

While job-relatedness and validity evidence are of utmost importance for perceived fairness, other structural components of the selection system have also proven vital to applicant reactions. Applicants seek consistency and objectivity in the evaluation process.[45,46] More simply, applicants want to be evaluated on the same playing field as every other applicant, with all candidates evaluated on the same criteria in an unbiased manner. Ensuring these structural characteristics can be very helpful in fostering positive applicant reactions. At the same time, however, structural characteristics are not enough to guarantee positive reactions to the selection system. Applicants also pay attention to the social nature of the selection process.

Social components of the selection process

Even if a selection system is job-related, consistent, objective, and demonstrates adequate validity evidence, this may be all for naught if applicants perceive disrespectful communication and discourteous social interaction during the selection process. The way in which applicants are treated can have just as much of an impact on the perceived fairness of the selection system as the structural qualities of the selection methods used.

In fact, **social validity** has been proposed as a counterpoint to the more traditional views of validity.[47] Focusing on interpersonal dignity and respect, social validity refers to the factors that make the selection system more socially acceptable to applicants. While this may overlap slightly with the structural components of selection systems, it is important enough to warrant its own discussion.

> **Social Validity:** The extent to which selection systems are perceived as socially acceptable.

Four characteristics have been proposed as contributing factors to the social validity of a selection system: information, participation, transparency, and feedback.[48] *Information* refers to the extent to which applicants are provided with relevant information pertaining to job requirements and organizational characteristics. Relevant organizational characteristics may include goals, culture, leadership, and opportunities for career development. Receiving this information can help the applicant make an informed decision on whether they wish to continue in the selection process, or self-select out.

The second component of social validity, *participation*, reflects the extent to which applicants have the opportunity to exert control over their situation and be actively involved in the decision process. In other words, applicants seek sufficient opportunity to showcase their relevant KSAOs. If an applicant feels he/she did not have the chance to demonstrate their competence during the selection process, they may develop negative reactions and perceive injustice in the selection system. In a similar vein, if an applicant is rejected for a position, they may seek the opportunity to be reconsidered for the same position, or a similar position in the future. This opportunity for reconsideration may lighten the initial blow of an undesirable selection decision.

Transparency refers to the clarity of the selection methods and evaluation criteria used. In other words, there should be little ambiguity regarding how and why the applicant is to be evaluated. This highlights the need for honest communication regarding the selection tests and procedures used, how the tests will be administered, and why they are used. To the extent that there is increased transparency in the selection process, this will likely enhance applicants' perceptions of face validity.

Finally, *feedback* refers to whether applicants receive information about their performance in the selection process. This entails both the content of the feedback as well as the way in which the feedback was delivered. Applicants should not only be informed of the selection decision (hired or not) but also provided with appropriate rationale for that decision. To further demonstrate the importance of feedback, think about some of the more memorable times in which you've received feedback – positive and negative – on your performance. Whether the feedback came from a parent, teacher, coach, director, or peer, a large part of what made the feedback memorable was probably the way in which it was delivered. Sometimes, positive feedback can come off as ingenuine and patronizing, whereas negative feedback may be viewed as enlightening and motivating. It all comes down to the respectfulness and capability of the communicator. Indeed, explanations have been shown to play an important role in the development of applicant fairness reactions.[49] Thus, feedback – and the way it is implemented – is an important part of establishing social validity.

When social validity is combined with more traditional forms of validity, applicants are more likely to have positive reactions to the selection process. To the extent that applicants are provided with relevant information pertaining to the job and organization, have the opportunity to adequately participate in the selection process, perceive transparency in the selection system, and receive timely and adequate feedback, social validity will be maximized.

Procedural rules for selection

Combining many of the factors discussed above, drawing on both structural and social components of the selection system, Gilliland (1993)[50] proposed ten procedural justice rules that selection systems should adhere to in order to ensure positive applicant reactions:

1. Job-relatedness: Selection systems should use tests and assessments that are directly relevant to the job in question.
2. Opportunity to perform: Applicants should be provided with a chance to demonstrate their true KSAOs and fully express themselves before the selection decision is made.
3. Reconsideration opportunity: Applicants should have the ability to challenge or modify the decision-making process (e.g., review their scores and possibly receive a second-chance).
4. Consistency: Tests and selection procedures should be standardized and administered in the same way across all applicants.
5. Feedback: Relevant information (regarding test performance) should be provided in a timely and efficient manner.
6. Selection information: Applicants should be provided with adequate justification for the selection decision.
7. Honesty: Applicants should be provided with truthful information throughout the selection process.
8. Interpersonal effectiveness of the administrator(s): Applicants should be treated with warmth and respect during the selection process.
9. Two-way communication: Applicants should have the opportunity to provide input or to have their views considered during the selection process.
10. Propriety of questions: Applicants should be asked appropriate, legal, and unbiased questions during the selection process.

To summarize, applicants expect to be evaluated based on consistent, objective, job-related methods in which they have the ability to accurately showcase their abilities.

Moreover, applicants seek transparency, honesty, and timeliness in communication, prefer to have some input with regard to the selection decision and the rationale for it, and look to be treated with dignity and respect throughout the selection process. When these structural and social conditions are met, applicants will have more positive reactions to the selection process and increased perceptions of fairness. Taking a look at this list, are there any other criteria you would like to see addressed when you apply for a job?

Summary

In this chapter, we described the construct of organizational justice, reviewed several individual differences and characteristics of the selection system that contribute to applicant reactions, and outlined the individual and organizational outcomes related to applicant reactions and justice perceptions. To the extent that an organization maximizes the face, content, criterion-related, and social validity of the selection process, organizational justice perceptions among applicants will increase and applicants will have a more positive reaction to the organization and its selection practices.

REVIEW QUESTIONS

1. What is organizational justice and why is it important within the selection context?
2. How do allocation rules and equity sensitivity impact organizational justice perceptions?
3. How do test perceptions, expectations, attributions, and personality contribute to the development of applicants' perceptions of the selection process?
4. How can organizations ensure the job-relatedness of their selection procedures?
5. What is social validity and why is it important to the selection process?
6. What are the individual and organizational outcomes associated with applicant reactions?

DISCUSSION QUESTIONS

1. Which dimension of organizational justice do you think is most important? Why?
2. How would you classify yourself with regard to equity sensitivity?
3. What is the most important thing organizations can do to ensure positive applicant reactions and perceptions of fairness in the selection process?
4. Has second-hand knowledge of an organization's hiring procedures influenced your perceptions of that organization? How so?
5. Would you add any rules to Gilliland's list? What do you think is missing?

Notes

1. Arvey, R. D., Strickland, W., Drauden, G., & Martin, C. (1990). Motivational components of test taking. *Personnel Psychology, 43*(4), 695–716.
2. Chan, D., Schmitt, N., DeShon, R. P., Clause, C. S., & Delbridge, K. (1997). Reactions to cognitive ability tests: The relationships between race, test performance, face validity perceptions, and test-taking motivation. *Journal of Applied Psychology, 82*(2), 300–310.
3. Hausknecht, J. P., Day, D. V., & Thomas, S. C. (2004). Applicant reactions to selection procedures: An updated meta-analysis. *Personnel Psychology, 57*(3), 639–683.
4. Truxillo, D. M., Bodner, D. E., Bertolino, M., Bauer, T. N., & Yonce, C. A. (2009). Effects of explanations on applicant reactions: A meta-analytic review. *International Journal of Selection and Assessment, 17*(4), 346–361.
5. McCarthy, J. M., Van Iddekinge, C. H., Lievens, F., Kung, M., Sinar, E. F., & Campion, M. A. (2013). Do candidate reactions relate to job performance or affect criterion-related validity? A multistudy investigation of relations among reactions, selection test scores, and job performance. *Journal of Applied Psychology, 98*(5), 701–719.
6. Truxillo, D. M., Bauer, T. N., McCarthy, J. M., Anderson, N., & Ahmed, S. M. (2018). Applicant perspectives on employee selection systems. In D. S. Ones, N. Anderson, C. Viswesvaran, & H. K. Sinangil (Eds.), *The SAGE handbook of industrial, work & organizational psychology: Personnel psychology and employee performance* (pp. 508–532). Sage Reference.
7. Hausknecht, J. P., Day, D. V., & Thomas, S. C. (2004). Applicant reactions to selection procedures: An updated meta-analysis. *Personnel Psychology, 57*(3), 639–683.
8. Anderson, N., Salgado, J. F., & Hülsheger, U. R. (2010). Applicant reactions in selection: Comprehensive meta-analysis into reaction generalization versus situational specificity. *International Journal of Selection and Assessment, 18*(3), 291–304.
9. Hausknecht, J. P., Day, D. V., & Thomas, S. C. (2004). Applicant reactions to selection procedures: An updated meta-analysis. *Personnel Psychology, 57*(3), 639–683.
10. Bauer, T. N., Truxillo, D. M., Sanchez, R. J., Craig, J. M., Ferrara, P., & Campion, M. A. (2001). Applicant reactions to selection: Development of the selection procedural justice scale (SPJS). *Personnel Psychology, 54*(2), 387–419.
11. Anderson, N., Ahmed, S., & Costa, A. C. (2012). Applicant reactions in Saudi Arabia: Organizational attractiveness and core-self evaluation. *International Journal of Selection and Assessment, 20*(2), 197–208.
12. Hausknecht, J. P., Day, D. V., & Thomas, S. C. (2004). Applicant reactions to selection procedures: An updated meta-analysis. *Personnel Psychology, 57*(3), 639–683.
13. Truxillo, D. M., Bodner, D. E., Bertolino, M., Bauer, T. N., & Yonce, C. A. (2009). Effects of explanations on applicant reactions: A meta-analytic review. *International Journal of Selection and Assessment, 17*(4), 346–361.
14. Bell, B. S., Wiechmann, D., & Ryan, A. M. (2006). Consequences of organizational justice expectations in a selection system. *Journal of Applied Psychology, 91*(2), 455–466.
15. Geenen, B., Proost, K., van Dijke, M., de Witte, K., & von Grumbkow, J. (2012). The role of affect in the relationship between distributive justice expectations and applicants' recommendation and litigation intentions. *International Journal of Selection and Assessment, 20*(4), 404–413.
16. Bell, B. S., Wiechmann, D., & Ryan, A. M. (2006). Consequences of organizational justice expectations in a selection system. *Journal of Applied Psychology, 91*(2), 455–466.
17. Walsh, B. M., Tuller, M. D., Barnes-Farrell, J. L., & Matthews, R. A. (2010). Investigating the moderating role of cultural practices on the effect of selection fairness perceptions. *International Journal of Selection and Assessment, 18*(4), 365–379.

18. Truxillo, D. M., Bauer, T. N., & Garcia, A. M. (2017). Applicant reactions to hiring procedures. In H. W. Goldstein, E. D. Pulakos, J. Passmore, & C. Semedo (Eds.), *The Wiley Blackwell handbook of the psychology of recruitment, selection and employee retention* (pp. 53–70). John Wiley & Sons Ltd.
19. Geenen, B., Proost, K., van Dijke, M., de Witte, K., & von Grumbkow, J. (2012). The role of affect in the relationship between distributive justice expectations and applicants' recommendation and litigation intentions. *International Journal of Selection and Assessment, 20*(4), 404–413.
20. Bauer, T. N., Truxillo, D. M., Sanchez, R. J., Craig, J. M., Ferrara, P., & Campion, M. A. (2001). Applicant reactions to selection: Development of the selection procedural justice scale (SPJS). *Personnel Psychology, 54*(2), 387–419.
21. Ababneh, K. I., Hackett, R. D., & Schat, A. C. H. (2014). The role of attributions and fairness in understanding job applicant reactions to selection procedures and decisions. *Journal of Business and Psychology, 29*(1), 111–129.
22. Truxillo, D. M., Bauer, T. N., McCarthy, J. M., Anderson, N., & Ahmed, S. M. (2018). Applicant perspectives on employee selection systems. In D. S. Ones, N. Anderson, C. Viswesvaran, & H. K. Sinangil (Eds.), *The SAGE handbook of industrial, work & organizational psychology: Personnel psychology and employee performance* (pp. 508–532). Sage Reference.
23. Greenberg, J. (1990). Organizational justice: Yesterday, today, and tomorrow. *Journal of Management, 16*(2), 399–432.
24. Truxillo, D. M., Bauer, T. N., & McCarthy, J. M. (2015). Applicant fairness reactions to the selection process. In R. S. Cropanzano & M. L. Ambrose (Eds.), *The oxford handbook of justice in the workplace* (pp. 621–640). Oxford University Press.
25. Colquitt, J. A. (2001). On the dimensionality of organizational justice: A construct validation of a measure. *Journal of Applied Psychology, 86*(3), 386–400.
26. Cropanzano, R., Bowen, D. E., & Gilliland, S. W. (2007). The management of organizational justice. *Academy of Management Perspectives, 21*(4), 34–48.
27. Huseman, R. C., Hatfield, J. D., & Miles, E. W. (1987). A new perspective on equity theory: The equity sensitivity construct. *Academy of Management Review, 12*(2), 222–234.
28. Davison, H. K., & Bing, M. N. (2008). The multidimensionality of the equity sensitivity construct: Integrating separate benevolence and entitlement dimensions for enhances construct measurement. *Journal of Managerial Issues, 20*(1), 131–150.
29. McCarthy, J. M., Bauer, T. N., Truxillo, D. M., Anderson, N. R., Costa, A. C., & Ahmed, S. M. (2017). Applicant perspectives during selection: A review addressing "so what?," "what's new?," and "where to next?" *Journal of Management, 43*(6), 1–33.
30. Arvey, R. D., Strickland, W., Drauden, G., & Martin, C. (1990). Motivational components of test taking. *Personnel Psychology, 43*(4), 695–716.
31. Chan, D., Schmitt, N., DeShon, R. P., Clause, C. S., & Delbridge, K. (1997). Reactions to cognitive ability tests: The relationships between race, test performance, face validity perceptions, and test-taking motivation. *Journal of Applied Psychology, 82*(2), 300–310.
32. Bell, B. S., Wiechmann, D., & Ryan, A. M. (2006). Consequences of organizational justice expectations in a selection system. *Journal of Applied Psychology, 91*(2), 455–466.
33. Ployhart, R. E., & Harold, C. M. (2004). The applicant attribution-reaction theory (AART): An integrative theory of applicant attributional processing. *International Journal of Selection and Assessment, 12*(1), 84–98.
34. Ryan, A. M., & Ployhart, R. E. (2000). Applicants' perceptions of selection procedures and decisions: A critical review and agenda for the future. *Journal of Management, 26*(3), 565–606.
35. Truxillo, D. M., Bauer, T. N., Campion, M. A., & Paronto, M. E. (2006). A field study of the role of Big Five personality in applicant perceptions of selection fairness, self, and the hiring organization. *International Journal of Selection and Assessment, 14*(3), 269–277.

36. Viswesvaran, C., & Ones, D. S. (2004). Importance of perceived selection system fairness determinants: Relations with demographic, personality, and job characteristics. *International Journal of Selection and Assessment, 12*(1), 172–186.
37. Hausknecht, J. P., Day, D. V., & Thomas, S. C. (2004). Applicant reactions to selection procedures: An updated meta-analysis. *Personnel Psychology, 57*(3), 639–683.
38. Honkaniemi, L., Feldt, T., Metsäpelto, R., & Tolvanen, A. (2013). Personality types and applicant reactions in real-life selection. *International Journal of Selection and Assessment, 21*(1), 32–45.
39. Geenen, B., Proost, K., van Dijke, M., de Witte, K., & von Grumbkow, J. (2012). The role of affect in the relationship between distributive justice expectations and applicants' recommendation and litigation intentions. *International Journal of Selection and Assessment, 20*(4), 404–413.
40. Truxillo, D. M., Bauer, T. N., & McCarthy, J. M. (2015). Applicant fairness reactions to the selection process. In R. S. Cropanzano & M. L. Ambrose (Eds.), *The oxford handbook of justice in the workplace* (pp. 621–640). Oxford University Press.
41. Bauer, T. N., Truxillo, D. M., Sanchez, R. J., Craig, J. M., Ferrara, P., & Campion, M. A. (2001). Applicant reactions to selection: Development of the selection procedural justice scale (SPJS). *Personnel Psychology, 54*(2), 387–419.
42. Gilliland, S. W. (1993). The perceived fairness of selection systems: An organizational justice perspective. *Academy of Management Review, 18*(4), 694–734.
43. Arvey, R. D., & Sackett, P. R. (1993). Fairness in selection: Current developments and perspectives. In N. Schmitt & W. Borman (Eds.), *Personnel Selection* (pp. 171–202). Jossey-Bass.
44. Hausknecht, J. P., Day, D. V., & Thomas, S. C. (2004). Applicant reactions to selection procedures: An updated meta-analysis. *Personnel Psychology, 57*(3), 639–683.
45. Bauer, T. N., Truxillo, D. M., Sanchez, R. J., Craig, J. M., Ferrara, P., & Campion, M. A. (2001). Applicant reactions to selection: Development of the selection procedural justice scale (SPJS). *Personnel Psychology, 54*(2), 387–419.
46. Gilliland, S. W. (1993). The perceived fairness of selection systems: An organizational justice perspective. *Academy of Management Review, 18*(4), 694–734.
47. Schuler, H. (1993). Social validity of selection situations: A concept and some empirical results. In H. Schuler, J. L. Farr, & M. Smith (Eds.), *Personnel selection and assessment: Individual and organizational perspectives* (pp. 11–26). Lawrence Erlbaum Associates, Inc.
48. Schuler, H. (1993). Social validity of selection situations: A concept and some empirical results. In H. Schuler, J. L. Farr, & M. Smith (Eds.), *Personnel selection and assessment: Individual and organizational perspectives* (pp. 11–26). Lawrence Erlbaum Associates, Inc.
49. Truxillo, D. M., Bodner, D. E., Bertolino, M., Bauer, T. N., & Yonce, C. A. (2009). Effects of explanations on applicant reactions: A meta-analytic review. *International Journal of Selection and Assessment, 17*(4), 346–361.
50. Gilland, S. W. (1993). The perceived fairness of selection systems: An organizational justice perspective. *Academy of Management Review, 18*(4), 694–734.

8 Judgment and decision-making in selection

LEARNING OBJECTIVES

- Know the definition of selection
- Understand the costs of a bad hire
- Know the models of judgment and decision-making
- Be able to compare and contrast the holistic versus mechanical approach in decision-making
- Understand the fallacy of intuition in hiring decision-making
- Know the various approaches in making hiring decisions
- Know the criteria for deciding which selection tools to use

In 2013, there were more than two million applicants to Google. For every 130 applicants, only one got hired, making getting a job at the "Happiest Company in America" almost ten times harder than getting admitted as a student to Harvard![1] To an applicant, this is surely an intimidating statistic. Consider, though, the daunting task of the hiring manager who has to weed through all those applicants. How would one decide whom to hire? As discussed in Chapter 4, effective recruitment may help attract many applicants, but we certainly do not want to hire *everyone* interested in working for us. Instead, we want to hire only those who best possess the KSAOs required of the job and who would fit within the group and organizational contexts. This process of identifying suitable candidates to fill job positions is referred to as **personnel selection** or just **selection**.[2]

> **Selection:** The process of identifying the most suitable individual from a pool of applicants for a job position.

In this chapter, we will examine the psychological processes used to help employers judge the qualifications of individual applicants as well as the process that employers use to decide who to hire.

The costs of a bad hire

Selection is one of the most important topics in personnel psychology. It is important because a poor hire could cost an employer a great deal of money. According to the U.S. Department of Labor, the average cost of a bad hiring decision can equal 30% of the individual's first-year potential earnings. The late ex-CEO of Zappos, Tony Hsieh, estimated that his own bad hires have cost the company over $100 million.[3]

The cost of making a bad hiring decision is more than just financial. To quote Ben Schneider in his presidential address to the Society for Industrial and Organizational Psychology almost three decades ago, "the attributes of people ... are the fundamental determinants of organizational behavior."[4] Put more aptly, "the people make the place," such that members of an organization "come to define the way that place looks, feels, and behaves." Hence, a poor hire could have ripple effects throughout the company. In a survey of 2,100 chief financial officers regarding the cost of bad hires, most were concerned about decreased employee morale (39%) and productivity (34%), with financial costs coming in third (25%).[5] Realizing that a poor hire can have a negative effect on the culture of Zappos, the company now offers new employees a $2,000 bonus to quit after their first week on the job![6]

A poor hiring decision also has implications for the individual who was chosen for the job. A comprehensive meta-analysis of various forms of fit and their outcomes showed decreased job satisfaction with poor person-job fit, lower organizational commitment with poor person-organization fit, and lower satisfaction with co-workers when there was a poor fit between the individual and team members.[7]

Selection as prediction

Selection is ultimately about making predictions about the future, specifically about the employees we have hired. How will they perform? How well will they get along with others in the organization? Will they steal from the company? How likely is it that they will be frequently absent or even quit? These questions remind us of a classic toy developed by Mattel in the 1950s. The Magic 8 Ball™, a novelty toy, is a plastic sphere resembling an eight ball with a transparent window. One would turn the ball upside-down, ask a *yes-no* question, and (voila!) the answer would be revealed in the window when the ball is turned over. The Magic 8 Ball is unfortunately but a toy; fortunately, though, there is a great deal of science to help us predict how individuals may behave in the future so we can avoid making bad hires and increase the odds employers will hire those who possess the traits and exhibit the behaviors their organizations want.

To make these predictions, we have to make judgments of applicants in order to decide whom to hire. **Judgment** refers to an evaluation of a person, object, or event in terms of its value or attractiveness.[8] In personnel selection, a hiring manager would make a judgment of how qualified a candidate is for a job. In contrast, a **decision** involves choosing between a set of alternatives. For example, a hiring manager faced with three top candidates has to decide whom to hire.

> **Judgment:** An evaluation of a person, object, or event in terms of its value or attractiveness.

> **Decision:** Choosing between a set of alternatives.

As noted by Huber, Neale, and Northcraft,[9] "the very nature of human resource management is a series of choices." Therefore, it is important for us to understand how people make judgments and decisions, so that aids may be developed to reduce any mistakes or address human shortcomings. The study of judgment and decision-making (JDM) spans many disciplines, from economics to cognitive psychology. Theory and research in this area have implications for any aspect of life that involves JDM, including medicine, criminal justice, public policy, and of course, personnel psychology. Below, we cover several of the major theories of JDM and key research findings as they pertain to personnel selection.

Models of judgment and decision-making

According to the **normative model of decision-making**, people are assumed to be *rational* decision-makers who would estimate the probability of any alternative and multiply this by its utility to determine the value of success. The decision-maker would then choose the alternative which yields the highest utility. This rational model of decision-making comes from the field of economics, and although useful in providing standards of evaluation,[10] it falls short of capturing how people actually make decisions. Take, for instance, a hiring manager interviewing an applicant. Would they ask all applicants who have been called in for the interview the same exact questions in the same order? Would they recall all responses of every applicant? Would all applicants be evaluated against the same standard? We I-O psychologists would be thrilled to hear this happens.

> **Normative Model of Judgment and Decision-making:** Model that proposes people are rational decision-makers who estimate the probability and value of uncertain outcomes, and choose the alternative with the highest utility.

In reality, however, the interviewer would have asked some questions of some candidates and not of others, and included some casual conversations. Very negative interviewee responses would be more likely to be remembered and considered in the final decision.[11] Strong candidates interviewed earlier in the day probably received higher ratings than those interviewed later.[12] This more realistic scenario reflects the idea of **bounded rationality**, proposed by Herbert Simon (one of only a few psychologists who have won the Nobel Prize – alas, in economics as there is none given in psychology). As an alternative to the rational model, this model proposes that our ability to make rational decisions is limited by our own cognitive resources, availability of information, and time.

> **Bounded Rationality:** Model of human judgment and decision-making which proposes that rational decision-making is constrained by limited cognitive resources, availability of information, and time.

> **Descriptive Model:** Model of decision-making that describes how people actually make decisions.

Taking the idea of bounded rationality even further, Daniel Kahneman (another psychologist with a Nobel Prize in economics) and Amos Tversky proposed the **descriptive model of decision-making**. As the name implies, this model *describes* how people actually make decisions, by illustrating common departures from normative standards. Many decisions involve predicting uncertain events. One way to make predictions is to assess the probability of their occurrence. However, assessing probabilities is quite a complex task for which most of us are not equipped in terms of time and resources. Hence, we rely on simple judgmental operations referred to as "heuristics." Put another way, heuristics are

Judgment and decision-making in selection

"mental shortcuts" we all take to navigate a rather complex world. In doing so, we can make judgments and decisions more quickly. However, this may result in errors and biases. Below is a discussion of heuristics and biases that commonly occur.

> **Heuristic:** Simple judgmental operation or mental shortcut used to quickly make judgments or decisions.

Let's start with a scenario Kahneman and Tversky presented to participants in one of their classic studies:

> Linda is 31 years old, single, outspoken, and very bright. She majored in philosophy. As a student she was deeply concerned with issues of discrimination and social justice and also participated in antinuclear demonstrations.

Which do you think is more probable: (1) Linda is a bank teller or (2) Linda is a bank teller and is active in the feminist movement? If your answer is that Linda is a bank teller and active in the feminist movement, then you are like the vast majority (over 80%) of participants. And you would be wrong, because probability-wise, there are many more bank tellers than bank tellers who are also feminists. (The former probability would include bankers who were feminists as well as bankers who did not identify as feminists, whereas the latter probability would include only bankers who were feminists and by definition must be lower than the former.) The heuristic just illustrated is called the *representativeness heuristic*, where we judge the probability of an occurrence by its similarity to a prototypical object or event. We think of feminists as having liberal views, therefore, align Linda with the feminist movement. This heuristic may be used to explain our reliance on stereotypes in judging others. For example, many studies demonstrate the existence of the "what-is-beautiful-is-good" belief that physically attractive individuals also possess other desirable traits. Subsequently, physically attractive individuals are more likely to be judged favorably and selected by hiring managers.[13]

> **Representativeness Heuristic:** Judging the probability of an occurrence by its similarity to a prototypical object or event.

> **Availability Heuristic:** Judging the probability of an occurrence by how easily it comes to mind.

The availability heuristic refers to how frequently we think something will occur simply by what we can remember. When making a final decision regarding which candidate to choose after interviews have been conducted, decision-makers tend to recall more negative information about candidates than positive information.[14]

Let's turn here to a quick question to see if you have been paying attention to your reading: How many students applied for admission to Harvard in 2013? The correct answer is 35,000 students vied to be in Harvard's class of 2017. However, if your answer was much higher and closer to two million, then we have successfully demonstrated the next heuristic. In other words, you may have been swayed by the statistic I had provided regarding the number of applicants to Google. This tendency to be swayed by an initial estimate is the anchoring bias. In one study, interviewers were provided scoring keys that contained either high, low, or no anchors.[15] Interviewers who were asked to rate applicants against "a score of 5 (5 = good)" provided higher ratings than those who were asked to rate applicants against "a score of 1 (1= poor)."

> **Anchoring:** Making estimations that are based upon an initial value.

At this point, let's summarize two of the major points made thus far about JDM. First, humans are generally not rational decision-makers as suggested. Second, and on the contrary, we rely on mental shortcuts that often result in errors and biases. The costs of poor decisions (i.e., making a bad hire) warrant a model that bridges the normative and descriptive models to help people actually be able to make good decisions. Prescriptive models of decision-making are "based on both the strong theoretical foundation of normative theory in combination with the observations of descriptive theory."[16] There is not one specific prescriptive model; rather, this framework captures a more applied approach to helping real-life decision-makers meet the standards of the normative model, by taking into consideration the limitations uncovered by the descriptive model.[17]

> **Comparing the Three Models of Judgment and Decision-making:**
>
> Normative: What people should do (in theory).
>
> Descriptive: What people actually do, or have done.
>
> Prescriptive: What people should and can do.

What about intuition?

An assumption underlying all the models of JDM covered earlier is the belief that *rationality* is the path toward good decision-making. In other words, the normative model assumes (albeit incorrectly) that people are rational decision-makers and espouses rationality as the standard. The descriptive approach suggests that this failure to be rational results in biases and errors in decision-making. The prescriptive approach sets rationality as the goal in any applied decision tools. But what about intuition? There are few other topics in selection decision-making that yields as many contradictions. A Google search using the keywords "intuition and hiring" yielded 42,100,000 hits. Below are some of them:

- When It Comes to Hiring, Don't Trust Your Intuition
- In Hiring, Algorithms Beat Instinct

- Intuition "Very Important" in Recruitment for 9 in 10 Leaders
- How Data Beats Intuition in Making Selection Decisions
- All Hiring Decisions Hinge on a Single Factor: Intuition
- Six Reasons to Recruit with Intuition

Such contradictions regarding the usefulness of intuition in hiring exist possibly for two reasons. First, there appears to be great confusion, if not disagreement, about what "intuition" means. In the popular press, terms such as "gut feelings," "awareness," and "expertise" have been used to mean intuition. To arrive at a more scientific definition of intuition as *affectively charged judgments that arise through rapid, non-conscious, and holistic associations*,[18] Dane and Pratt gathered the numerous, various definitions of intuition from the philosophical and social scientific literature.[19]

You may have read the news about the pilot who safely landed U.S. Airways Flight 1549 on the Hudson River in 2009 after the plane's both engines shut down. Would recounts of this event be more exciting if the pilot talked about how his extensive training had prepared him? Or, would it be more interesting to hear about how his instinctive, quick reaction saved 155 lives? Analyses of this event reveal that both intuition and extensive training of the pilot were crucial. However, intuition is not effective in all decision-making situations.[20] In predicting which applicants will be effective employees, a meta-analysis of 17 studies showed the superiority of rational versus intuition decision-making.[21] More specifically, the "mechanical" approach, which involves applying an algorithm to applicant scores, was compared to the "holistic" approach, which uses human judgment or intuition. Results indicated that a simple equation outperformed human decisions by at least 25%, across a large number of candidates at all job levels.

What about expertise?

In his article, *Stubborn Reliance on Intuition and Subjectivity in Employee Selection*, Scott Highhouse argued that the "myth of expertise" is one of the reasons intuitive selection decision-making has appeal. People tend to believe in their own skill in judging others, despite evidence suggesting that the same heuristic and biases identified in the descriptive model are committed by even those with years of hiring experience. (Ironically, overconfidence itself is one of the well-known biases in the JDM literature.) Kahneman himself likens "intuition" with "expertise."[22] However, he states that intuition cannot be improved: "I've been studying intuition for 45 years, and I'm no better than when I started. I make extreme predictions. I'm over-confident. I fall for every one of the biases."

Which selection tools should we use?

Although industrial-organizational psychologists have yet to develop the magic selection ball, decades of research have yielded numerous tools that allow us to predict future work behavior. As noted by Highhouse, "the greatest technological achievement in industrial and organizational (I–O) psychology over the past 100 years is the development of decision aids ... that substantially reduce error in the prediction of employee performance." In the next several chapters, we will discuss these selection tools that help hiring decision-makers accurately judge applicants and choose the best one, thereby avoiding the numerous costs of making a bad hire. While more details will be provided regarding each of these selection tools in upcoming chapters, we provide a framework here that will help you decide which selection tool should be used. In an ideal scenario with unlimited resources, one could consider using many selection tools in order to provide as comprehensive of an evaluation of a job applicant as possible. However, selection costs money, so employers must be thoughtful about which tool to use. Moreover, as an applicant, you may not necessarily want to jump through too many hoops in order to be considered for a position. Hence, below is a list of five criteria that should be taken into consideration when deciding which selection tool should be used to hire the best applicants:

- Validity: How related is performance on the selection tool to a future outcome, such as job performance? Refer to Chapter 5 which covers validity.
- Potential adverse impact/Legal issues: Are members of a protected class less likely to get hired based upon outcomes of the tool? Are there concerns regarding invasion of privacy? Refer to Chapter 2 which covers legal issues.
- Response distortion (Faking): How possible is it for an applicant to "lie" when responding?
- Applicant reactions: How do applicants feel about the selection tool? Would they feel that it is fair? Refer to Chapter 7 which covers fairness and applicant reactions.
- Practicality: How much would the selection tool cost the organization? How much time would it take to administer?

In addition to using the above criteria to determine how "good" a selection tool is, we could also conduct a utility analysis, which could let us know the financial benefits of using a specific selection tool.[23] While there are several utility analysis techniques, one common way is to calculate the net dollars gained from using the selection tool. A few studies have been conducted to see if presenting a utility analysis will convince hiring managers to utilize these more rational, mechanical approaches when making selection decisions. Results have been mixed. One early study found that such information may actually turn managers off from using these tools.[24] While subsequent studies have failed to replicate this negative effect,[25] the "utility" of utility analysis remains up in the air.

Which selection plan should we use?

As mentioned earlier, we must be selective about which selection tools we would want to use and relying on various criteria to assess the tools will help us make our decision. That said, it is wise to use more than one selection tool because not any one tool can capture the many knowledge, skills, and abilities required to perform a job. Consider, for example, a fairly simple job such as a grocery bagger. The bagger needs to have, among other requirements, hand dexterity, physical strength, and must be conscientious and friendly. To assess these skills, abilities, and traits, several selection tools could be used, including a physical ability test, structured interview, and personality test. When several selection tools are used, the hiring decision-maker must plan an overall strategy. There are several options possible. One is a hurdle approach, in which the applicant is assessed on one selection tool first then only moves on if they pass. In this example, the applicant could first be given a personality test, and then only if they meet a desired minimum score, be invited to take part in the physical ability test, and then if they do well enough, move onto the structured interview. An advantage of the hurdle approach is that it will ultimately cost less for the organization as the applicant pool gets reduced after each stage; there is less cost per application for administration and assessment. Putting the less costly (in both time and money) selection tool earlier can keep costs lower as we are assessing more applicants at that stage. A disadvantage is that an applicant, who might otherwise have been qualified, may be ruled out by poor performance on just one of the selection tools. A remedy to this concern is to assess applicants on all the selection tools. This approach may allow an applicant to compensate for doing poorly on one selection tool by doing well on another. For example, if the applicant does poorly on the personality test, they may still be considered for the job if they did well on the physical ability test and structured interview. Of course, putting applicants through all the selection tools will cost more time and money for the employer and may not ultimately net a financial benefit. Moreover, a compensatory approach may not be at all appropriate if the job requires all the knowledge, skills, and abilities being assessed by each of the selection tools. In summary, we encourage you to think about the entire selection process and these various approaches as we will be discussing specific selection tools in the next several chapters.

REVIEW QUESTIONS

1. What is the definition of personnel selection?
2. What are the costs of a bad hire?
3. Compare and contrast the models of judgment and decision-making.
4. What are the various heuristics and biases in judgment and decision-making?
5. What does research say about the holistic versus mechanical approach in decision-making?
6. How useful is intuition in hiring decision-making?
7. How useful is expertise in hiring decision-making?
8. What are the criteria to decide which selection tool(s) to use?
9. What are the several approaches to a selection plan?

DISCUSSION QUESTIONS

1. If you were a hiring manager, would you prefer a mechanical approach or holistic approach to decision-making when selecting your employees? Explain your answer.
2. If you were a job applicant, would you prefer the employer use a mechanical or holistic approach in decision-making when selecting employees? Explain your answer.
3. Do you agree or disagree with the perspective that humans are irrational decision-makers?
4. What decisions have you made for which you relied solely upon intuition? What were the outcomes of your decisions?
5. What decisions have you made for which you relied solely upon the rational approach? What were the outcomes of your decisions?
6. Of the five criteria used to decide which selection tool to use, which criterion do you think is most important, and why? Which criterion do you think is least important, and why?
7. Think of a specific job and imagine you have to create a selection plan to select applicants for that job. Which approach would you take?

Notes

1. http://www.forbes.com/sites/stanphelps/2014/08/05/cracking-into-google-the-15-reasons-why-over-2-million-people-apply-each-year/
2. http://www.apadivisions.org/division-31/publications/articles/california/bobrow.pdf
3. http://www.businessinsider.com/tony-hsieh-hiring-wrong-people-2014-1#ixzz3h0wEE9lt
4. Schneider, B. (1987). The people make the place. *Personnel Psychology, 40,* 437–453.
5. http://www.shrm.org/hrdisciplines/staffingmanagement/articles/pages/morale-productivity-bad-hires.aspx#sthash.rw5Yq0Pa.dpuf
6. https://www.businessinsider.com/zappos-tony-hsieh-paid-new-workers-to-quit-the-offer-2020-11
7. Kristof-Brown, A., Zimmerman, R. D., & Johnson, E. C. (2005). Consequences of individuals' fit at work: A meta-analysis of person-job, person-organization, person-group, and person-supervisor fit. *Personnel Psychology, 58*(2), 281–342.
8. Dalal, R. S., Bonaccio, S., Highhouse, S., Ilgen, D. R., Mohammed, S., & Slaughter, J. E. (2010). What if industrial-organizational psychology decided to take workplace decisions seriously? *Industrial and Organizational Psychology: Perspectives on Science and Practice, 3*(4), 386–405.
9. Huber, V. L., Neale, M. A., & Northcraft, G. B. (1987). Decision bias and personnel selection strategies. *Organizational Behavior and Human Decision Processes, 40*(1), 136–147.
10. Baron, J. (2012). The point of normative models in judgment and decision making. *Frontiers in Psychology, 3,* 577. https://doi.org/10.3389/fpsyg.2012.00577
11. Dipboye, R. (1994). Structured and unstructured selection interviews: Beyond the job-fit model. In G. R. Ferris (Ed.), *Research in personnel and human resources management: Vol. 12* (pp. 79–123). JAI Press Inc.

12. Simonsohn, U., & Gino, F. (2013). <u>Daily horizons: Evidence of narrow bracketing in judgments from 9000 MBA admission interviews.</u> *Psychological Science, 24*(2), 219–224.
13. Hosoda, M., Stone-Romero, E., & Coats, G. (2003). The effects of physical attractiveness on job-related outcomes: A meta-analysis of experimental studies. *Personnel Psychology, 56*(2), 431–462.
14. Constantin, S. W. (1976). An investigation of information favorability in the employment interview. *Journal of Applied Psychology, 61*(6), 743–749.
15. Kataoka, H. C., Latham, G. P., & Whyte, G. (1997). The relative resistance of the situational, patterned behaviour and conventional structured interviews to anchoring effects. *Human Performance, 10*(1), 47–63.
16. Dillon, M.S. (1998). Descriptive decision making; comparing theory with practice, Department of Management Systems, University of Waikato, New Zealand.
17. David E. Bell, Howard Raiffa, & Amos Tversky (Eds.). (1988). *Decision making: Descriptive, normative and prescriptive interactions*. Cambridge University Press.
18. Dane, E., Rockmann, K. W., & Pratt, M. G. (2012). When should I trust my gut? Linking domain expertise to intuitive decision-making effectiveness. *Organizational Behavior and Human Decision Processes, 119*(2), 187–194.
19. Dane, E., & Pratt, M. G. (2007). Exploring intuition and its role in managerial decision making. *The Academy of Management Review, 32*(1), 33–54.
20. Dane, E., & Pratt, M. G. (2007). Exploring intuition and its role in managerial decision making. *The Academy of Management Review, 32*(1), 33–54.
21. Kuncel, N. R., Klieger, D. M., Connelly, B. S., & Ones, D. S. (2013). Mechanical versus clinical data combination in selection and admissions decisions: A meta-analysis. *Journal of Applied Psychology, 98*(6), 1060–1072.
22. http://engineering.nyu.edu/news/2012/03/13/end-intuition-daniel-kahneman-speaks-14th-annual-lynford-lecture
23. Cronshaw, S. F., & Alexander, R. A. (1985). One answer to the demand for accountability: Selection utility as an investment decision. *Organizational Behavior and Human Decision Processes, 35*, 102–118.
24. Latham, G. P., & Whyte, G. (1994). The futility of utility analysis. *Personnel Psychology, 47*(1), 31–46.
25. Carson, K. P., Becker, J. S., & Henderson, J. A. (1998). Is utility really futile? A failure to replicate and an extension. *Journal of Applied Psychology, 83*(1), 84–96.

9 Ability tests

LEARNING OBJECTIVES

- Learn about different types of ability tests, including cognitive ability, clerical ability, physical ability, mechanical ability, and job knowledge tests
- Learn about the validity and reliability of these different types of ability tests
- Learn about the advantages and disadvantages of including ability measures in pre-employment selection

You have likely already taken a lot of ability tests, especially as a K–12 student. The United States in particular is a country that tests its students frequently. Early ability assessments test reading capacity to determine the appropriate level of instructions as well as identify the need for remedial training. You likely also took the ACT or SAT, a test that decided whether you were able to gain admittance to a college or university of your choice, and for many of you, you are studying for the Graduate Record Examination (GRE) so that you can gain admittance into a graduate program (perhaps in I-O psychology!) of your choice. Finally, for many jobs that you might have applied for, you might have assessed basic mathematical ability, typing skills, or knowledge about mechanics.

One of the most robust findings in personnel psychology has been that ability tests, in particular cognitive ability tests, predict success on the job for nearly every occupation and job type, and in general they are some of the most predictive of success compared to nearly every other type of predictor.[1] In addition, testing for specific types of abilities required for different jobs is important as well. For example, if a company wants to hire a mechanic, it is crucial that an applicant has a basic understanding of mechanical principles. Although ability tests have high validity, there are some challenges with their use because they also tend to have significant adverse impact, thus providing a dilemma for organizations on validity versus adverse impact.

In this chapter, we will review some of the basic findings about ability tests, and will discuss cognitive ability tests, clerical ability tests, physical ability tests, mechanical ability tests, and job knowledge tests.

Cognitive ability tests

Applicants are often surprised to be given tests of basic arithmetic when applying for jobs that seemingly do not require basic math to be done on a daily basis. In fact, who really needs to do basic arithmetic any more with calculators close by on our smartphones? And vocabulary similarly often seems less important in a world where definitions are just a click away on online dictionaries. Many entry-level selection tests incorporate tests of basic ability even though candidates often fail to see the connection between the content of the items and the content of the job that they will eventually do. These tests are popular, though, because research has consistently shown that cognitive ability is one of the top predictors of job success *across nearly all types of jobs*. This is likely because people with higher cognitive ability are able to learn and apply job-related information and techniques more quickly, on average, than those with lower cognitive ability.

John Hunter and Frank Schmidt in a series of meta-analyses conducted in the 1970s and 1980s demonstrated that cognitive ability tests were the best predictors (except work samples) across all levels of jobs, including those with high complexity (e.g., managers and data analysts) and those with low complexity (e.g., assembly line factory workers). Validities are slightly higher for jobs high in complexity than those lower in complexity though cognitive ability is predictive of all criteria related to job performance, including supervisor ratings, promotion, tenure, and training success.[2] Recent research has shown cognitive ability tests to be useful in predicting performance adaptation, which is a measure of how much someone can adapt their approaches to changes in the work environment, a skill that seems especially important given the rate for which the workplace is changing.[3] That researcher found that cognitive ability was most predictive in performance adaptation in highly dynamic situations ($r = .31$), even more so than relevant personality tests.

One dilemma with cognitive ability tests is how to best measure it. Psychologists have debated the nature of intelligence throughout the history of the field, often with little consensus on what it is.[4] There are a large number of theories about intelligence and each one of these theories has potentially different implications for how to measure it. One could spend a whole semester digging into the particular theories of intelligence, though we will focus on one important distinction in cognitive ability measurement, in particular broad versus specific traits.

Types of measures

One common refrain in measurement is the notion of broad versus narrow traits, a theme that we encountered in job performance measurement and one that we will visit again in the next chapter when talking about personality measurement. In the context of cognitive ability, the debate goes back to the early days of measurement when Charles Spearman and LL Thurstone argued whether you should just focus on a general factor of intelligence (Spearman's choice) or more narrow measures of cognitive ability (Thurstone's preference). g, as proposed by Spearman, was identified as the general or first factor for which nearly all mental abilities load on when conducting a factor analysis. Although more specific factors (such as verbal, spatial, and numerical) are likely to show up in a factor analysis, there is a general factor that all items load on.

General intelligence, g, is the first factor that is related to nearly all measures of intelligence.

Specific Factors of Intelligence. Measures of intelligence that are narrowly focused on a particular type of content domain (e.g., mathematical ability or spatial ability).

Until recently, the general conclusion was that a general measure of cognitive ability, typically label g, was the most predictive and useful measure to use in applied settings. The "not much more than g" argument was that once g was included in a prediction equation, specific factors failed to add incremental prediction in job performance[5] and training performance.[6] More recent research, however, shows that well-chosen narrow measures of cognitive ability can provide incremental prediction.[7] Specifically, specific factors that are relatively less correlated with g are more useful in providing incremental validity. Traits such as visual processing, general knowledge, and processing speed were the most useful narrow traits. This research shows that if you can only include a single measure of cognitive ability, then g would be the best choice. However, if you want to maximize prediction, a measure of *g* combined with well-chosen narrow traits would be helpful. The takeaway message from this research is that specific abilities tailored toward a particular job can be useful.

Popular measures of *g*

Given the importance of *g*, we review several popular tests of general intelligence, including the Raven's Advanced Progressive Matrices (RAPMs) and the International Cognitive Ability Resource (ICAR).

Raven's Advanced Progressive Matrices. The RAPMs were developed initially by John Raven to measure cognitive ability using non-verbal items, thus minimizing cultural differences and reducing the reliance on vocabulary.[8] The test includes 36 items that are arranged in ascending difficulty and the test is usually administered as a power test, that is administered without time limit, though in some cases time limit of 40–60 minutes has been used. A shortened 12-item version of the RAPM has been developed for those who wish to cut down administration time significantly.[9] There is also an additional version of the Raven's test that can be administered to clinical populations, useful for clinical psychologists who are using cognitive tests for clinical diagnoses and tests of impairment.

International Cognitive Ability Resource (ICAR). The ICAR is a public-domain measure that was developed to spur research and provide a common tool for researchers to use when measuring cognitive ability.[10] There are four facets or subdimensions of the ICAR, Letter and Number Series, Matrix Reasoning, Three-Dimensional Rotation, and Verbal Reasoning, and there is a 16-item version of the ICAR that combines four items from each dimension into an overall score, which itself has shown significant correlations with SAT and ACT scores as well as other measures of achievement and cognitive ability. The project was designed to be ongoing with the creation of additional items and measures as well as the ability for potential users to share validity data. Although this test might not be appropriate for personnel selection given that all items are publicly available and hence could be easily compromised for job applicants, the test could help advance organizational research on cognitive ability by providing a free tool that has established reliability and validity for researchers who wish to incorporate measures of cognitive ability in their research.

Challenges using tests of cognitive ability

Although cognitive ability tests tend to have some of the highest validity of all predictors for a wide variety of jobs, they also tend to have high adverse impact for some of predicted classes (refer Chapter 2). For example, one analysis[11] found about a standard deviation lower on tests of general cognitive ability for African-Americans compared to Whites, with Latino/a groups scoring half a standard deviation lower compared to Whites on the same tests. However, Asian-Americans tended to score .2 standard deviation units higher on these tests than Whites, and there were no meaningful differences between men and women on tests of general intelligence. Older Americans tended to score .4 standard deviation units lower than younger Americans. These mean differences across groups highlight that if you use a test of general cognitive ability, everything else equal, you will hire disproportionately more White, Asian, and younger applicants and fewer African-American, Latino/a, and older applicants. Given the importance that most businesses have in terms of hiring diverse employees, companies are often placed in a dilemma of choosing validity or diversity. It should be noted that these mean differences are for tests of general cognitive ability. Tests measuring specific constructs of cognitive ability tend to have less adverse impact, even though they may often also have less validity.

Given the importance of hiring diverse employees, there has been considerable attention paid toward strategies that help companies resolve the validity-diversity dilemma. In this section, we will briefly review these strategies. The first strategy is to use *banding*. Banding takes into account the uncertainty of individual test scores and creates ranges of equivalence for which all test scorers who are within a particular band are treated equivalently. Instead of using top-down selection, which requires organizations to choose the top-scoring candidate and then the second-highest applicant, banding gives organizations more flexibility. For example, on a test that ranges from 0 to 100, people within the 88–100 range (i.e., band) may be treated as equal during the selection process. Once bands are formed, organizations may randomly choose within a band or even choose based on protected class status, though the latter is risky legally as our court system tends to outlaw systems that explicitly use race. Usually, the key statistic used to create bands is the standard error of measurement which incorporates the reliability of the test along with test variability, in an effort to quantify the range of uncertainty that is present in all individual test scores.

Test Score Banding. Ranges of test scores that are created, typically based on the standard error of measurement, take into account the inherent uncertainty of individual test scores. Applicants who fall within the same band are treated as equivalent.

Test banding is not without controversy; however, with some I-O psychologists advocating that even though at the individual level scores may be statistically equivalent, in general, scores that are higher than scores that are lower should be treated as such.[12] In general, the debate about banding within I-O psychology has been substantial,[13] though we believe that the logic behind the tool (treat scores that are statistically equivalent as equivalent) is one that should be considered.

Add non-cognitive predictors to the test battery

In addition to test banding, I-O psychologists have advocated adding tests to the selection battery that measure features that have less adverse impact. For example, personality traits (we will discuss more in the next chapter) tend to have modest validity with job performance criteria and they tend to have minimal adverse impact across race. The logic is that by adding tests without adverse impact to a battery that has a test with substantial adverse impact, the overall adverse impact will be decreased. Research shows, however, that adding a personality test to a test battery that has cognitive ability tends not to reduce adverse impact substantially.[14]

Other solutions to reducing adverse impact

Another strategy that has been proposed to reduce adverse impact is to make sure that there are good training materials freely and widely available to help test takers prepare for taking your test. The logic is that affluent applicants may do better on your exam because they feel more comfortable taking standardized tests (and have more experience taking them) and so if you can make sure that all applicants are prepared in advance, organizations may help all candidates score better, especially those prone to anxiety. Most of the data that has been collected on the role of coaching has been in the educational domain, though the small amount of research in the employment literature shows modest reductions in adverse impact for race after coaching.[15] This is a low-cost way of reducing adverse impact while also reducing anxiety among test takers, hence also likely improving validity.

A related solution is dealing with *stereotype threat*, a concept proposed by Steele that posits that in some situations a stereotype related to a group becomes more salient and for those group members, the increased saliency of the stereotype causes stress and anxiety, thus causing a reduction in performance.[16] Stereotype threat has been used as an explanation for mean differences between Blacks and Whites as well as men and women on cognitive ability tests. In the original research, Steele and Aronson placed students in a non-threat condition (i.e., participants were told that problem-solving tests were not diagnostic of ability) or a threat condition (i.e., participants were told that the same tests measured verbal ability). In that experiment, after controlling for SAT, Black students in the threat condition performed significantly worse than Blacks in the non-threat condition, worse than Whites in the threat condition, and similar to Whites in the non-threat condition. As pointed out by Tomeh and Sackett,[17] accounting for stereotype threat does not eliminate Black-White differences on tests, though the research body does show that reducing the threat in testing can make differences smaller. Therefore, some recommendations are to make sure test takers feel at ease during the testing (prior exposure to items can help) as well as minimize the saliency of race and sex. Therefore, if an organization is collecting demographic information about applicants, make sure to collect that information after testing is completed so that race or sex is not made salient.

Stereotype Threat. A state of anxiety or stress for specific group members caused by the heightened saliency of their group membership in particular situations.

Clerical skills

If you are hiring for a job that requires lots of typing and data entry, it makes sense that one of the best predictors would be a test of clerical ability. There are several typical forms of these clerical tests: production tests that test the speed and accuracy of typing as well as other tests that focus on proofreading ability. Typically, these tests have a large speeded component in that applicants are asked to type as much as they can within a short amount of time, or they are given material to proofread and are given a short amount of time to catch as many errors as possible. An assumption of a speeded test is that given enough time, nearly all respondents should be able to answer all items correctly (e.g., find all the errors), but that a strict time limit tests a respondent's ability to complete tasks quickly. Other examples of speeded tests are basic arithmetic tests that include a large number of simple arithmetic items, more than that could be completed by most applicants. Speeded tests are useful in predicting success on jobs where time is important, though they present challenges with a traditional item analysis given that all items are roughly equal in difficulty.

Speeded Test. All items are roughly of the same ability. The tests are administered with a strict time deadline so that the final score is the number of items completed.

A recent study used a comparing-and-checking test that was administered without a time limit, where job applicants had to identify whether two sets of typically encountered stimuli (e.g., website URLs, email addresses, and names) were identical or different. When administered without a time limit, the test was correlated with personality measures of attention to detail and perfectionism, as well as supervisor ratings of performance on detailed tasks.[18]

In a meta-analysis of the predictive validity of different types of predictors of clerical performance, Weitzel et al. found that performance tests (i.e., tests of typing skill and document production) had the highest corrected validity ($r = .56$) with tests of general mental ability ($r = .52$) and perceptual speed ($r = .50$) to be the highest,[19] although general clerical aptitude tests, tests of verbal ability, quantitative ability, and reasoning were also quite high. They compared validities of these tests with validities conducted on meta-analyses done prior to 1980 and found that most tests maintained their validity, though the validity of quantitative ability tests decreased slightly, perhaps due to the ubiquity of calculators for most clerical staff. Verbal ability, performance tests, and reasoning, however, had slightly increased validity over that time. Whetzel et al. reasoned that the nature of clerical performance has changed significantly over time with the nature of the job rising in complexity as computers are able to handle more mundane aspects of the job. Whetzel's analysis makes us realize that tests need to adapt to the changing nature of work, though in most cases, tests of basic abilities will maintain validity.

Mechanical aptitude tests

When hiring for jobs that require specific mechanical knowledge, it may make sense to hire individuals who have the specific skills needed to operate mechanical equipment or the aptitude to learn mechanical tasks quickly. We all know individuals who can quickly figure out how to repair a lawn mower or a car engine with minimal reliance on any reference or guidebooks, whereas others (including myself) freeze at the thought of doing simple mechanical tests. There are a series of tests that have been developed to predict performance on mechanical jobs. The Bennett Mechanical Comprehension Test and the Ramsay Mechanical Aptitude Test (RMAT) are two tests that have been used frequently in hiring.

Bennett Mechanical Comprehension Test II (BMCTII). The Bennett measures mechanical comprehension, spatial visualization, knowledge of basic physical and mechanical principles, and technical dedication of how machinery works.[20] The current version of the test has 55 items that cover ten topic areas and applicants are given 25 minutes to complete the test. One study investigated the role of the Bennett in conjunction with general cognitive ability tests in predicting success in manufacturing jobs and found that the Bennett provided was the best predictor of job performance and that other aptitude and ability tests did not provide incremental validity.[21]

Ramsay Mechanical Aptitude Test (RMAT). The RMAT is a 36-item test designed for hiring employees who need to know or learn job activities related to production and maintenance. It has four content areas, including household objects, work: production and maintenance, school: science and physics, and hand and power tools. The test has been found to correlate significantly ($r = .40$, $p < .01$) with the GPA of post-secondary technical school students and correlates highly with other tests of mechanical job knowledge.[22]

Physical ability tests

To be successful on some jobs, you need a certain amount of ability to lift and carry large objects. For example, firefighters need to be able to carry people out of burning rooms to safety and so to be a successful firefighter you will need a certain amount of strength. For other jobs, you may need eye-hand coordination or a certain amount of physical dexterity. Joyce Hogan in pioneering work done on physical ability tests found three general factors that underlie physical ability measurement: *muscular strength, cardiovascular endurance,* and *movement quality*. The latter includes coordination, balance, and flexibility.[23]

Three Categories of Physical Abilities. Muscular strength, cardiovascular endurance, and movement quality (flexibility, balance, and coordination).

Arvey et al. developed physical ability tests used for hiring police officers to measure endurance and strength. Tests that assessed strength include grip strength, the dummy drag test (i.e., how fast can you drag a dummy a specified distance), the dummy wrestle test (i.e., how fast can you make a series of rolls and rotations simulating wrestling a suspect to the ground), lifting and carrying, and pushing and pulling. Endurance tests include an obstacle course, sit-ups, bench dips, and a one-mile run.[24] Some tests such as the 100-yard dash as well as the dummy drag and dummy wrestle test loaded on both factors suggesting that the dimensions of strength and endurance are correlated.

Besides helping organizations find individuals who are physically able to do the job, there may be several positive unintended consequences of using physical ability tests for hiring. First, everything else equal, insurance costs may be lower for individuals who score higher on physical fitness exams, though organizations should not hire based on this alone because as we mention next, there are Americans with Disabilities Act concerns when hiring based on physical fitness. Second though, a recent study suggests that physical fitness is negatively related to deviance.[25] In a series of three creative studies, researchers tested the idea that physical fitness is itself positively related to self-control capacity such that people who are in good physical shape are less likely to suffer from loss of self-control, which itself inhibits deviant behavior. They found that military recruits who scored higher on physical fitness tests engaged in less deviant behavior during training as reported by fellow recruits. Example deviant behaviors included taking shortcuts during training and lying to protect oneself. In a sample of service employees, they were able to test their conceptual model which did find that ego depletion did mediate the relation between physical fitness and deviance.

Challenges using physical ability tests

Although all tests need to be examined for differences for protected classes, physical ability tests are especially susceptible to sex differences. In a comprehensive meta-analysis, Courtright et al. found that women tend to score lower on muscular strength tests and cardiovascular endurance, though for movement quality there were no differences.[26] The differences in strength ($d = 1.81$) and endurance ($d = 2.01$) are quite large, larger than nearly any other types of adverse impact found for other tests and protected classes. Given these large differences, using physical ability tests that measure strength and endurance will likely result in adverse impact against women. One analysis of a midwestern police agency found only 28% of all women applicants passed their physical ability test, whereas 93% of all men applicants passed the test.[27]

Given these sex differences, it is crucial for those using physical ability tests to link the abilities that the test measures to demonstrable performance on the job. In addition, performance on physical ability tests can be impacted by physical disabilities, thus opening up the use of these tests to claims under the Americans with Disabilities Act. To address these concerns, it seems prudent when using physical ability tests to set minimum qualifications that candidates need to pass instead of using the tests in a top-down manner. These qualifications should be set based on a careful job analysis that shows the typical weight that is needed to be carried or the speed and distance traveled in pursuits on foot. Using the physical ability tests in a top-down manner (i.e., always selected the strongest or fastest) is likely to exacerbate sex differences compared to requiring candidates to exceed a minimum standard and not differentiating between candidates in other ways.

Summary

In this chapter, we considered a wide range of ability tests, including tests of cognitive ability, mechanical ability, clerical ability, and physical abilities. These tests often show some of the highest validities of all predictors, though in many cases they also show substantial adverse impact. To use these tests, then, requires significant validation work to demonstrate job-relatedness. In this chapter, too, we reviewed strategies that organizations can use to minimize adverse impact and increase fairness, specifically in relation to cognitive ability testing and physical ability testing.

Another challenge with ability testing is that not all ability tests are the same and so within a particular type of ability, there can be substantial variation in the types of content and material covered on each exam. This makes it important to understand the theoretical framework that underlies each construct. Again, it is important to match the constructs being measured by a particular test to particular jobs. Relying on the label of a particular test without digging into the content of the items as well as the theoretical models of the test can cause lots of problems.

REVIEW QUESTIONS

1. What is the difference between a general factor model of intelligence and one that focuses on specific factors?
2. Describe research on adverse impact and cognitive ability tests.
3. What are methods to reduce adverse impact for ability tests?
4. Describe the different types of ability tests and how they might be useful for personnel selection.

DISCUSSION QUESTIONS

1. What are the societal implications of relying on ability tests for hiring purposes?
2. If you were developing a selection battery, what role would you give to ability tests?
3. What types of jobs do you think it is appropriate to use physical ability tests?
4. How do existing laws governing bias and discrimination influence your views on using ability tests for hiring?

Notes

1 Hunter, J. E. (1986). Cognitive ability, cognitive aptitudes, job knowledge, and job performance. *Journal of Vocational Behavior, 29*(3), 340–362.
2 Hunter, J. E., & Hunter, R. F. (1984). Validity and utility of alternative predictors of job performance. *Psychological Bulletin, 96*(1), 72–98. https://doi.org/10.1037/0033-2909.96.1.72; Schmidt, F.L. (2002). The role of general cognitive ability and job performance: Why there

cannot be a debate. *Human Performance, 15*(1–2), 187–210. https://doi.org/10.1080/08959285.2002.9668091

3   Stasielowicz, L. (2020). How important is cognitive ability when adapting to changes? A meta-analysis of the performance adaptation literature. *Personality and Individual Differences, 166*, 110178.

4   Thorndike, R. M. (1997). The early history of intelligence testing. In D. P. Flanagan, J. L. Genshaft, & P. L. Harrison (Eds.). *Contemporary intellectual assessment: Theories, tests, and issues* (pp. 3–16). The Guilford Press.

5   Ree, M. J., Earles, J. A., & Teachout, M. S. (1994). Predicting job performance: Not much more than g. *Journal of Applied Psychology, 79*(4), 518.

6   Ree, M. J., & Earles, J. A. (1991). Predicting training success: Not much more than g. *Personnel Psychology, 44*(2), 321–332.

7   Nye, C. D., Ma, J., & Wee, S. (2022). Cognitive ability and job performance: Meta-analytic evidence for the validity of narrow cognitive abilities. *Journal of Business and Psychology, 37*, 1119–1139.

8   https://www.pearsonassessments.com/

9   Arthur Jr, W., & Day, D. V. (1994). Development of a short form for the Raven Advanced Progressive Matrices Test. *Educational and Psychological Measurement, 54*(2), 394–403.

10 Condon, D. M., & Revelle, W. (2014). The international cognitive ability resource: Development and initial validation of a public-domain measure. *Intelligence, 43*, 52–64.

11 Hough, L. M., Oswald, F. L., & Ployhart, R. E. (2001). Determinants, detection and amelioration of adverse impact in personnel selection procedures: Issues, evidence and lessons learned. *International Journal of Selection and Assessment, 9*(1–2), 152–194.

12 Schmidt, F. L. (1995). Why all banding procedures in personnel selection are logically flawed. *Human Performance, 8*(3), 165–177.

13 Campion, M. A., Outtz, J. L., Zedeck, S., Schmidt, F. L., Kehoe, J. F., Murphy, K. R., & Guion, R. M. (2001). The controversy over score banding in personnel selection: Answers to 10 key questions. *Personnel Psychology, 54*(1), 149–185.

14 Ryan, A. M., Ployhart, R. E., & Friedel, L. A. (1998). Using personality testing to reduce adverse impact: A cautionary note. *Journal of Applied Psychology, 83*(2), 298.

15 Hough, L. M., Oswald, F. L., & Ployhart, R. E. (2001). Determinants, detection and amelioration of adverse impact in personnel selection procedures: Issues, evidence and lessons learned. *International Journal of Selection and Assessment, 9*(1–2), 152–194.

16 Steele, C. M., & Aronson, J. (1995). Stereotype threat and the intellectual test performance of African Americans. *Journal of Personality and Social Psychology, 69*(5), 797; Steele, C. M. (1998). Stereotyping and its threat are real. *American Psychologist, 53*(6), 680–681. https://doi.org/10.1037/0003-066X.53.6.680

17 Tomeh, D. H., & Sackett, P. R. (2022). On the continued misinterpretation of stereotype threat as accounting for Black-White differences on cognitive tests. *Personnel Assessment and Decisions, 8*(1), 1.

18 Stevenor, B. A., Zickar, M. J., Wimbush, F., & Beck, W. (2022). The attention to detail test: Measurement precision and validity evidence for a performance-based assessment of attention to detail. *Personnel Assessment and Decisions, 8*(1), 6. https://doi.org/10.25035/pad.2022.01.006

19 Whetzel, D. L., McCloy, R. A., Hooper, A., Russell, T. L., Waters, S. D., Campbell, W. J., & Ramos, R. A. (2011). Meta-analysis of clerical performance predictors: Still stable after all these years. *International Journal of Selection and Assessment, 19*(1), 41–50.

20 https://www.talentlens.com/recruitment/assessments/bennett-mechanical-comprehension-test.html

21 Muchinsky, P. M. (1993). Validation of intelligence and mechanical aptitude tests in selecting employees for manufacturing jobs. *Journal of Business and Psychology, 7*(4), 373–382.
22 https://www.ramsaycorp.com/product/?id=2133
23 Hogan, J. C. (1991). Physical abilities. In M. D. Dunnette & L. M. Hough (Eds.). *Handbook of industrial and organizational psychology* (pp. 753–831). Consulting Psychologists Press.
24 Arvey, R. D., Landon, T. E., Nutting, S. M., & Maxwell, S. E. (1992). Development of physical ability tests for police officers: a construct validation approach. *Journal of Applied Psychology, 77*(6), 996.
25 Tai, K., Liu, Y., Pitesa, M., Lim, S., Tong, Y. K., & Arvey, R. (2022). Fit to be good: Physical fitness is negatively associated with deviance. *Journal of Applied Psychology, 107*(3), 389.
26 Courtright, S. H., McCormick, B. W., Postlethwaite, B. E., Reeves, C. J., & Mount, M. K. (2013). A meta-analysis of sex differences in physical ability: Revised estimates and strategies for reducing differences in selection contexts. *Journal of Applied Psychology, 98*(4), 623.
27 Birzer, M. L., & Craig, D. E. (1996). Gender differences in police physical ability test performance. *American Journal of Police, 15*(2), 93–108.

10 Non-cognitive tests

LEARNING OBJECTIVES

- Gain knowledge of the history of personality test development
- Learn the Big Five personality traits and their relations with job-related criteria
- Learn about faking on personality tests and ways to minimize its effects
- Gain understanding of other non-cognitive measures such as emotional intelligence, biodata, integrity testing, and situational judgment testing

The tests in the previous chapter were generally most useful in predicting whether someone had the skills and abilities to be able to do a particular job. One limitation of those tests, however, is that ability tests often fail to measure whether someone has the motivation to perform at a high level on their job. Or whether they will steal from an employer, or are likely to quit their job after a bad day. In addition, some jobs require important non-cognitive skills such as the ability to interact pleasantly with strangers and the need to act self-confidently when presenting information. In this chapter, we will review personality tests as well as their usage in organizations. In addition, we will review emotional intelligence tests, biographical data, as well as tests used to measure integrity.

History of personality tests

Personality tests were initially developed by the U.S. military during World War I to identify soldiers who were likely to fall susceptible to "shell shock" when facing enemy combat fire for the first time. R.S. Woodward developed the Psychoneurotic Tendencies scale that asked military recruits a series of questions such as "Do you ever get so angry that you see red?" and "Do you tire of people easily?" After the war, Woodward marketed the scale to private industry, marketing the scale as a way for companies to avoid hiring temperamental and hot-headed employees.[1] In fact, during the 1930s, companies were worried about the threat of unionization and falsely believed that unions were caused by employees who were angry and maladjusted. After President Franklin Delano Roosevelt signed the National Labor Relations Act of 1935, it was no longer legal for employers to ask directly about union proclivities of applicants, and so employers turned to newly marketed personality tests to try to screen out potential union-friendly employees[2] (these tests were not successful in doing so despite their marketing efforts). After the Woodward effort, additional scales were developed and marketed to industry such as the Bernreuter Personality Inventory and the Humm Wadsworth Temperament Scale.[3] All of these tests focused mostly on a dimension of adjustment-maladjustment, a dimension partially influenced by anti-union proponents as mentioned by clinical psychologists who became interested in personality measurement and developed tests such as the Minnesota Multiphasic Personality Inventory (MMPI).

Personality testing had its ups and downs in private industry, though it suffered significantly in the mid-1960s when personnel psychologist Dr. Robert Guion attacked the tests as having insignificant validity for predicting job performance. One challenge that Guion noted was that each personality test relied on its own theory and structure of personality so that some tests had five traits, others six or even 16. And the nature of the traits differed across tests, making it challenging to have generalizable findings. After Guion's critiques, personality testing went through period of disuse in industry until the early 1990s when two meta-analyses published nearly simultaneously showed that a new taxonomy of personality, the Big Five, resulted in tests that showed modest validity in predicting job performance across a variety of jobs.[4] In particular, conscientiousness was the most useful predictor, demonstrating modest validity ($r \sim .20$) for most jobs. In addition, extraversion was found to be an important predictor of job performance.

Big Five

The Big Five was developed in the 1950s and 1960s by a group of personality psychologists, including John Digman who factor analyzed a variety of personality items and found that a five-factor solution was commonly identified across a variety of factors. Paul Costa Jr. and Robert McCrae built on this original research and developed a five-factor solution personality inventory, the NEO-PI, that was the driver of much of the original validity work applying the Big Five to work-related samples. The five personality traits are openness to experience, conscientiousness, extraversion, agreeableness, and neuroticism. (Yes, the acronym OCEAN is an easy way to make sure you remember them all correctly!)

Openness to Experience: People high in openness to experience like to travel, experience new cuisines and new ideas, and are relatively more open to challenging pre-existing ideas. People who are low in openness to experience crave familiarity and find comfort predictable things. I (Zickar) am extremely high in openness to experience and so I would prefer to try the new restaurant in town even if I suspect that the food will not be that good because I crave new experiences. Those low in openness, however, may think, "Why try anything besides Applebee's? I know I'll get a good burger there!"

Openness to experience has been a tough construct to measure and to relate to job performance. In general, the correlations between openness and performance tend not to be significant and so the trait is not often used in personnel selection. Some research, however, shows that there is a positive correlation between openness and expatriate performance. That finding makes sense in that those who are likely to perform successfully in jobs in other countries are likely to be those who are more sensitive to the norms and cultures of other countries and more willing to adapt in those situations.

Some personality inventories use the term, intellectance, for this factor, with those scales tending to measure items that relate to intellectual pursuits. For example, people high in intellectance are more likely to read challenging literature, be interested in word puzzles and games, and like to try new hobbies where they can learn new skills. Intellectance is conceptualized differently than intellectual ability in that it is the tendency to try cognitively challenging tasks, whereas cognitive ability is having the actual ability to perform those tasks well. One challenge, though, is that even though intellectance and cognitive ability are conceptually independent, there is often a modest positive correlation between the two, making it less likely that intellectance would provide incremental validity above and beyond cognitive ability measures.

Openness to Experience: The degree to which individuals crave and appreciate trying new things and experiencing new ideas.

Conscientiousness: Individuals high in conscientiousness are hard-working, detail-oriented, and responsive to deadlines and rules. Individuals low in conscientiousness are care-free, sloppy, and averse to regulations and deadlines. The one consistent finding in the Big Five literature is that conscientiousness is a valid predictor of job success across all types of jobs. That makes sense because for nearly all jobs, working hard is a prerequisite for success as is dedication and attention to detail. Individuals who are low in conscientiousness are more likely to be absent, tardiness, and to miss deadlines. Individuals high in conscientiousness are internally driven and are more likely to follow rules and regulations, key traits useful for nearly all jobs.

It is hard to think of a job for which conscientiousness would not be useful. Some have speculated that for artists, low conscientiousness may actually be preferred because artists need to be open to the moment and to break rules and conventions. The research, however, has not supported that. Even for artists, working hard and regularly turns out to be important for success.

Conscientiousness: The degree to which individuals work hard, follow rules, and pay attention to details.

Extraversion: People high in extraversion enjoy being around other individuals, tend to be more assertive, and find it easy to make new friends. Individuals low in extraversion, otherwise known as introverts, tend to prefer solitude or being around a small number of individuals they already know and tend to be more passive in social situations. One key difference between introverts and extraverts is that the latter gain energy from being around groups of individuals and the former get emotionally drained being around large groups of individuals for a long period of time. In addition, introverts tend to be fine being around individuals who they already know and for whom they can engage in personal conversations, whereas extraverts enjoy being surrounded by people who they do not know well and get energy from small talk.

Extraversion is an important predictor of job performance for jobs in which sustained interaction with strangers is important, though would be less important for jobs in which interaction with strangers is less important. For some sales jobs, extraversion would be crucial, especially those that require cold-calling of individuals with whom the salesperson has no personal connection. Door-to-door salespersons, who must knock on the door of strangers to try to get them to purchase a product, would benefit from high extraversion. Introverts who perform that job would likely be emotionally wiped out after a few interactions and be less likely to perform well over time. For other jobs, though, that involve fewer social interactions, there tends to be little relation between extraversion and job performance. Take the job of a college professor. Although there are significant numbers of interactions between students and the professor, over the course of the semester as the professor and students get to know each other, introverts are likely to feel more comfortable interacting with their students. The key differentiator might be the first day of class, where extraverts would be energized to meet a crop of new students, whereas introverts might experience a sense of heightened anxiety. Over time, though, students are likely to realize less of a difference.

Extraversion: The degree to which individuals get energy by being around other individuals and the degree of assertiveness that individuals have in social settings.

Agreeableness: People high in agreeableness tend to be kind, empathetic, and altruistic, whereas people who are low in agreeableness tend to be grumpy, selfish, and lacking empathy. Imagine you are prepared to turn in an assignment for a class and right before returning to campus to hand in the paper, you get a call that some emergency has happened that will require you to return home. Later that day once the emergency has resolved, you email your professor and explain the scenario and why you were late. A professor who is high in agreeableness will tend to be empathetic and kind and quite possibly grant you an extension, whereas a professor low in agreeableness would likely reply that there are no exceptions to the deadline and express little sympathy for whatever it was that you experienced.

In terms of predictiveness, agreeableness tends to have modest positive correlations for jobs that require human interaction. Jobs such as school teacher, therapist, and customer sales representatives would all be jobs where someone who is low on agreeableness would likely not fare as well as someone moderate to high in agreeableness. Although there is no specific research on this, we can speculate, however, that there might be a few jobs such as debt collector in which being low on agreeableness might be an asset.

Agreeableness: The degree to which individuals are empathetic, kind, and altruistic.

Neuroticism: People high in neuroticism experience lots of strong emotions and feel deeply anxiety and fear. People low in neuroticism (also reframed as emotional stability) typically experience a sense of calm in high pressure situations. Neuroticism is related to performance in specific types of jobs and is used to screen for jobs that require a calm sense of presence. For example, police, airplane pilots, and firefighters need to maintain calmness in the face of pressure and so hiring someone high in neuroticism would likely create problems. For most jobs, though, the relation between neuroticism and job performance is not significant. For example, for the role of a psychology professor, having a professor who has some preclass anxiety is unlikely to result in a meaningful decrease in performance.

One challenge in using neuroticism in hiring is that extreme levels of neuroticism may be associated with psychological disorders such as generalized anxiety disorder and hence would be protected under the Americans with Disabilities Act (ADA).[5] Therefore, employers who screen for neuroticism should be careful to link their usages to a job analysis and to avoid personality inventories that assess the extreme ranges of neuroticism.

Neuroticism-Emotional Stability: The degree to which individuals experience fear and anxiety on a regular basis.

Alternatives to the Big Five: Although the Big Five has dominated personality measurement, several points need to be made. First, different personality instruments often use different labels for different personality traits. For example, the Hogan Personality Inventory (HPI) has a measure of Prudence that is their proprietary measure of conscientiousness. In addition, some instruments use slightly different structures, such as the HPI breaking the traditional Big Five dimension of extraversion into two separate dimensions of Sociability and Ambition. These tweaks of the Big Five factor structure are not a repudiation of the overall structure but minor refinements. In general, the Big Five structure continues to be a useful framework.

Although the Big Five are viewed as a universal framework, researchers have developed additional factors and scales that do not fall cleanly within the Big Five taxonomy. Specifically, the HEXACO model includes the Big Five though with slightly different labels (e.g., emotionality instead of emotional stability), though it adds an additional dimension Honesty-Humility, which includes a moral component that is not directly measured by the Big Five traits. The HEXACO model also includes four facets per each of the six factors. This notion of facets of larger traits is something that is also common in traditional Big Five measures. For some purposes, researchers may wish to have more narrow dimensions of personality traits and the facets allow one to focus. For example, the HEXACO model posits four facets underneath openness to experience: aesthetic appreciation, inquisitiveness, creativity, unconventionality. You can imagine some jobs for which inquisitiveness might be important but perhaps aesthetic appreciation would be less relevant (perhaps a librarian). In this case, the overall trait of openness to experience may not be relevant, though the specific targeted facet may be useful.

Personality Trait Facet: A specific dimension of personality that is subsumed under a larger dimension that is narrow and homogeneously defined.

Besides the HEXACO trait of Honesty-Humility, other researchers have posited personality traits and characteristics not measured by the Big Five and these include religiosity, eroticism, frugality, conservatism, masculinity-femininity, and humor.[6] Although those traits may be useful for researchers looking to fully understand personality, they are less relevant for predicting workplace behavior.

Another framework that has gathered momentum in the personality literature is the concept of the Dark Triad. Researchers posited that most personality traits, especially those in the Big Five, as well as the accompanying personality tests used in I-O psychology settings, relate to personality in a normal range. That is, the variation captured by these personality tests is well within the range of individuals not considered to have psychological disorders. Paulhus and Williams,[7] however, posited that there are psychological traits that they called *subclinical* which are important in predicting workplace outcomes. Subclinical traits are traits that are related to psychological disorders though they measure levels of the traits that do not rise themselves to the level of psychological disorders.

Subclinical Personality Traits: Personality traits that measure characteristics related to psychological disorders, though in a range below what is considered clinically relevant.

Paulus and Williams proposed three traits that comprise the Dark Triad: Narcissism, Machiavellianism, and Psychopathy. Each of these traits had significant previous research on them, though combining the traits into a comprehensive framework was an important contribution.

Work on the Dark Triad was consistent with Robert and Joyce Hogan's work on the Dark Side of leadership.[8,9] The Hogans developed the Hogan Development Survey (HDS), which took traits based on personality disorders and adapted items to measure variation related to the personality disorders but again at a subclinical level. The HDS is often used for leadership coaching, helping managers understand their limitations and blindspots and is predicated on an understanding that many leaders fail because they have significant limitations that they cannot overcome.[10] Remember a particularly bad manager that you have had and you will likely identify someone who has significant derailers. The Dark Triad is an attempt to understand the personality dimensions of those failures and the HDS is one measure that has been used to identify significant derailers.

One challenge with using subclinical personality traits, and personality traits in general, is the ADA that precludes including medical information in hiring decisions.[11] I-O psychologists have been concerned that job applicants could challenge the use of personality tests in hiring as indirectly screening for psychological disorders. For example, someone high in clinical depression may score low on emotional stability and thus be denied employment. Therefore, although subclinical traits are designed not to measure abnormal levels of personality traits, researchers urge caution in using personality measures designed to measure Dark Side traits for hiring.[12] That does not mean that the Dark Triad, and other subclinical traits, would not be useful for testing theories in work context, though caution should be used when hiring.

Faking

One concern that has persisted throughout the history of personality testing is that applicants can misrepresent themselves in order to get hired for a job.[13] And so if you are interested in a sales job and you are asked the question "Do you like talking with strangers?" you might be likely to respond "strongly agree" even though in real life you often get overwhelmed when talking with strangers. You would not be alone if you thought about distorting your responses to get a job. In one study, 47% of respondents admitted to exaggerating positive characteristics and 62% admitted to deemphasizing negative characteristics.[14] To address the problem of faking and distortion, test developers have tried a variety of techniques to prevent faking from occurring as well as to identify those who do fake.

Preventing faking

To the extent that you can keep applicants from distorting their responses in the first place, you can avoid many of the problems of identifying who was faking and then figuring out how to deal with those responses. To prevent faking, test developers have generally used two types of strategies: applicant warnings and difficult-to-fake items.

With applicant warnings, test developers include some kind of statement that responses are being monitored and if people are caught distorting their responses, they will not be considered for hiring. For example, one set of researchers included this warning[15]:

> It is critical to note that these inventories have items which are designed to detect faking.
>
> Research has shown that these questions are able to identify individuals who provide inaccurate information about themselves.

Warnings reduce faking. In one study, scores on the Big Five traits were substantially lower for those who were warned about faking compared to those who were not, with *d* statistics ranging from .27 to .76.[16] There is some concern that applicant warnings may impact justice perceptions regarding the fairness of the personality test, though that concern likely depends on the severity of the warning. For example, in one experiment, respondents after completing 25 items were given this warning:

You have been flagged as being dishonest.
If you continue to answer dishonestly, then you will be automatically disqualified from winning the $50.

This highly visible and direct warning reviewed fairness perceptions.[17] General warnings at the beginning of a test tend to result in little to no reduction in applicant reactions.[18]

Besides warnings, another strategy is to write items that are difficult to fake. One approach to writing difficult items is to write items for which it is difficult to determine the underlying trait. Some items are obvious, such as "I enjoy going to parties," which is clearly an item that measures extraversion. Subtle items were originally developed for the popular clinical measure of personality, the MMPI.[19] For an example of a subtle item, Holden and Jackson use the "I would enjoy the occupation of a butcher" as an item that does not have any obvious substantive content, though individuals who endorse this item are likely to be higher in sadism.[20] Individuals high in sadism may be more likely to endorse this item than an item low in subtlety such as "I often have sadistic thoughts." The research on subtle items, however, suggests that they lack face validity and therefore may be problematic when asking applicants to complete these items[21] and they also often perform worse psychometrically, having lower item discrimination values.[22] Therefore, item subtlety is not a feasible solution to the problem of faking.

A more promising solution to preventing faking is forced-choice personality inventories. Forced-choice personality inventories have been around for a long time and are designed to prevent faking by presenting two items of roughly similar social desirability. Respondents are forced to choose which of the two items best describe them. For example, I may ask you, "Would you rather go to a large party" or "Read a complex Russian novel." At least for some people, attending large parties may be enjoyable and for others, reading a complex Russian novel may be fun. By themselves, there is no single obvious answer. Individuals who are high in extraversion may choose the party, whereas those low in extraversion may choose the novel. Individuals low in the intellectual component of openness to experience may dread the novel and choose the party. Although forced-choice items were used periodically since the 1950s, they failed to catch on because of the problem of *ipsativity*.

Ipsative measurement refers to types of measures that allow individuals to make choices that describe how they feel, without any reference to a normative group. For example, if I ask you to choose which color you like better, blue or red, you may choose red even though you do not like either color much, you just dislike red slightly less than you dislike blue. However, a friend of yours may love both of those colors and choose red only because she likes it somewhat more than she likes blue. In both cases, we know that each person prefers red to blue, but we still do not understand whether they like red at a rate higher than the general population or not. Ipsative measurement is useful in vocational assessment where we want to know what type of occupation an individual is most interested in compared to other types of occupations. The within-person comparison is useful in that case in which we do not care whether your engineering interest is higher than your neighbor's engineering interest. Given that the test will be used for occupational guidance, we want to know that your engineering interest is higher than your interest in being a social worker and a librarian.

Ipsative Measurement: Scales used to measure within-person variation, comparing the level of standing on one trait with the level of standing of other traits within a single person.

In the early 2000s, a group of researchers used item response theory, a complex psychometric device, to extract normative information from forced-choice items.[23,24,25] In this series of studies, by varying the presentation of items so that some items have choices across a variety of traits and others have choices within a single trait, it is possible to turn forced-choice items into normative measurement. The algorithms are statistically complicated and beyond the scope of this textbook, though the work has revitalized forced-choice measurement so that it has become a useful tool for personality assessment for hiring.

Normative Measurement: Scales used to measure between-person variation, allowing researchers to compare standings on the same trait across individuals.

Given that recent psychometric work has salvaged forced-choice personality measurement, the question remains whether the tests are useful in preventing applicants from faking. Cao and Drasgow conducted a meta-analysis comparing the differences between forced-choice respondents in high-stakes situations (e.g., hiring) compared to those in low-stakes situations (e.g., experimental research).[26] Overall, they found a negligible effect size with high-stakes respondents having a $d = .06$ difference compared to low-stakes respondents. Digging into their results deeper, respondents in high-stakes were able to have slight success in faking traits that are often viewed as job desirable such as conscientiousness ($d = .23$) and extraversion ($d = .16$), though there was no difference for neuroticism ($d = .00$). Their results show that forced-choice methodologies reduce the level of score inflation, though forced-choice tests likely do not eliminate the problem of faking.

Identifying fakers

Another strategy to addressing faking is to embed methods of identifying individuals who fake within the measures themselves. Once individuals have been flagged as faking, test administrators may use that information in hiring decisions, ranging from verifying suspect information, discounting scores, to the extreme of refusing to hire. There are a variety of scales and techniques used to identify fakers.[27] Social desirability scales were first created in the 1950s and relied on items that appeared to be high in value to nearly everyone.[28] Items such as "Before voting I thoroughly investigate the qualifications of all the candidates" and "I like to gossip at times [reverse-scored]" were two items on the popular Marlowe-Crowne Social Desirability Scale.[29] The logic is that individuals who respond to a large number of these items are likely to be exaggerating the truth or professing what some people have called "unlikely virtues." Paulhus expanded on the early work to identify two factors related to social desirability. *Self-deceptive denial* refers to an unconscious tendency that most individuals engage in to present oneself in a favorable light. *Impression management*, however, is a conscious effort by individuals to improve their standing to others.[30] The important contribution here is to note that socially desirable responding has both unconscious and conscious motivations.

Research is mixed on whether social desirability is negative, benign, or even a positive attribute. In a classic meta-analysis, Ones et al. found that social desirability was positively related to training performance ($\rho = .22$) but unrelated to job performance ($\rho = .01$) and counterproductive work behavior ($\rho = -.03$).[31] It turns out that the skill of being able to see what is the positive answer for an item is unrelated to job performance and not associated with negative work behaviors. And the skill of social desirability is marginally related to performance in training situations, likely when putting on a positive face is helpful.

Another challenge with social desirability scales, or any kind of scale designed to identify lying or deception, is the problem of *false positives*. The phrase false positive comes from the signal detection literature which tries to quantity and understands mistakes that people use when detecting stimuli. False positives are detecting a stimulus when in fact it does not exist. In the case of faking detection, it would be the error of falsely identifying an honest respondent as someone who is a liar. These false accusations can be especially damaging, unjustly penalizing honest respondents. Zickar and Drasgow found using traditional social desirability scales that significant amounts of false positives occurred when using social desirability scales to identify faking.[32]

Other methods of addressing faking have been proposed, including using reaction times to predict who is faking[33] as well as using psychometric modeling such as item response theory to predict who is deviating from normative models[34]; it seems like in every decade, there will be a new technique offering hope in eliminating faking. In general, these methods create false positive problems and also suffer from the faking problem itself. Many techniques designed to catch fakers can themselves be faked, which has happened with social desirability tests. Sophisticated test takers can find information online on how to respond to items to evade detection, rendering these scales which were marginally useful in the first place, even less effective.[35]

So what to do about faking? Just like in medicine, prevention is the best cure. Preempting faking by applicant warnings can be helpful, though again it should be noted that many sophisticated test takers now realize that these warnings are empty threats. We think a simple warning such as this will be helpful:

Please respond honestly on this personality test. We will be evaluating the accuracy of your responses

If social desirability scales are included in a measure, for individuals who receive high scores on these scales, we recommend that you verify that information in personal interviews with the candidate as well as with reference checking. Personality characteristics can be especially useful in understanding and predicting job performance and organizations should embrace using personality tests, despite their limitations, in personnel selection.

Emotional intelligence

Do you have friends who seem clueless in interpersonal interactions, unable to read social cues and body language, unable to interpret the emotional undertones of everyday conversation? Psychologists have conjectured about emotional intelligence for a long time and whether it is a personality trait or an ability trait and whether it can even be scientifically measured.[36] Salovey and Mayer formulated the first rigorous model of emotional intelligence, a model that includes three components, the ability to accurately appraise the emotions of self and other, the regulation of emotions, and finally the ability to utilize emotions.[37] Since that initial publication, the research on emotional intelligence has skyrocketed with over 4,000 titles in Amazon using the phrase emotional intelligence and many publications.

Joseph and Newman came up with their own cascading model of emotional intelligence that builds on the work of Salovey and Mayer.[38] They propose that first individuals must perceive emotions accurately and second, once perceived emotions must be properly understood, and finally this leads to emotional responses and regulations. The term cascading is used because the three components work in a hierarchical manner with perception preceding understanding preceding regulation. Joseph and Newman propose that conscientiousness, cognitive ability, and emotional stability are the key components in this process with conscientiousness related to emotional perception, cognitive ability related to emotion understanding, and emotional stability related to emotion regulation. In their meta-analysis, Joseph and Newman found that there was a modest incremental validity of emotional intelligence measures that were what they labeled mixed-ability measures. In the literature, there is a distinction between ability-based measures of emotional intelligence and self-report measures of emotional intelligence. For ability measures of EI, the individual might need to identify what the underlying emotion is in an image that is presented to him or her.[39] For a self-report measure, individuals may assess their level of emotional ability through direct questions such as "How accurate are you in gauging peoples' feelings toward you?" A mixed approach would include elements of both components and was found to be superior by Joseph and Newman in their comprehensive meta-analysis.

Joseph and Newman also provided preliminary evidence that for jobs that require high emotional labor (e.g., customer service jobs), the relation between emotional intelligence and job performance was higher than for jobs with low emotional labor requirements (e.g., a desk clerk with minimal customer contact). Joseph and Newman's research shows that emotional intelligence is a useful construct that can help understand and predict job performance for some jobs, that emotional intelligence is related to personality and cognitive ability but also distinct, and that emotional intelligence is the solution for hiring. With regard to the last point, some self-described experts have proffered that emotional intelligence is twice as important as cognitive intelligence,[40] a finding that the data just do not support.

Situational judgment tests

Another type of non-cognitive assessment that has been popular is the situational judgment test (SJT). A typical SJT item gives a work-related scenario to an individual and then asks them to choose from a variety of options how they would respond to that situation. Here is a hypothetical item:

You are working hard to meet a deadline when one of your close coworkers, Bob, pops by to tell you that he has been experiencing depression and is finally seeing a therapist. He seems to really want to talk though you realize that you have such limited time to make your deadline. How do you respond to this situation?

A. Ignore your project for the moment and listen to Bob for as long as it takes.
B. Tell Bob that you are busy and would like to chat with him but at some later time.
C. Explain to Bob that you are working against a deadline and ask to schedule a time to chat at a later date.
D. Tell Bob that this sounds important and that he better call the Employee Assistance Hotline.

This is probably like a workplace scenario that you are likely to encounter in your work-life, one that might be challenging to navigate. The question is what is the right answer. From an employer's perspective, the answer seems that C might be the best answer. B seems as if you would show lack of empathy or understanding of Bob's conversation. D might be a decent answer. A seems like from an employer's perspective that it is ignoring the deadline. C seems to express the importance of Bob's situation while expressing the importance of the deadline. This scenario, though, like many workplace scenarios, does not seem to have a single correct answer.

There are lots of different formats for SJTs as well as ways to score them. Some tests focus on choosing the best answer, what McDaniel et al. called "knowledge SJTs," whereas others focus on choosing the answer that would best describe how you would respond in the situation, what McDaniel et al. label "behavior tendency SJTs."[41] They found in their meta-analysis that instruction type did not make a difference and that SJTs had incremental validity beyond personality tests and cognitive ability tests. In general, SJTs tend to be strong predictors of job performance, particularly for managers. Salter and Highhouse concluded that SJTs were efficient measures of common sense for managerial selection.[42] A recent meta-analysis found that SJTs were useful in predicting success in selecting medical applicants for postgraduate education with incremental validity above knowledge and cognitive ability tests.[43]

In terms of scoring SJTs, one can take a rational approach, choosing best responses based on theory or test developer judgment. I would be using a rational approach by concluding that C was the best answer in the hypothetical item. An empirical approach could be used, though, in which we administer that item to a series of employees and then compare job performance data across options. It may be that people who chose option A are actually better managers and if so, the empirically keyed approach would use that as the correct answer.

Another take on the SJT is to use a video to present the scenario, hiring actors to role play the setting, adding a level of realism to the assessment. Olson-Buchanon and colleagues developed a video-based assessment of conflict-resolution skills and found that the assessment scored using an empirical approach correlated significantly with supervisor ratings of conflict-resolution skills ($r = .26$) and was unrelated to cognitive ability. Finally, there was no adverse impact on women in the assessment tool.[44] Although most research shows minimal differences between video-based and paper-and-pencil versions of SJT in terms of validity,[45] video-based assessment adds some enhanced realism to assessment that may make it attractive to some organizations.

Biodata

Assessing candidates on biographical data is one of the earliest methods in personnel selection, particularly being used in the insurance industry since the 1930s with life insurance sales representatives being hired on tools like the Career Profile which attempts to assess the number of leads and connections someone has in the community based on objective life experiences (e.g., the number of community organizations that someone is active in)[46] and assessing commitment to the organization as well as life stability. Application forms, often called weighted application forms, that included items about education, hobbies, and accomplishments were often turned into scores that were used to predict whether someone was going to be successful or not.

Biodata, as biographical data assessment is typically called, has been one of the historically strongest predictors of job performance.[47] Considerable effort has gone into developing techniques for scoring biodata, with the primary ones being a rational scoring approach which uses theory (and often common sense) to figure out the way to score items and empirical keying which uses data to make scoring decisions. In the later approach, a validation sample is needed where incumbents complete a battery of items common in application blanks and then items that are correlated with positive job performance are scored positively, whereas items correlated negatively with job performance would be given negative weightings. Empirical keying can be challenging in that you need a large sample to avoid capitalizing on chance.[48] As will be talked about in Chapter 12, advances in machine learning as well as access to large databases may make empirical keying more sophisticated in the future.

In a recent meta-analysis, Speer and colleagues found that empirically scored biodata inventories had impressive validities ($r = .44$), whereas rationally keyed biodata inventories validities were lower ($r = .24$).[49] Interestingly, they also found that biodata scores were only modestly correlated with cognitive ability as well as Big Five personality trait scores, thus suggesting that biodata measures should be used in applicant hiring. Another benefit of empirically keyed biodata inventories is that they are often less fakeable.

Integrity tests

Most of the predictors that we have studied so far have aimed to predict job performance, whether that is measured by the number of items produced or sold, or the quality of teaching or therapy (see Chapter 6 for measuring job performance). Integrity tests, however, are designed to predict whether employees will engage in counterproductive work behavior or engage in moral lapses. Counterproductive work behaviors might include stealing from an employer, clocking in before starting work, using work supplies for personal goals, and giving friends discounts that were not warranted. There are two basic types of integrity tests, *overt* measures and *personality-based* measures. Overt measures ask candidates directly whether they have engaged in the past in counterproductive work behaviors. Personality-based measures are more covert in that they do not directly ask whether candidates have stolen from their employer but ask about personality characteristics that are likely to be correlated with such behavior.

In a comprehensive meta-analysis, Van Iddekinge and colleagues found that integrity tests were modestly correlated with job performance ($r = .15$), though more successful in predicting counterproductive work behavior ($r = .32$).[50] They found minimal differences between overt tests ($r = .14$ across all criteria) and personality-based tests ($r = .18$) suggesting that conceptual differences between the tests make minimal differences in terms of prediction. In terms of practical differences, Cooper, Slaughter, and Gilliland found that using an overt-based integrity test, IntegrityFirst resulted in a significant reduction in workers' compensation claims.[51] The IntegrityFirst measure includes direct items about employee theft, drug use, and workplace aggression. They found that integrity scores across a variety of samples were related to the amount of malingering (i.e., faking or exaggerating injuries) as well as with safety compliance. The large body of research suggests that including a measure of integrity is useful, especially for jobs in which the incidents of counterproductive work behavior is high (e.g., retail) or the cost of malfeasance could be extremely damaging (e.g., account clerks).

Summary

In this chapter, we reviewed a large amount of literature on personality testing and other types of non-cognitive measures such as emotional intelligence, integrity testing, and biodata. Employers get that personality and these other characteristics matter. We certainly take into account personality characteristics when choosing a romantic partner (some online dating platforms even assess personality and attempt to match on this) and friends, and we would all agree that integrity is an important characteristic in a partner as well. Therefore, it makes sense that employers are motivated to assess these characteristics in potential employees as well. There are several themes throughout this chapter. First, it is essential to use job analyses as well as relevant empirical research to link non-cognitive traits to job performance. In terms of personality, traits will be useful for predicting performance on some jobs but likely irrelevant for other jobs (excluding conscientiousness which is important for all jobs). Second, non-cognitive traits are often difficult to assess given that respondents are often able to figure out what the correct answer is on assessments. Therefore, reliance on a single measure is often fraught with challenges. We discussed several options on resolving the faking problem, however, and believed that employers benefit from including non-cognitive measures despite their challenges.

REVIEW QUESTIONS

1. How are each of the Big Five traits related to job performance?
2. What are alternatives to the Big Five?
3. What are potential solutions to the problem of applicant faking?
4. What are the advantages and disadvantages of normative and ipsative measurement?
5. What are the different ways of scoring Biodata?

DISCUSSION QUESTIONS

1. Do you think it is unethical for applicants to fake on personality tests?
2. In what cases should organizations use integrity tests?
3. What value do personality tests have for organizations? What danger do they pose?
   a. Do you believe that emotional intelligence is in fact actually a type of intelligence?

Notes

1. Gibby, R. E., & Zickar, M. J. (2008). A history of the early days of personality testing in American industry: An obsession with adjustment. *History of Psychology, 11*(3), 164.
2. Zickar, M. J. (2001). Using personality inventories to identify thugs and agitators: Applied psychology's contribution to the war against labor. *Journal of Vocational Behavior, 59*(1), 149–164.
3. Lussier, K. (2018). Temperamental workers: Psychology, business, and the Humm-Wadsworth Temperament Scale in interwar America. *History of Psychology, 21*(2), 79.
4. Barrick, M. R., & Mount, M. K. (1991). The big five personality dimensions and job performance: A meta-analysis. *Personnel Psychology, 44*(1), 1–26; Tett, R. P., Jackson, D. N., & Rothstein, M. (1991).

Personality measures as predictors of job performance: A meta-analytic review. *Personnel Psychology, 44*(4), 703–742.

5 Melson-Silimon, A., Harris, A. M., Shoenfelt, E. L., Miller, J. D., & Carter, N. T. (2019). Personality testing and the Americans with Disabilities Act: Cause for concern as normal and abnormal personality models are integrated. *Industrial and Organizational Psychology, 12*(2), 119–132.

6 Paunonen, S. V., & Jackson, D. N. (2000). What is beyond the big five? Plenty! *Journal of Personality, 68*(5), 821–835.

7 Paulhus, D. L., & Williams, K. M. (2002). The dark triad of personality: Narcissism, Machiavellianism, and psychopathy. *Journal of Research in Personality, 36*(6), 556–563.

8 Hogan, R., & Hogan, J. (2001). Assessing leadership: A view from the dark side. *International Journal of Selection and Assessment, 9*(1–2), 40–51.

9 Hogan, R., Kaiser, R. B., Sherman, R. A., & Harms, P. D. (2021). Twenty years on the dark side: Six lessons about bad leadership. *Consulting Psychology Journal: Practice and Research, 73*(3), 199–213.

10 Hogan, R. (1994). Trouble at the top: Causes and consequences of managerial incompetence. *Consulting Psychology Journal: Practice and Research, 46*(1), 9.

11 Melson-Silimon, A., Harris, A. M., Shoenfelt, E. L., Miller, J. D., & Carter, N. T. (2019). Personality testing and the Americans with Disabilities Act: Cause for concern as normal and abnormal personality models are integrated. *Industrial and Organizational Psychology, 12*(2), 119–132.

12 Melson-Silimon, A., Harris, A. M., Shoenfelt, E. L., Miller, J. D., & Carter, N. T. (2019). Personality testing and the Americans with Disabilities Act: Cause for concern as normal and abnormal personality models are integrated. *Industrial and Organizational Psychology, 12*(2), 119–132.

13 Zickar, M. J., & Gibby, R. E. (2006). A history of faking and socially desirable responding on personality tests. In Peterson, M.H. & Griffith, R.L. (Eds.), *A closer examination of applicant faking behavior* (pp. 21–42). Information Age Publishing.

14 Donovan, J. J., Dwight, S. A., & Hurtz, G. M. (2003). An assessment of the prevalence, severity, and verifiability of entry-level applicant faking using the randomized response technique. *Human Performance, 16*(1), 81–106.

15 Burns, G. N., Filipkowski, J. N., Morris, M. B., & Shoda, E. A. (2015). Impact of electronic warnings on online personality scores and test-taker reactions in an applicant simulation. *Computers in Human Behavior, 48*, 163–172.

16 Mcfarland, L. A. (2003). Warning against faking on a personality test: Effects on applicant reactions and personality test scores. *International Journal of Selection and Assessment, 11*(4), 265–276.

17 Burns, G. N., Filipkowski, J. N., Morris, M. B., & Shoda, E. A. (2015). Impact of electronic warnings on online personality scores and test-taker reactions in an applicant simulation. *Computers in Human Behavior, 48*, 163–172.

18 Mcfarland, L. A. (2003). Warning against faking on a personality test: Effects on applicant reactions and personality test scores. *International Journal of Selection and Assessment, 11*(4), 265–276.

19 Wiener, D. N. (1948). Subtle and obvious keys for the Minnesota multiphasic personality inventory. *Journal of Consulting Psychology, 12*(3), 164.

20 Holden, R. R., & Jackson, D. N. (1979). Item subtlety and face validity in personality assessment. *Journal of Consulting and Clinical Psychology, 47*(3), 459.

21 Holden, R. R., & Jackson, D. N. (1979). Item subtlety and face validity in personality assessment. *Journal of Consulting and Clinical Psychology, 47*(3), 459.

22 Zickar, M. J., & Ury, K. L. (2002). Developing an interpretation of item parameters for personality items: Content correlates of parameter estimates. *Educational and Psychological Measurement, 62*(1), 19–31.

Min, H., Zickar, M., & Yankov, G. (2018). Understanding item parameters in personality scales: An explanatory item response modeling approach. *Personality and Individual Differences, 128*, 1–6.

23 Heggestad, E. D., Morrison, M., Reeve, C. L., & McCloy, R. A. (2006). Forced-choice assessments of personality for selection: Evaluating issues of normative assessment and faking resistance. *Journal of Applied Psychology, 91*(1), 9.

24 Brown, A., & Maydeu-Olivares, A. (2011). Item response modeling of forced-choice questionnaires. *Educational and Psychological Measurement, 71*(3), 460–502.

25 Lee, P., Joo, S. H., Stark, S., & Chernyshenko, O. S. (2019). GGUM-RANK statement and person parameter estimation with multidimensional forced choice triplets. *Applied Psychological Measurement, 43*(3), 226–240.

26 Cao, M., & Drasgow, F. (2019). Does forcing reduce faking? A meta-analytic review of forced-choice personality measures in high-stakes situations. *Journal of Applied Psychology, 104*(11), 1347.

27 Zickar, M. J., & Gibby, R. E. (2006). A history of faking and socially desirable responding on personality tests. In Peterson, M.H. & Griffith, R.L. (Eds.), *A closer examination of applicant faking behavior* (pp. 21–42). Information Age Publishing.

28 Edwards, A. L. (1957). *The social desirability variable in personality assessment and research.* The Dryden Press.

29 Crowne, D. P., & Marlowe, D. (1960). A new scale of social desirability independent of psychopathology. *Journal of Consulting Psychology, 24*(4), 349.

30 Paulhus, D. L. (1988). *Assessing self-deception and impression management in self-reports: The Balanced inventory of desirable responding.* University of British Columbia. Unpublished manual.

31 Ones, D. S., Viswesvaran, C., & Reiss, A. D. (1996). Role of social desirability in personality testing for personnel selection: The red herring. *Journal of Applied Psychology, 81*(6), 660.

32 Zickar, M. J., & Drasgow, F. (1996). Detecting faking on a personality instrument using appropriateness measurement. *Applied Psychological Measurement, 20*(1), 71–87.

33 Fine, S., & Pirak, M. (2016). Faking fast and slow: Within-person response time latencies for measuring faking in personnel testing. *Journal of Business and Psychology, 31*(1), 51–64.

34 Zickar, M. J., & Sliter, K. A. (2012). Searching for unicorns: Item response theory-based solutions to the faking problem. *New perspectives on faking in personality assessment* (pp.113–130).

35 https://www.seattletimes.com/seattle-news/health/faking-your-type-to-pass-a-personality-test/

36 Spector, P. E. (2005). Introduction: Emotional intelligence. *Journal of Organizational Behavior, 26*(4), 409; Landy, F. J. (2005). Some historical and scientific issues related to research on emotional intelligence. *Journal of Organizational Behavior, 26*(4), 411–424.

37 Salovey, P., & Mayer, J. D. (1990). Emotional intelligence. *Imagination, Cognition and Personality, 9*(3), 185–211.

38 Joseph, D. L., & Newman, D. A. (2010). Emotional intelligence: An integrative meta-analysis and cascading model. *Journal of Applied Psychology, 95*(1), 54.

39 Caruso, D. R., Mayer, J. D., & Salovey, P. (2002). Relation of an ability measure of emotional intelligence to personality. *Journal of Personality Assessment, 79*(2), 306–320.

40 Goleman, D. (1995). *Emotional intelligence: Why it can matter more than IQ.* Bantam Books.

41 McDaniel, M. A., Hartman, N. S., Whetzel, D. L., & Grubb III, W. L. (2007). Situational judgment tests, response instructions, and validity: A meta-analysis. *Personnel Psychology, 60*(1), 63–91.

42 Salter, N. P., & Highhouse, S. (2009). Assessing managers' common sense using situational judgment tests. *Management Decision, 47*(3), 392–398.

43 Webster, E. S., Paton, L. W., Crampton, P. E., & Tiffin, P. A. (2020). Situational judgement test validity for selection: A systematic review and meta-analysis. *Medical Education, 54*(10), 888–902.

44 Olson-Buchanan, J. B., Drasgow, F., Moberg, P. J., Mead, A. D., Keenan, P. A., & Donovan, M. A. (1998). Interactive video assessment of conflict resolution skills. *Personnel Psychology, 51*(1), 1–24.

45 Webster, E. S., Paton, L. W., Crampton, P. E., & Tiffin, P. A. (2020). Situational judgement test validity for selection: A systematic review and meta-analysis. *Medical Education, 54*(10), 888–902.

46 McManus, M. A., & Kelly, M. L. (1999). Personality measures and biodata: Evidence regarding their incremental predictive value in the life insurance industry. *Personnel Psychology, 52*(1), 137–148.

47 Hunter, J. E., & Hunter, R. F. (1984). Validity and utility of alternative predictors of job performance. *Psychological Bulletin, 96*(1), 72.

48 Cucina, J. M., Caputo, P. M., Thibodeaux, H. F., & Maclane, C. N. (2012). Unlocking the key to biodata scoring: A comparison of empirical, rational, and hybrid approaches at different sample sizes. *Personnel Psychology, 65*(2), 385–428.

49 Speer, A. B., Tenbrink, A. P., Wegmeyer, L. J., Sendra, C. C., Shihadeh, M., & Kaur, S. (2022). Meta-analysis of biodata in employment settings: Providing clarity to criterion and construct-related validity estimates. *Journal of Applied Psychology, 107*(10), 1678–1705.

50 Van Iddekinge, C. H., Roth, P. L., Raymark, P. H., & Odle-Dusseau, H. N. (2012). The criterion-related validity of integrity tests: An updated meta-analysis. *Journal of Applied Psychology, 97*(3), 499.

51 Cooper, D. A., Slaughter, J. E., & Gilliland, S. W. (2021). Reducing injuries, malingering, and workers' compensation costs by implementing overt integrity testing. *Journal of Business and Psychology, 36*(3), 495–512.

11 Behavioral and observational measures

LEARNING OBJECTIVES

- Understand the value of behavioral and observational measures as a selection tool
- Appreciate the controversy surrounding drug testing within the selection context
- Understand the purpose(s) of using reference checks and background checks
- Know the differences between structured and unstructured interviews
- Understand what work sample tests entail and when they may be used
- Recognize the various exercises utilized within assessment centers

Behavioral and observational measures

How confident would you feel if your instructor for this class asked you to change a tire? Juggle? Do a cartwheel? Sing Pharrell Williams' hit song "Happy"? Now imagine that your classmates were instructed to formally evaluate you as you performed each activity! Although your confidence may vary depending on the activities mentioned, you would likely experience at least a little nervousness regardless of the activity chosen. In this scenario, your behavior is, quite literally, put on the spot. This is the essence of behavioral and observational measures. While ability tests (Chapter 9) and non-cognitive tests (Chapter 10) serve as indirect indicators of your future behaviors, there are several selection tools meant to formally assess your actual behavior as an indicator of future on-the-job performance. This chapter will review behavioral and observational methods used by organizations in the selection process.

Drug testing

Let's start with one of the more controversial behavioral screening tools: **drug testing**. These tests are used to indicate recent drug use. The logic behind drug testing is that drug use can be dangerous and is associated with negative consequences for both the user and the organization. However, the fairness and legality of drug testing have been called into question, with particular attention paid to the accuracy of certain drug testing procedures and one's right to privacy.[1] Given the controversial nature of this assessment method, there are potential advantages and disadvantages associated with its implementation.

> **Drug Testing:** Procedures implemented to examine whether a person has recently used a drug.

The case for drug testing

There is a large amount of evidence demonstrating the negative side effects associated with illicit drug use. The most important of these include alterations in one's thinking and decision-making, impaired reasoning ability, and a dulling of one's senses. Given these effects, it is not surprising that drug use has been shown to impact both cognitive and psychomotor performance.[2] In the workplace, drug abuse by employees has been linked to increased absences, inattention while at work, increased risk for accidents and injuries, increased health care use/cost, and increased turnover.[3,4] As a result, many employers screen employees for drug use as part of the hiring process. Furthermore, the Drug-free Workplace Act of 1988 stipulates that a drug-free workplace policy is required for any organization receiving federal grant money.

There are three primary drug testing strategies. Drug testing may be used (1) as a pre-hire screening tool, (2) as part of post-accident evaluation, or (3) randomly to ensure compliance with specified drug use policies. Random drug testing is typically reserved for occupations in which performance-enhancing drugs may provide a competitive advantage, such as professional sports. For most jobs, after an employee is hired, the employer must have reasonable suspicion before requiring an employee to take a drug test. Therefore, pre-employment and post-accident drug testing are the most common methods used within organizations. Regardless of the type of drug testing implemented, French et al. (2004) suggest that simply having a drug testing program in place is associated with lower probability of worker drug use.[5] Given the known side effects of drug use, and paired with the demonstrated empirical links to workplace outcomes, the efficacy of drug testing as an evaluation tool seems pretty clear-cut, right? Not so fast.

Issues to consider when drug testing

The consequences of a failed drug test may include removal from employment consideration, termination, rehabilitation, or losing unemployment benefits. Accordingly, important decisions about a person's work status (and life in general) are made on the basis of drug test results. Perhaps the most controversial aspect of drug testing is the possibility for a false positive – when a drug test detects the presence of a banned/restricted substance even though the person has not actually taken the substance. A variety of prescribed and over-the-counter medications, foods, and other substances may contribute to a false positive. Indeed, there are numerous examples of individuals testing positive for substances in an initial urine test only to be exonerated with a more thorough and sophisticated follow-up drug test. Unfortunately, one of the most common drug testing procedures used within organizations – urinalysis – is prone to a higher percentage of false positives.[6] For example, you may have heard that ingesting poppy seeds can lead to a failed drug test. Indeed, opiates may be detected in urine samples for as long as two days after eating a muffin containing poppy seeds, thereby leading to a positive drug test.[7] Alternatively, if hair or blood samples are used, poppy seeds are much less likely to result in a false positive. Obviously, an applicant would be unhappy to learn that they were removed from consideration due to their muffin flavor preferences!! Given that the method(s) used for drug testing may impact the likelihood of a false positive, employers should have procedures in place to ensure that initial results of a drug test – particularly urinalysis – are accurate. This typically requires more complex and expensive drug testing procedures, but these are necessary given the ramifications associated with a failed drug test.

Another important issue regarding drug testing lies in the fact that drug tests can indicate substance use, but they are not necessarily indicators of impairment (i.e., intoxication or withdrawal).[8] Most people will agree that being under the influence of drugs *while at work* constitutes a problem. However, for certain drugs (e.g., marijuana), the use of the drug can be traced within the body for days, and sometimes weeks after use. Thus, the drug test may occur well after the effects of the drug have worn off. This adds an additional layer of complexity to drug testing. What should be done when a worker uses drugs recreationally on the weekends (which is legal in many states), but not at work? Should the employer have any say over what an individual does during his/her leisure time if it is ambiguous as to whether it is impacting their performance at work? There are, of course, competing perspectives on this issue, and this represents a question that HR professionals must consider when deciding whether to use drug testing as a screening tool.

A final consideration is what to do if/when an employee fails a drug test. Pre-employment testing is relatively straightforward. If the employer makes a job offer contingent upon passing an illicit drug test, the employer is justified in rescinding the offer if the applicant tests positive. For current employees, however, the situation is much more complicated due to variations in state law. For example, in some states, an employer cannot fire someone for the first failed drug test if the employee agrees to attend a rehabilitation program.[9] In any case, whatever decisions are made with regard to positive drug tests, it is crucial that the employer remains consistent in their handling of all similar cases, treating each case with the same standardized procedures and ensuring the fairness of their drug testing policies. Moreover, it is important for organizations to be cognizant of how the Americans with Disabilities Act (ADA) treats drug addiction. Specifically, a person who is addicted to drugs is protected under the ADA as long as he/she is not *currently* using illegal drugs.[10]

Now that you have some background information on drug testing, what do you think? Should applicants be required to pass a drug test before being hired? After being involved in a work accident? Randomly? This has been, and will continue to be a contentious issue for the foreseeable future, especially given the changing state-level legislation when it comes to certain psychoactive drugs (i.e., marijuana). Next, we'll move on to a more common – and less controversial – pre-employment screening device.

Reference and background checks

Think about three people whom you would trust to provide an opinion on your potential for future success. If you are like most people, you would only consider those who will provide a positive evaluation of your ability, character, and work habits. Asking for references is a common method of pre-employment screening, and is usually part of a formal job application. A **reference check** occurs when employers contact applicant's previous employers, supervisors, co-workers, or educators to acquire information related to the applicant's KSAOs.[11] References can be asked to provide either a verbal or written evaluation of an applicant's suitability for hire. A popular form of a reference check, often used within educational settings, is the **letter of recommendation**. This entails a written narrative expressing an opinion regarding an applicant's potential for success. Whether verbal or written, the purpose of reference checks is to gather information related to the applicants' past behavior and performance.

> **Reference Check:** The practice of contacting previous colleagues or acquaintances to gain information about a job applicant.

> **Letter of Recommendation:** A written document expressing an opinion on an applicant's suitability for a given position.

One simple benefit of a reference check is that it provides a relatively quick and easy way to weed out applicants who should *not* move forward in the selection process. For example, if each reference raises concerns about the applicant's ability to succeed in the position they applied for, this should obviously serve as a red flag for the organization. In addition to spotting blatant red flags, references that have known the applicant for a long period of time may be able to provide specific and detailed information about the person's past performance and competencies, thereby expanding upon the qualifications listed on a resume. This information can offer additional evidence of an applicants' fit for a given position. When multiple references are contacted, the opinions of each reference can be compared to determine if there is a consensus regarding the applicant's potential for success.

Even with the potential benefits, there are several issues that limit the validity and usefulness of reference checks and letters of recommendation as a selection tool. For example, references may gloss over applicant shortcomings, overemphasize positive characteristics, or provide ambiguous responses. Lenient evaluations are especially likely if the reference fears any form of legal ramifications from rejected applicants who become resentful over not being selected. Even though references have legal protection to express their honest and truthful opinion (i.e., qualified privilege), the simple threat of litigation – in the form of a defamation of character lawsuit – is enough to cause some references to sensor or moderate their responses to some degree. Another potential problem deals with the structure of the reference check process itself. If there is little direction given to references regarding the competencies and skills relevant to the position for which the applicant has applied, the information provided by the reference may be irrelevant to the job, and therefore unusable from a selection standpoint. Additionally, if the applicant is allowed to choose their own references, as is often the case, this almost ensures that the reviews will be universally positive and it will be difficult to discriminate between applicants. Finally, the competence, lexical ability, or writing style of the recommendation writer may impact the perception of an applicant.[12] Thus, a mediocre applicant with a highly persuasive wordsmith as a reference may appear better than a superior applicant with a less lyrically gifted reference. Despite their flaws, reference checks and letters of recommendation remain a relatively common screening tool in the job application process.

Reference checks and letters of recommendation may be used as a part of a broader, more thorough evaluation of one's past. A **background check** is the formal process of investigating whether an applicant is unqualified for a job due to a history of suspicious behavior. Specifically, background checks verify that an individual is who they claim to be. Depending on the job, background checks may be used to consider one's criminal record, driving record, credit history, education, and/or work history.[13,14] The underlying assumption behind these background checks is that past behavior is a good predictor of future behavior. A primary reason for conducting background checks is to ensure that the organization is hiring a safe, honest, and qualified employee.

> **Background Check:** The process of verifying the information provided by a job candidate.

Checking an applicant's educational credentials, work history, and personal references is relatively straightforward in that employers simply seek to verify the information an applicant has provided on the job application. While it is easy to simply trust the information provided by applicants, it is not uncommon for people to engage in fraudulent behavior, misrepresent their credentials, or lie on an application. Even among high-profile positions, there are several examples of "leaders" lying about their academic credentials. For example, Marilee Jones worked at the Massachusetts Institute of Technology for 28 years – and even served as the dean of admissions for ten years – before being forced to resign as a result of lying on her application (she claimed that she had three degrees, when in actuality she had none). Similarly, David Tovar, former Vice President of corporate communications at Walmart, and Scott Thomson, former CEO of Yahoo, were both forced to resign as a result of exaggerating their educational background on their resumes. As such, the background check represents a quick way to confirm that applicants have actually attended the institutions listed and worked with the references they have provided.

While credit history and driving records are indicators of an applicant's general trustworthiness, the importance and relevance of these checks are job-dependent. For example, credit checks are more pertinent to jobs that involve access to money or sensitive customer data, such as accounting positions and any job dealing with money. For these positions, it is especially important that applicants are trustworthy and demonstrate fiscal responsibility. Driving records, on the other hand, are more applicable to positions that involve operation of a motor vehicle, such as a truck driver or cab driver. At the same time, one's driving record may be relevant to any employee who is expected to commute a considerable distance to work, as the employee is expected to reliably show up to work on time.

Criminal background checks provide evidence of more severe disciplinary problems such as sexual harassment, violence, or fraud. Although not every crime would automatically disqualify an applicant from being hired, this information will help the organization make an informed decision. If an applicant has a history of criminal behavior that would be disruptive or counterproductive for the job in question, this is important information for the employing organization to consider in the selection process. Regardless of the type of background check utilized by the organization, it is important that any information collected and used as part of the selection process be job-related, as indicated by a thorough job analysis. Employers should be wary though of potential adverse impact issues when using criminal background checks, given racial disparities in our justice system.[15]

In summary, reference and background checks serve the purpose of confirming the accuracy of information reported on the job application. These methods, alone, are not especially effective in determining the best candidate for a given job.[16,17] Rather, reference and background checks often serve as a useful initial screening tool to reveal whether there are any glaring issues that would prevent the applicant from being an effective member of the organization. Accordingly, reference and background checks are typically used in combination with additional behavioral measures, such as the interview.

Interviews

The most prevalent and popular behavioral measure is the job interview. Nearly every organization uses the interview method in some shape or form. Interviews are used to predict future performance based on applicant's verbal responses to a series of questions. Although all interviews follow a similar general procedure, the content of the questions asked within an interview can vary greatly. For example, imagine you are interviewing for your dream job. Below are two common approaches to beginning your interview:

1. Tell me about yourself.   2. Tell me why you are a good fit for this position.

Think carefully about how you would answer each question. Believe it or not, the subtle difference between these two introductory questions can potentially impact the trajectory of an interview, the questions asked within the interview, and the rating provided by the interviewer. This is especially the case if an unstructured interview format is used. To understand how the structure of an interview – or lack thereof – can greatly impact the hiring decision, let's explore the interview process in more depth.

Interview structure

An **unstructured interview** has the appearance and feel of a casual conversation between the interviewer and the applicant. A hallmark of unstructured interviewers is the mentality of "I'll see where it goes" on the part of the interviewer. As a result, the interviewer is free to ask any questions he sees fit, thereby tailoring each interview to the specific person he is interviewing and subjectively deciding what topic(s) to pursue and which avenues to explore.

> **Unstructured Interview:** Assessment procedure that is developed and implemented arbitrarily, with little to no uniformity across applicants.

Take, for example, the familiar phrase "Tell me about yourself." This is a common way to begin an unstructured interview. After hearing the applicant's response, the interviewer will focus on what she finds most interesting or relevant, and then develop follow-up questions on the fly based on her subjective sense of where the interview should go next. This may not sound problematic at face value, but this format ensures that each applicant interview will follow a different path – with a different subset of questions – based on the nature of the applicants' responses and the personal whims of the interviewer. Furthermore, the follow-up questions asked by the interviewer may or may not be job-related.

Perhaps the applicant begins their response to "tell me about yourself" by expressing that they are a hard worker but then veers into non-job-related territory with a summary of their interests and hobbies, their affinity for local sports teams, and ends by sharing a picture of their beloved pet cat. The majority of this information is neither useful nor relevant. After hearing this, a good interviewer will steer the conversation back toward job-relevant characteristics. In a worst-case scenario, the interviewer latches on to a piece of non-job-relevant information and indulges the applicant with additional irrelevant questions. Getting off topic obviously represents a major problem if the interviewer wants to ensure that the selection decision is completely job-related, but can even lead to some dicey territory with regard to the *legality* of the questions being asked. For example, if the informal nature of the unstructured interview takes the conversation to a place where families and holidays are discussed, these issues are not only irrelevant but can also be illegal when or if they are used in the selection context.

Even if an interviewer stays focused on job-relevant topics for the entirety of each unstructured interview, she is resigned to making holistic comparisons across multiple candidates who were asked different sets of questions. This is problematic, particularly due to the lack of formal scoring within unstructured interviews. Given that there is no standard scoring system used for evaluating applicant responses, the interviewer is forced to clinically combine multiple pieces of subjectively interpreted information after the interview has taken place. These interpretations are often based on the interviewers' supposed expertise at reading people and/or their "gut feeling" about the candidate. The lack of standardization in the evaluation process, paired with the differing sets of questions asked of each candidate, makes it extremely difficult to make objective comparisons between competing candidates. As a result, this approach is not as effective or useful as the structured interview.

A **structured interview** has three key features that set it apart from the unstructured interview. First, all questions are strictly job-relevant and stem from a job analysis. Second, each applicant applying for a given position is asked the same set of questions. Third, a formal rating/scoring system is used to evaluate applicant responses to each question. Thus, the interviewer has a series of questions that have been prepared in advance, resists the urge to stray away from that set of standardized questions, and systematically scores applicant responses to each question based on predetermined criteria. These three features address the most egregious concerns associated with unstructured interviews.

> **Structured Interview:** Assessment procedure where all applicants are asked the same set of job-related questions and are formally evaluated on their responses to each question.

As you might guess, a structured interview looks and feels much different than an unstructured interview. When it comes to beginning an interview, "tell me why you are a good fit for this position" is a nice alternative to the infamous "tell me about yourself." Opening an interview with this phrase ensures that the interview begins on a job-related note and makes it much less likely for the applicant to get side-tracked with non-job-relevant information. This is one of the most important distinctions between structured and unstructured interviews. When the unstructured interview format is used, questions may not necessarily remain job-related throughout the entire interview. In a structured interview, all questions are inherently job-related. This is accomplished through careful consideration of the question development process.

Two specific types of structured interview strategies – *behavioral interviewing* and *situational interviewing* – demonstrate the value of formal, behavior-based interview questions. **Behavioral interview items** ask job-related questions focused on applicants' past experiences. **Situational interview items**, in contrast, ask job-related questions focused on hypothetical future behavior. Each type of question is typically associated with a job-relevant KSAO to be evaluated. For example, let's say someone was interviewing for a management position, and two of the key requirements for the job are conflict resolution and decisiveness. Behavioral interview items may ask about a time when the applicant had to resolve a conflict or be decisive in the past. Situational interview items, on the other hand, would ask about how the applicant would respond to a future job-relevant scenario involving conflict resolution or decisiveness. Here are a couple of examples of each type of question:

Conflict resolution

Behavioral: "Tell me about a time when you were in conflict with a coworker and how the situation was resolved"
Situational: "What would you do if you were confronted by an angry and dissatisfied customer? What steps would you take to resolve the issue?"

Decisiveness

Behavioral: "Give me an example of a time you made an unpopular decision. Explain how you implemented that decision effectively"
Situational: "As a manager, you've made an unpopular decision. What actions would you take to ensure that morale in your department is not negatively impacted?"

> **Behavioral Interview Items:** Structured interview questions focused on applicant behavior in previous job-related situations.
>
> **Situation Interview Items:** Structured interview questions focused on how applicants would respond in future job-related scenarios.

A structured interview would consist of a series of predetermined questions such as these. After the candidate responds to a given question, the interviewer would rate the candidate's response on a formal rating scale based on established criteria, and then move on to the next question. This pattern would repeat until the interview is complete. You may be thinking to yourself that structured interviews don't sound like much fun. You're not necessarily wrong. Although a structured interview may be perceived as less fun or enjoyable than an unstructured interview – by both the interviewer and the interviewee – the organization associated with structured interviews allows for a more objective comparison of the competing applicants. This is the name of the game when it comes to employee selection. Thus, the "fun" comes when the best candidate is selected for the job in the most fair and objective way possible (Table 11.1).

Empirical evidence supports the use and value of structured interviews, consistently demonstrating that structured interviews are superior at predicting future performance when compared to unstructured interviews.[18,19,20] In reality, an interview may be completely unstructured, semi-structured (in that there are a few standard questions, but follow-up questions may differ), or completely structured. Research evidence shows that the more structured, the better. Even so, there still remains quite a bit of resistance to fully structured interviews, with many HR professionals preferring the unstructured interview format.[21] Given the hesitance to incorporate the structured interview, it is important to understand the many potential biases that may arise as part of the interview process, and how structured interviews help to prevent these biases from shaping the selection decision.

Biases associated with the interview process

Before an interview even begins, there are several biases that may arise as a result of first impressions. It is a well-established finding that we tend to like and prefer people who are similar to us. This is a simple fact of being human. Consequently, initial preconceived notions (positive or negative) about an applicant may develop from the information provided on the job application, the candidate's physical appearance, or both. This **similarity bias** can occur due to perceived similarities with regard to the applicant's demographic

Table 11.1 Characteristics of unstructured and structured interviews

Unstructured	Structured
The factors evaluated by the interview are implicit and vary across candidates.	The factors evaluated are explicit, based on job analysis, and are the same for each candidate.
Questions are not necessarily job-related.	Questions are job-related.
Questions vary from interview to interview for the same job.	The same questions are asked of all candidates for the same job.
There is no system or guide for evaluating interview results.	There is a pre-developed system for evaluating interview results.
Interviewers may be untrained.	Interviewers have received the same training.

characteristics, personality, educational background, work history, or apparent shared interests or hobbies. While the similarity bias may not be overly problematic in an informal everyday setting, it should not impact the selection process. Another potential area for bias related to first impressions is the perceived attractiveness of the candidate. Though obviously not job-relevant, it has been shown that attractive people are perceived as more competent than less attractive people.[22] Finally, some research has even suggested that the quality of an initial handshake can be related to interviewer hiring recommendations.[23] All of these biases may arise *before the candidate is asked any questions*, and can even influence the types of questions asked during the interview itself (if using an unstructured interview).

> **Similarity Bias:** A preference/liking of people who are more similar to oneself.

During the interview, interviewers may seek information that confirms their first impressions of the candidate. This is known as **confirmation bias**, and may happen intentionally or unintentionally. Confirmation bias can plague the best, most well-intentioned interviewers. For example, if an interviewer has a negative first impression about a candidate based on the initial handshake, they may ask different questions – and interpret applicant responses differently – in order to confirm their initial negative impressions. In contrast, if the interviewer has a positive first impression of an applicant, this may lead the interviewer to do less questioning and more "selling" of the company to the candidate.[24] This reiterates the importance of using a structured set of questions, as opposed to developing questions on the fly.

> **Confirmation Bias:** A tendency to seek out and interpret evidence in a way that confirms one's existing beliefs.

Another factor that may bias an interviewers' perceptions is non-verbal communication. Interviewers may misinterpret non-verbal cues such as posture, eye contact, and general nervousness. If an interviewer places more emphasis on the mannerisms of the candidate than on their qualifications and responses to job-related questions, this is problematic. Similarly, interviewers may place too much focus on superficial qualities, such as extraversion and verbal skills, rather than job-relevant KSAOs. Because interviews are inherently a verbal task, verbal skills may be taken into consideration by the interviewer regardless of whether they are necessary for the job in question. Structured interviews seek to reduce this potential bias by developing job-related questions and using a formal rating system to carefully evaluate applicants' responses to each question individually.

Finally, the use of non-job-related questions is a major concern and area for potential bias. As noted by Zhang (2021), some organizations use oddball and/or unorthodox interview questions to assess applicants while also trying to demonstrate the unique culture of the organization.[25] Although these questions may be perceived as more likeable, they are virtually useless for recruiting and selection decisions. In fact, some research has even suggested that people who would consider using oddball/brainteaser interview questions in the hiring process tend to be more narcissistic, sadistic, and less socially competent.[26] As such, oddball interview questions may indicate more about the interviewer than the interviewee.

After the interview is over, interviewers may use their intuition to make clinical, holistic comparisons between candidates, possibly seeking to "read between the lines" of what happened within the interview.[27] Intuition can impact not only the interviewers' overall gut feeling about a candidate but also the interpretation of applicant's responses to each specific question. For example, let's say a candidate was asked why they left their previous job, and their response focused on a conflict they had with their boss. While one interviewer may view this as a sign of confidence and initiative on the part of the applicant, another interviewer may view this as a sign of entitlement and insubordination. This demonstrates the importance of standardizing the evaluation process with a formal scoring system, and making sure that each interviewer has the same frame of reference for evaluating each interview question.

As you can see, there are many areas where bias may arise in the interview process. Structured interviews are not only better at predicting performance but have also been shown to reduce the biases that may arise while using an unstructured interview format.[28] Although bias cannot be completely eliminated from the interview process, the structured interview seeks to make the interview process as objective as possible. The less structured the interview, the more likely it is to suffer from many of the biases presented above.

Summary

At its best, an unstructured interview may approximate the content of a structured interview. At its worst, an unstructured interview will lack organization and forethought on the part of the interviewer, venture down several non-job-related (and possibly illegal) topic areas, and prevent the possibility of objective comparisons between applicants due to the inconsistency of the questions asked within each interview. Although not perfect, it is clear to see the value and improvements provided by the structured interview format.

Work sample test

A work sample test is exactly what it sounds like. While most assessment methods measure indirect indicators of one's potential for completing work activities, the work sample test has applicants actually perform a small portion of the job. For example, as part of the selection process, a professor may be required to present a lecture to a room full of students, a plumber may be asked to fix a leaky faucet, or an accountant may be asked to balance a petty cash ledger. The applicant is evaluated based on their proficiency at completing the task(s) in question. As can be seen from these examples, this method of assessment is inherently job-related.

> **Work Sample Test:** An assessment that evaluates a candidate's ability to execute important job tasks.

Given its direct relation to the job of interest, it is not surprising that work sample tests yield high content and criterion-related validity. In fact, work sample tests have proven to be one of the best *single* predictors of job performance.[29,30] Furthermore, these tests are hard to fake and are typically well-received by applicants due to their job-relatedness. An added advantage of this method is that it provides a realistic job preview for applicants, thereby allowing applicants to evaluate their own suitability for hire.[31] Because this assessment is a genuine sample of the job for which one is applying, it is hard to argue against the validity of this method.

While the work sample test has many obvious advantages, developing a work sample test can be quite costly and time-consuming to administer. Moreover, although this method is highly useful for jobs in which work tasks can be completed in a short period of time, they are less efficient at predicting performance for jobs in which tasks may take days or weeks to complete. Work sample tests are also less feasible when work tasks are dangerous or difficult to replicate in a contained physical environment. Under these circumstances, applicants may be asked to complete simulations that mimic the work tasks as closely as possible in an environment where there is no inherent danger or risk involved to applicants or assessors. Finally, while work sample tests are adept at measuring a candidate's ability to perform a task, they should not necessarily be used to assess job skills or abilities that applicants would be expected to learn later on the job and/or as part of their standard job training. Thus, work sample tests may not be the best option for candidates without job experience.[32]

Assessment centers

Imagine combining all the previously mentioned behavioral assessments into an extended period of intense behavioral evaluation. This is the gist of an assessment center. Broadly, an assessment center provides a detailed evaluation of several applicants on a variety of job-relevant KSAOs. More specifically, assessment centers use multiple assessors to evaluate a group of job candidates at the same time and place using multiple behavioral evaluation methods. Candidates are judged based on their proficiency in a variety of work sample tests, simulations, and group exercises. The goal of the assessment center is to demonstrate whether a person is the right fit for a particular position. The assessment center may be used to assess external candidates applying for a given position, or internal

Behavioral and observational measures

incumbents applying for a promotion. Due to the cost and complexity of developing an assessment center, this method is primarily used for higher-profile managerial positions.

> **Assessment Center:** An evaluation method in which multiple assessors evaluate multiple candidates on multiple behavioral dimensions.

Several behavioral measures are employed within an assessment center. **In-basket exercises** are meant to mimic some of the day-to-day concerns a manager must face as part of their job. These exercises require candidates to review a series of job-related circumstances (emails, paperwork, memos, phone messages), determine how to prioritize each task, and decide how they would respond to each issue in an appropriate manner. The candidate is then evaluated based on the quality of the decisions they made, as well as the manner and order in which the decisions were carried out.

> **In-Basket Exercise:** An exercise in which candidates are asked to prioritize and respond to various daily tasks that may be encountered on the job.

Another common behavioral assessment is the **role play**, in which candidates act out a situation they would encounter on the job. The role play is different from the in-basket exercise in that it evaluates candidates as they partake in complex social interactions that may be encountered within the workplace. For example, let's assume you were a candidate in a role play scenario, and you were assigned the role of "new vice president of sales" for a particular company. In the role play exercise, you must interact with a regional sales manager who has been with the company for several years. This person is upset with a recent change in the sales strategy at your company. As this is the first interaction between yourself and the regional manager, the goal for your role play exercise may be to lay the groundwork for a productive relationship with the regional sales manager, explain the reasoning for the change in sales strategy, and lay out sales goals for the future. Sounds easy, right? Now, imagine that the person enacting the role of the regional sales manager has been instructed to be difficult and combative in your social interactions. All the while, as your role play scenario is taking place, you are being evaluated by multiple assessors on your ability to effectively manage the situation and interact with the sales manager in a diplomatic manner. In an actual assessment center evaluation, there may be multiple role plays where you are expected to navigate a variety of different social situations.

> **Role Play:** An exercise in which candidates take on a particular role and act out a situation they would encounter on the job.

Assessment centers may also use exercises that allow the applicants to interact with one another. The **leaderless group discussion** is a practice in which applicants are put into a small group with the goal of discussing and resolving a job-relevant issue. For example, the candidates may be asked to discuss strategies for improving worker motivation and morale, or how to reduce employee turnover in a particular department. A key aspect of this exercise is that none of the applicants are assigned the role of the leader. While the applicants are discussing the problem and brainstorming solutions, assessors are observing the applicants and rating them on several behavioral dimensions (e.g., cooperativeness, persuasiveness, communication skills, and critical thinking ability). The goal of this exercise is to evaluate how each candidate handles themselves within the group, what role each individual enacts within the group, and who emerges as a leader.

> **Leaderless Group Discussion:** An exercise in which multiple applicants are placed in a group and asked to discuss a job-related issue.

In addition to the exercises described above, applicants may also be asked to deliver a presentation, go through a series of interviews, or take a battery of psychological tests. All the exercises are meant to provide an indication of the applicant's job-related proficiency. The end result of an assessment center is a comprehensive profile of each applicant's suitability for hire based on a thorough evaluation of several behavioral dimensions. As evidenced by the variety of exercises involved, applicants are placed under a great deal of scrutiny by the assessors. Similarly, there is a great deal of burden placed on the assessors, themselves, as they rate multiple people on multiple behavioral dimensions. As such, training assessors and providing a standard frame of reference for evaluation are crucial in order to ensure the reliability of assessor ratings.[33]

Similar to work sample tests, a primary benefit of assessment centers is that they have a high degree of content validity – they look and feel like the job for which one is applying. Assessment centers have also been shown to be significantly related to work performance, thereby demonstrating criterion-related validity.[34] A unique aspect of the assessment center is that it is perhaps one of the only selection methods that can provide in-depth feedback to applicants on a variety of behavioral dimensions. Accordingly, assessment centers can serve as a valuable tool for applicant development, particularly when evaluating internal candidates for promotion. Despite the benefits of using assessment centers, the major drawback is the cost and complexity associated with this method. Given the time and resources required, assessment centers are rarely used in typical selection contexts.

Summary

In this chapter, we reviewed several behavioral measures used to predict on-the-job performance. Specifically, drug tests, reference checks, and background checks may be used as initial screening tools to weed out unqualified applicants based on previous behavior.

Interviews may be used to gain more insight into how an applicant is likely to perform on the job but can also suffer from several areas of potential bias. Structured interviews take several steps to reduce these biases, thereby allowing for more objective comparisons between applicants. Finally, work sample tests and assessment centers provide more detailed evaluations of how applicants are likely to perform specific, job-related tasks and activities. Behavioral measures can be a powerful predictor of future performance, particularly when paired with other cognitive and non-cognitive selection tests.

REVIEW QUESTIONS

1. How are behavioral and observational measures different from cognitive and non-cognitive measures?
2. Why is drug testing controversial when used as a measure of employee selection?
3. What are the pros and cons associated with reference checks and background checks?
4. What are the differences between structured and unstructured interviews?
5. Why are unstructured interviews more prone to bias?
6. What is the difference between a work sample test and an assessment center?
7. What exercises are involved in an assessment center?
8. When is an assessment center likely to be used?

DISCUSSION QUESTIONS

1. Would you recommend using drug testing as part of the employee selection process? Why or why not?
2. What value can be gained through reference checks and background checks?
3. If you were interviewing for a job, would you prefer an unstructured or a structured interview? Why?
4. Given its content and criterion-related validity, should a work sample test be used in the selection process for every job? Why or why not?
5. For which jobs would you recommend using an assessment center? For which jobs would you recommend *not* using an assessment center?

Notes

1 Hickox, S. (2017). It's time to rein in employer drug testing. *Harvard Law and Policy Review, 11*, 419–462.
2 Frone, M. R. (2013). *Alcohol and illicit drug use in the workforce and workplace.* American Psychological Association.

3 Goplerud, E., Hodge, S., & Benham, T. (2017). A substance use cost calculator for US employers with an emphasis on prescription pain medication misuse. *Journal of Occupational and Environmental Medicine, 59*(11), 1063–1071.
4 Larsen, S. L., Eyerman, J., Foster, M. S., & Gfroerer, J. C. (2007). *Worker substance use and workplace policies and programs.* U.S. Department of Health and Human Services.
5 French, M. T., Roebuck, M. C., & Alexandre, P. K. (2007). To test or not to test: Do workplace drug testing programs discourage employee drug use? *Social Science Research, 33*(1), 45–63.
6 Saitman, A., Park, H., & Fitzgerald, R. L. (2014). False-positive interferences of common urine drug screen immunoassays: A review. *Journal of Analytical Toxicology, 38*(7), 387–396.
7 Thevis, M., Opfermann, G., & Schänzer, W. (2003). Urinary concentrations of morphine and codeine after consumption of poppy seeds. *Journal of Analytical Toxicology, 27*(1), 53–56.
8 Hickox, S. (2017). It's time to rein in employer drug testing. *Harvard Law and Policy Review, 11,* 419–462.
9 Nagele-Piazza, L. (2020). *Workplace drug testing: What to do when employees fail.* Society for Human Resource Management. https://www.shrm.org/resourcesandtools/legal-and-compliance/state-and-local-updates/pages/what-to-do-when-an-employee-fails-a-drug-test.aspx
10 *Are employees undergoing treatment for drug and alcohol addictions covered under the ADA?* (2022). Society of Human Resource Management. https://www.shrm.org/resourcesandtools/tools-and-samples/hr-qa/pages/adadrugsandalcohol.aspx
11 *Conducting background investigations and reference checks.* (2021). Society of Human Resource Management. https://www.shrm.org/resourcesandtools/tools-and-samples/toolkits/pages/conductingbackgroundinvestigations.aspx
12 Templer, A. J., & Thacker, J. W. (1988). Credible letters of reference: How you read them is important. *Journal of Managerial Psychology, 3,* 22–26.
13 Nagele-Piazza, L. (2020). *Workplace drug testing: What to do when employees fail.* Society for Human Resource Management. https://www.shrm.org/resourcesandtools/legal-and-compliance/state-and-local-updates/pages/what-to-do-when-an-employee-fails-a-drug-test.aspx
14 Brody, R. G. (2010). Beyond the basic background check: Hiring the "right" employees. *Management Research Review, 33*(3), 210–223.
15 https://law.fiu.edu/2020/04/10/the-disparate-impact-of-criminal-background-checks-as-hiring-criteria/
16 Muchinsky, P. M. (1979). The use of reference reports in personnel selection: A review and evaluation. *Journal of Occupational Psychology, 52*(4), 287–297.
17 Brody, R. G. (2010). Beyond the basic background check: Hiring the "right" employees. *Management Research Review, 33*(3), 210–223.
18 Schmidt, F. L., & Hunter, J. E. (1998). The validity and utility of selection methods in personnel psychology: Practical and theoretical implications of 85 years of research findings. *Psychological Bulletin, 124*(2), 262–274.
19 Schmidt, F. L., & Zimmerman, R. D. (2004). A counterintuitive hypothesis about employment interview validity and some supporting evidence. *Journal of Applied Psychology, 89*(3), 553–561.
20 Huffcutt, A. I., & Arthur, W. (1994). Hunter and Hunter (1984) revisited: Interview validity for entry-level jobs. *Journal of Applied Psychology, 79*(2), 184–190.
21 Highhouse, S. (2008). Stubborn reliance on intuition and subjectivity in employee selection. *Industrial and Organizational Psychology, 1*(3), 333–342.
22 Jackson, L. A., Hunter, J. A., & Hodge, C. N. (1995). Physical attractiveness and intellectual competence: A meta-analytic review. *Social Psychology Quarterly, 58*(2), 108–122.
23 Stewart, G. L., Dustin, S. L., Barrick, M. R., & Darnold, T. C. (2008). Exploring the handshake in employment interviews. *Journal of Applied Psychology, 93*(5), 1139–1146.

24 Dougherty, T. W., Turban, D. B., & Callender, J. C. (1994). Confirming first impressions in the employment interview: A field study of interviewer behavior. *Journal of Applied Psychology, 79*(5), 659–665.
25 Zhang, D. C. (2022). Horse-sized ducks or duck-sized horses? Oddball personality questions are likeable (but useless) for organizational recruitment. *Journal of Business Psychology, 37*, 215–233.
26 Highhouse, S., Nye, C. D., & Zhang, D. C. (2018). Dark motives and elective use of brainteaser interview questions. *Applied Psychology, 68*(2), 311–340.
27 Highhouse, S. (2008). Stubborn reliance on intuition and subjectivity in employee selection. *Industrial and Organizational Psychology, 1*(3), 333–342.
28 Levashina, J., Hartwell, C. J., Morgeson, F. P., & Campion, M. A. (2014). The structured employment interview: Narrative and quantitative review of the research literature. *Personnel Psychology, 67*(1), 241–293.
29 Schmidt, F. L., & Hunter, J. E. (1998). The validity and utility of selection methods in personnel psychology: Practical and theoretical implications of 85 years of research findings. *Psychological Bulletin, 124*(2), 262–274.
30 Roth, P. L., Bobko, P., & McFarland, L. A. (2005). A meta-analysis of work sample test validity: Updating and integrating some classic literature. *Personnel Psychology, 58*(4), 1009–1037.
31 Callinan, M., & Robertson, I. T. (2000). Work sample testing. *International Journal of Selection and Assessment, 8*(4), 248–260.
32 Callinan, M., & Robertson, I. T. (2000). Work sample testing. *International Journal of Selection and Assessment, 8*(4), 248–260.
33 Woehr, D. J., & Arthur, Jr., W. (2003). The construct-related validity of assessment center ratings: A review and meta-analysis of the role of methodological factors. *Journal of Management, 29*(2), 231–258.
34 Arthur, Jr., W., Day, E. A., McNelly, T. L., & Edens, P. S. (2003). A meta-analysis of the criterion-related validity of assessment center dimensions. *Personnel Psychology, 56*(1), 125–153.

12 New waves of assessment

LEARNING OBJECTIVES

- Learn about Big Data and Data Science
- Understanding how organizations are using social media and game-based assessments for personnel selection
- Understand the benefits and challenges of unproctored internet testing
- Learn about recent research on remote video interviewing, including asynchronous interviewing
- Learn an appreciation of the potential advantages and downsides of the increased role of technology in selection and human resources (HR)

Throughout much of the 20th century, pre-employment testing was relatively uninfluenced by technology as most tests were administered via paper with respondents answering with pen or pencil on sheets that were either hand-scored or eventually machine-scored. Sometime around the 1980s, though, with the development of relatively affordable personal computers, testing became highly influenced by technology. Early versions of computerized tests used computers merely as a page-turner and recording device, though as computers became more flexible and complex, tests better incorporated advanced technology such as graphical and video components that were not possible in earlier paper-and-pencil tests. Finally, with the advent and then mass availability of the internet, the potential for mass testing became possible even though that brought about challenges as well. In this chapter, we will review some of the ways that technology has transformed personnel selection. These areas include virtual reality (VR), mining social media information, game-based assessments, unproctored internet testing, video interviewing, and data mining. Before digging into specific types of assessments, we wanted to introduce the concept of Big Data and related concepts.

Big Data and Data Science

The phrase *Big Data* refers to the capacity that organizations now have to collect enormous amounts of data. For example, most retail organizations now collect data on customer purchases using rewards cards and can predict likely purchases and provide relevant coupons that are based on predicting what you might buy using your past purchase history. With the internet, huge amounts of text data can be mined to generate algorithms to predict what the next word will be when typing a memo or a text message. Big Data can also be useful in performance management of existing employees as well as the selection of future employees.

> **Big Data:** Very large data sets that can be analyzed, often in an exploratory manner, to identify and uncover trends and insights.

Data scientists are statistics experts who are able to generate insights from Big Data by using statistical algorithms to develop predictions and understandings. The phrase data scientist is unregulated and so people who call themselves data scientists may have a background in mathematics and statistics, or they may be industrial-organizational psychologists who have a special skillset in dealing with large data sets.

> **Data Scientist:** Someone employed to analyze complex large data sets, typically from a digital domain, to identify trends and insights that typically help provide business insights.

As our data sets get bigger and algorithms become more sophisticated, more and more universities are creating Data Science programs to train future data scientists. Also, organizations are more likely to hire people into positions with titles such as Data Analytics or even HR Data Analytics, and so if you are training to be an I-O psychologist, you will benefit from taking statistics classes that allow you some specialty in this area. One challenge with using Big Data has been described as a Skills Gap, in which the technical requirements for assembling, manipulating, analyzing, and interpreting large data sets are often beyond the skillsets of most I-O psychologists, and so we encourage you to do everything you can in order to become proficient in this area. Given the trend toward Big Data, more and more organizations will be seeking candidates with this skillset.

In this chapter, we will outline several ways that Big Data and data scientists are influencing the practice of pre-employment testing specifically and HR in general. Key to Big Data is the use of machine learning algorithms which rely on sophisticated statistical techniques to generate predicted outcomes from complex data sets.

> **Machine Algorithm:** A generic term that describes a process used by artificial intelligence systems to generate predictions based on a large amount of input data.

One of the ways that machine learning algorithms are being used is in creating new assessments. New approaches use text mining assessments to create a bank of items that are similar to pre-existing items, thus making it possible for test developers to create alternative forms of existing tests or to create larger test banks that have similar formats. The technology that is used is called *natural language processing* (NLP), which analyzes large amounts of textual data to learn how certain words go together to predict underlying meanings and connotations. Therefore, NLP algorithms can use knowledge gleaned from large amounts of textual data to create items that are semantically similar to existing items.[1] Although the technology is just emerging, this would be a large boon to test developers who often struggle to write new items. Test developers should still examine items that computer algorithms generate, though, as a proportion of the generated items are likely to not make sense. In addition to creating new items and test forms, NLP methods could be used to analyze job advertisements to identify similar jobs for the purposes of developing comparable compensation packages, as well as analyzing resumes and open-ended interviews to identify candidates likely to succeed. Also, as will be described in this chapter, machine learning algorithms may be used to analyze social media data (often called web-scraping) to better understand candidates.

Analyzing social media data

According to Pew Research, in 2021, 84% of all Americans from 18 to 29 years of age used at least one social media site per day[2] with 72% of all Americans using at least one social media site regularly. People use social media sites to connect with others, to share personal updates, to express their political views (and to comment on others), to sell products, look for jobs, and to sell products whether as part of a job or a "side hustle." In short, many of us, through various platforms, lead part of our lives on social media platforms. As social media use has proliferated, it is no surprise that psychologists have started studying social media use. Researchers have studied social media addiction,[3] cyberbullying,[4] and social support seeking.[5] I-O psychologists and organizational researchers have also studied how social media can be used in various aspects of pre-employment hiring.

Early (at least early in social media research, that is 2010) research found that there were modest correlations between self-reports of personality and observer raters of Facebook profiles.[6] Back and colleagues had participants fill out a Big Five personality measure and then granted access to researchers to observe their Facebook page. Observer ratings of the Big Five personality traits ranged from $r = .41$ for Openness to $r = .13$ for Neuroticism; all correlations were significant except for Neuroticism suggesting that observers could capture valid personality information by scouring peoples' Facebook pages. Since that publication, the practice of **cybervetting** has proliferated with roughly 70% of HR recruiters reporting that they check out social media profiles before hiring.[7]

> **Cybervetting:** Using online information to evaluate job candidates.

Although the practice has progressed, there are obstacles for using social media for hiring purposes. Some of the obstacles relate to practical issues. Some individuals are easy to find on social media, whereas others might be hard to identify. For example, there are apparently only two Michael Zickars in the world; my cyber-doppelganger has a PhD in mathematics and lives in Switzerland. However, if you were trying to find John Scott (who is currently the Chief Operating Officer at APT Metrics), there are over 100 entries for John Scott on Wikipedia alone, with many more entries on common social media sites. Others use nicknames to disguise their identity, whereas some people are not on social media at all. In addition, many people will have private profiles so that it is difficult to collect significant amounts of data on many individuals.

Other problems with cybervetting are that human raters may be overly influenced by non-relevant information in either positive or negative ways. For example, a rater may see that an applicant likes the same professional sports team and has an overly positive reaction to the candidate, or conversely, the rater may see that the applicant posted a positive article about a politician that the rater despises, which may cloud the observer's rating. Another problem is that the rater may see information related to protected classes. For example, the candidate may share that they attend the First United Methodist Church, or that they are expecting their third child in two months.

One solution for handling such concerns is using web-scraping to collect data so that human observers do not use protected classes. Then, computerized algorithms can be used to score web-scraped data to identify information that is likely to be related to job performance. Tay and colleagues describe how machine learning can be used to analyze text-mined data from social media platforms.[8] Another strategy to ensure fairness would be to only consider social media platforms that are already designed to focus on job-related information. Researchers have investigated whether information from LinkedIn can be used to predict personality scores and future job performance. In a recent study, researchers found correlations between characteristics on LinkedIn hypothesized to be related to Big Five traits.[9] For example, people who had a portrait photograph that was judged to be more artistic were higher on Openness to Experience, whereas people who were higher on Extraversion were more likely to have a high number of connections. Correlations between LinkedIn profile features tended to be small to moderate in size, though in aggregation these indicators could be used to understand someone's personality. Research on predicting job performance, however, is less supportive with a study of financial services professionals finding no correlation between different types of LinkedIn profiles and objective performance as judged by sales metrics.[10] Clearly, more research is needed on trying to understand how behavior in the social media realm is related to behavior and performance on the job.

Game-based assessments

Gaming is big business and video gaming in some form is a part of life of a large number of peoples' lives. In the United States, 65% of all Americans reported playing video games on at least one platform.[11] Test developers have started introducing game elements into assessments to make them more engaging to respondents. Test-taker fatigue and burnout has become a serious problem that becomes a barrier to assessment. Candidates who are responding to a gamified assessment are likely to be more engaged and likely to continue with the assessment longer than they might if the assessment was in a typical multiple-choice format. In fact, Landers and Sanchez catalog claims about game-based assessments, including better applicant reactions, improvement measurement, decreased bias, and increased perceived fairness.[12] As will be made clear, though, the practices of making assessments more game-based vary widely throughout the assessment industry, as do the results.

Landers and Sanchez[13] distinguish three types of ways that test developers can use gaming to enhance assessments. *Game-based assessment* has players engaged in what they call a "core gameplay loop" with the assessment of trait information. *Gameful design* uses game elements to help guide the creation of assessments. They use the term *gamification* to refer to the practice of adapting existing assessments to include game elements.

In general, assessments can be placed on a continuum to the degree that gaming has been incorporated into the assessment. Game-based assessments would provide rich and engaging elements that incorporate some assessment into them, whereas gamified assessments might take traditional assessments and add some gaming elements. For example, an existing cognitive ability exam might be gamified by presenting it as a type of game, using the process of *game-framing*[14] or a multiple-choice personality test could be converted into a game by converting the test into a type of story, a process called *storification*.[15] Assessments that are successfully treated as games will be viewed by participants as fun and embrace the goals of the game as non-trivial and achievable and would be willing to play the game voluntarily.[16] One challenge with game-based assessments is that the more successfully an assessment includes gaming elements, the more challenging it may be to collect job-related information that is reliable and valid. Psychometric theory has evolved in the context of multiple-choice and Likert-type items and so assessment of reliability and validity needs to adapt to the changing world of assessments.

In addition to pre-employment testing, gaming elements have influenced learning in general[17] and employee training and development specifically.[18] Just like how gaming can work its way into assessments in different ways, in terms of employee training, gaming elements can be incorporated into training through badges and leaderboards, trying to create competition among employees just as in games, or gaming elements can be embedded into the training itself, creating role playing and stories that might be more engaging than traditional stories. A review of 34 studies of gaming within education and learning found higher engagement, increased participation, and a reduction in the gaps between high-scoring and low-scoring participants. In a creative study linking gaming elements to psychological theory, Landers, Bauer, and Callan[19] found that leaderboards were effective in that they worked similar to goal setting in that leaderboards helped participants in a brainstorming experiment increase task performance similar to the level of those who set difficult goals.

As technology has evolved, testing has evolved along with that technology. The research on incorporating gaming into testing shows that the promise of technology is vast, though the actual benefits are often less than is promised. To achieve promised outcomes, I-O psychologists need to better collaborate with technology partners.

Unproctored internet testing

One challenge with internet testing is the challenge of administering tests in an unproctored environment. Early testing efforts assumed that test takers were in a standardized environment that included a quiet workspace and strict time limits along with no access to ancillary information (e.g., no cheat sheets) that might help provide insight into particular answers. This standardization was important in that the strict requirements tried to eliminate sources of variance that might be related to test performance beyond the construct of interest. In addition, with proctored examination, it is relatively easy to verify test-taker identity by checking with an authorized identification card; with unproctored internet testing, the person who is completing the assessment may not be who you think it is!

With the wide-scale accessibility of the internet, organizations realized that they could administer tests remotely using web-based administration. In pre-internet days, applicants would have to travel potentially long distances to take a test on a pre-arranged basis in a space that was reserved for testing. These spaces were generally proctored as well, costing additional staff time. Applicants might be reluctant to spend time and money to travel for testing purposes for a job that they might not receive and companies were hesitant to pay travel expenses for applicants who the companies were unsure they would hire. Online internet testing opened up the potential applicant pool to anyone who had a reliable internet connection, though it created new problems. Until recently, the possibility of proctoring online exams was unlikely, though with recent advances in video monitoring software, proctoring online administered exams is now possible.

A whole body of research examined the effectiveness of unproctored internet exams, studying their validity and reliability compared to traditionally administered proctored exams, as well as examining the amount of people who were likely to fake or cheat in the exams. In general, the research is supportive of the general use of unproctored internet testing. In a meta-analysis, the validity of unproctored internet administered noncognitive tests was nearly identical to the validities of in-person administered tests.[20] With ability tests, a recent meta-analysis found that the mean difference between unproctored internet tests versus proctored assessments was $d = .20$, suggesting that the mean differences are somewhat higher for the unproctored internet testing for ability tests. These results suggest on ability tests that there are some respondents who did indeed fake or cheat. To minimize the influence of cheating in unproctored internet testing, companies have used a variety of practices. One strategy includes conducting selection in multiple stages with unproctored internet tests administered early on the process; candidates who do well on those tests are then later administered a test, perhaps as part of an onsite interview, in a more proctored setting to confirm the earlier test score. In addition, Gibby et al. recommend when administered unproctored internet tests to (1) use adaptive tests so that different candidates receive different items, (2) include instructions to respond honestly, and (3) give candidates strict time limits per item to minimize the time candidates could use to look up answers.[21] With recent upgrades in technology, remote proctoring of exams is now possible and feasible with video software such as Zoom along with internet cameras and facial recognition software. These features allow companies to feel more confident that candidates who complete the exams are in fact the person they think they are testing, and that test takers do not rely on ancillary information to complete knowledge and ability items. We are not aware, however, of research on these remote-proctored exams to see how applicants react to them or whether the validities of tests under these situations are equivalent to other situations. As technology adapts, research must play catch up!

Remote interviews

The COVID-19 pandemic has transformed personnel selection, accelerating the use of technology in ways that were already occurring beforehand, though increasing the use of remote technology in ways that might have taken years for organizations to adapt to in normal times. The use of video-based technology to conduct interviews is one area that has perhaps received the most attention. Many activities of life that seemed to demand or profit from in-person contact were moved remotely, including many of the classes that you were likely part of, as well as psychotherapy and counseling, academic conferences, and, relevant to this chapter, pre-employment interviews. As video conferencing software became more accessible and better, companies had begun to use tools such as Skype and Zoom to conduct interviews, though during the pandemic the use of asynchronous video interviews (AVI) became more prevalent. In AVIs, applicants respond to a series of questions by recording answers using video technology. The interview is one-way in that respondents speak into the recording and there is no possibility of having a conversation with the interviewer.

> **Asynchronous Video Interviews:** Video interviews in which candidates are asked pre-arranged questions and record their answers using a camera and video recording device. There is no direct interaction between the candidate and the interviewer.

AVIs became popular during the pandemic when a large number of jobs needed to be filled, though organizations were reluctant to have in-person interactions with candidates, and travel was limited. There are several challenges and concerns with AVIs, and they largely revolve around applicant reactions and the quality of the information provided by the one-way interview. Although little empirical work has been done on AVIs, Lukacik, Bourage, and Roulin[22] provide suggestions on how to improve perceived fairness to applicants. The first has to do with preparation time. In some AVIs, candidates are given little to no time (10 seconds or less) between the presentation of the question and the need to respond. In other cases, candidates may be given a longer period of time, such as 1 minute, to be used to formulate thoughts and structure their answers. In addition, some AVIs allow candidates to re-record answers so that if they record an answer and realize that they had made mistakes or stumbled over words, they have the opportunity to delete their initial responses and record a second effort. Finally, some AVIs require individuals to answer all items in one sitting without interruptions, though others allow individuals to take breaks and return to the platform at their own leisure. All of these features are hypothesized to result in the AVIs being perceived as more fair. It is interesting to note that these features – allowing more preparation time, the possibility to have a second chance, and taking breaks – are not present in face-to-face interviews but are thought to be important in AVIs given the sterility involved in AVIs.

Another challenge with AVIs is how to score the videos that are recorded. Given the videos are recorded, it is possible to have multiple raters watch the videos and score responses on rubrics related to assessing KSAOs designed to predict job performance, similar to how traditional structured interviews are scored. Another possibility, due to the fact that all video responses are already recorded on a computer, is using some kind of machine learning algorithm to score items. With the high accuracy of voice to text systems, as well as the ability of computer algorithms to identify non-verbal characteristics such as facial expressions and body language, it is possible for computers to score these videos, further removing humans from the interview process. Although research is still in its infancy on the reliability and validity of these computerized scoring algorithms, what research is out there shows promise. Hickman and colleagues[23] found modest reliability and validity for machine learning scored algorithms when the algorithms were trained on human observer ratings of interview performance done as part of a mock interview process. That is, when trained raters provided a series of evaluations of candidate Big Five scores, machine learning algorithms were able to generate algorithms that could provide close approximations to the observer reports of the interviews. This is important because these algorithms could be used to score AVIs, saving considerable human time. Future research, however, needs to be conducted to replicate Hickman and colleagues' findings and to see how well machine learning algorithms can perform with interviewees who are really applying for jobs.

Virtual reality

VR uses computer technology to allow users to immerse themselves in a world different from the one that they are presently in. Typically, VR uses technological devices to mimic different virtual worlds using input and output devices such as 3D visual glasses to project alternative worlds and data gloves to determine the exact positioning of fingers and hands.[1] Although VR has been proposed to be used in HR applications to both improve pre-employment hiring as well as training, a recent review of VR in human resource management found that little empirical work has been done in pre-employment assessment.[24] In the training domain, VR has been used to help new employees learn to navigate difficult conditions that might be unsafe in the real world, such as having miners learn how to cope with unsafe mining conditions and having airplane pilots learn how to navigate difficult weather conditions.

In terms of pre-employment testing, the promise of VR would be to provide realistic work samples to test how individuals may perform in conditions that mimic, via technology, actual working conditions. These assessments could test how individuals perform in stressful situations, thus allowing organizations to test whether individuals can perform well in a situation that would not be possible to mimic during the interview session. In addition to testing under stress, another benefit of VR technology would be that test takers might be more engaged in completing assessments. However, VR technology requires more cost as well as an interface between testing experts and technology specialists. These latter impediments are likely one of the reasons that VR technology has yet to catch on in pre-employment testing. As we will see with other technological advances though, as VR technology becomes more accessible, the integration with pre-employment testing is likely to occur.

Summary

Technology has infiltrated nearly every aspect of our lives and so it should be no surprise that technology has had a huge impact on assessment, specifically, and personnel practices in general. As mentioned repeatedly in this chapter, this influence of technology has benefits while also presenting challenges. To succeed as an I-O practitioner today, it is important to be familiar with advances in technology, and to develop collaborations with experts who possess skills that most I-O psychologists would not have. The future is exciting and will keep us busy!

REVIEW QUESTIONS

1. How is machine learning impacting personnel selection?
2. What are concerns that organizations should have with the practice of cybervetting?
3. What are advantages and disadvantages of using unproctored internet testing?
4. What does the research tell us about how asynchronous video interviews work?

DISCUSSION QUESTIONS

1. Should organizations check social media of applicants before hiring?
2. How have you cleaned up your own social media for the purposes of getting a job?
3. What are the dangers of using machine learning in the context of personnel selection?
4. Would you be more or less likely to apply for a job that used an asynchronous video interview? A gamified assessment? Virtual reality?

Notes

1. Hernandez, I., & Nie, W. (in press). The AI-IP: Minimizing the guesswork of personality scale item development through artificial intelligence. *Personnel Psychology*.
2. https://www.pewresearch.org/internet/fact-sheet/social-media/
3. Hou, Y., Xiong, D., Jiang, T., Song, L., & Wang, Q. (2019). Social media addiction: Its impact, mediation, and intervention. *Cyberpsychology: Journal of Psychosocial Research on Cyberspace*, 13(1), 1–17.
4. Whittaker, E., & Kowalski, R. M. (2015). Cyberbullying via social media. *Journal of School Violence*, 14(1), 11–29.
5. Oh, S., & Syn, S. Y. (2015). Motivations for sharing information and social support in social media: A comparative analysis of Facebook, Twitter, Delicious, YouTube, and Flickr. *Journal of the Association for Information Science and Technology*, 66(10), 2045–2060.
6. Back, M. D., Stopfer, J. M., Vazire, S., Gaddis, S., Schmukle, S. C., Egloff, B., & Gosling, S. D. (2010). Facebook profiles reflect actual personality, not self-idealization. *Psychological Science*, 21(3), 372–374.
7. Wilcox, A., Damarin, A., & McDonald, S. (2022). Is cybervetting valuable? *Industrial and Organizational Psychology*, 15(3). https://doi.org/10.31219/osf.io/f52a7
8. Tay, L., Woo, S. E., Hickman, L., & Saef, R. M. (2020). Psychometric and validity issues in machine learning approaches to personality assessment: A focus on social media text mining. *European Journal of Personality*, 34(5), 826–844.

9. Fernandez, S., Stöcklin, M., Terrier, L., & Kim, S. (2021). Using available signals on LinkedIn for personality assessment. *Journal of Research in Personality, 93*, 104122.
10. Cubrich, M., King, R. T., Mracek, D. L., Strong, J. M., Hassenkamp, K., Vaughn, D., & Dudley, N. M. (2021). Examining the criterion-related validity evidence of LinkedIn profile elements in an applied sample. *Computers in Human Behavior, 120*, 106742.
11. https://www.statista.com/statistics/499703/share-consumers-ever-play-video-games-by-age-usa/
12. Landers, R. N., & Sanchez, D. R. (2022). Game-based, gamified, and gamefully designed assessments for employee selection: Definitions, distinctions, design, and validation. *International Journal of Selection and Assessment, 30*(1), 1–13.
13. Landers, R. N., & Sanchez, D. R. (2022). Game-based, gamified, and gamefully designed assessments for employee selection: Definitions, distinctions, design, and validation. *International Journal of Selection and Assessment, 30*(1), 1–13.
14. Collmus, A. B., & Landers, R. N. (2019). Game-framing to improve applicant perceptions of cognitive assessments. *Journal of Personnel Psychology, 18*(3), 157.
15. Landers, R. N., & Collmus, A. B. (2022). Gamifying a personality measure by converting it into a story: Convergence, incremental prediction, faking, and reactions. *International Journal of Selection and Assessment, 30*(1), 145–156.
16. Landers, R. N., & Sanchez, D. R. (2022). Game-based, gamified, and gamefully designed assessments for employee selection: Definitions, distinctions, design, and validation. *International Journal of Selection and Assessment, 30*(1), 1–13.
17. Dicheva, D., Dichev, C., Agre, G., & Angelova, G. (2015). Gamification in education: A systematic mapping study. *Journal of Educational Technology & Society, 18*(3), 75–88.
18. Armstrong, M. B., & Landers, R. N. (2018). Gamification of employee training and development. *International Journal of Training and Development, 22*(2), 162–169.
19. Landers, R. N., Bauer, K. N., & Callan, R. C. (2017). Gamification of task performance with leaderboards: A goal setting experiment. *Computers in Human Behavior, 71*, 508–515.
20. Beaty, J. C., Nye, C. D., Borneman, M. J., Kantrowitz, T. M., Drasgow, F., & Grauer, E. (2011). Proctored versus unproctored internet tests: Are unproctored noncognitive tests as predictive of job performance? *International Journal of Selection and Assessment, 19*(1), 1–10.
21. Gibby, R. E., Ispas, D., McCloy, R. A., & Biga, A. (2009). Moving beyond the challenges to make unproctored internet testing a reality. *Industrial and Organizational Psychology, 2*(1), 64–68.
22. Lukacik, E. R., Bourdage, J. S., & Roulin, N. (2022). Into the void: A conceptual model and research agenda for the design and use of asynchronous video interviews. *Human Resource Management Review, 32*(1), 100789.
23. Hickman, L., Bosch, N., Ng, V., Saef, R., Tay, L., & Woo, S. E. (2022). Automated video interview personality assessments: Reliability, validity, and generalizability investigations. *Journal of Applied Psychology, 107*(8), 1323.
24. Ferreira, P., Meirinhos, V., Rodrigues, A. C., & Marques, A. (2021). Virtual and augmented reality in human resource management and development: A systematic literature review. *IBIMA Business Review, 2021*. https://doi.org/10.5171/2021.926642

13 Performance evaluation

LEARNING OBJECTIVES

- Know the purposes of performance evaluation
- Know the characteristics of good performance evaluation measures
- Understand the importance of fairness in performance evaluations
- Understand rater errors in performance ratings
- Understand the effects of rater training
- Know what multisource feedback is and understand practical guidelines for its use
- Distinguish performance evaluation from performance management

The previous several chapters have focused on how organizations can predict whether applicants will turn out to be employees who are likely to perform well. In this chapter, we turn our attention to how the performance of said employees can be evaluated. Also called *performance appraisal*, performance evaluation is the process by which employee performance is measured and documented. Let's start by discussing the purposes that performance evaluations serve for organizations and employees.

> **Performance Evaluation (Performance Appraisal):** The process by which employee performance is measured and documented.

Purposes of performance evaluations

Think about a time in your life as an employee when you were evaluated by your boss. How did the evaluation help you? Perhaps a positive evaluation helped you get that deserved raise or promotion. Perhaps a less-than-positive evaluation helped you understand where you need to improve to be a more effective worker. Now, think about your boss. How did providing the evaluation help them do their job and benefit the organization? As a positive evaluation helped you get that raise or promotion, conducting that evaluation allowed your boss to be able to base their decisions on performance-related information. If providing the less-than-positive evaluation helped you identify areas of weakness to improve your future performance, then your improved performance also benefits the organization. Documenting the evaluation also helps the organization provide a legal defense should you believe your low evaluation was because you were discriminated against and you decided to sue the company. In short, performance evaluations can benefit both the employee and the organization. Below, we elaborate on the variety of purposes that measuring and documenting performance serves for both parties:

1. **As Criteria in Validation Studies.** This purpose of performance evaluation, as criterion data in criterion-related studies, is covered at length in Chapter 5 and Chapter 6. Hence, we will not discuss again the nuts and bolts of validation in this chapter. However, to reiterate the necessity of performance evaluation for this purpose, imagine that organizations have all decided to do away with formal evaluations of their employees. This means that no employees are evaluated; hence, no data on performance are gathered. Think for a moment about what this would mean for criterion-related studies. That is correct – without performance evaluation data, we would be lacking an important criterion variable. This means that we lack important evidence on which to base the validity of our selection predictor.
2. **To Make Formal Personnel Decisions.** Performance evaluation data serve as the basis for a number of personnel decisions, including pay raises, promotion, disciplinary action, and termination. In a 2000 survey conducted by the SHRM and Personnel Decisions International (PDI, an I-O consulting firm), respondents rank-ordered the

Table 13.1 Objectives of performance management system

Objectives	Average rank
Provide information to employees about their performance	2.8
Clarify organizational expectations of employees	2.8
Identify developmental needs	3.7
Gather information for pay decisions	4.0
Gather information for coaching	4.2
Document performance for employee records	4.6
Gather information for promotion decisions	5.2
Source: SHRM/PDI 2000 Performance Management Survey	

top objectives for their performance evaluation systems; indeed, gathering information for pay and promotion decisions fell in the top five listed purposes. See Table 13.1.

3. **To Provide Legal Justification for Personnel Decisions.** While we focused only on discrimination law in selection in Chapter 2, do know that Title VII of the Civil Rights Act of 1964 and other statutes state that any personnel practice which adversely affects protected classes is unlawful unless business necessity justifies the practice.[1] Should charges of discrimination arise when critical personnel decisions such as pay and termination are made, performance evaluations provide the evidence needed to justify these decisions. In a review of 115 federal district court opinions, researchers found that the existence of a formal appraisal system and documentation of poor performance were two of the factors significantly related to judicial rulings which benefited the defendant organization.[2]

4. **To Clarify Job Duties and Expectations.** Role ambiguity refers to vague job expectations, such that employees do not have a clear sense of what is expected of them.[3] This role stressor is found to be related to a number of negative outcomes for the organization, including lower performance,[4] decreased citizenship behaviors,[5] and propensity to quit.[6] Negative consequences for the individual have also been found, such as lower job satisfaction[7] and greater emotional exhaustion.[8] Performance evaluations can help clarify expectations, roles, responsibilities, and duties to employees.

5. **To Provide Feedback to Employees.** While many of the reasons for conducting formal performance evaluations are personnel decision-related, this fifth purpose is focused more on the employee. In the 2000 SHRM/PDI survey, the top-ranked objective provided by respondents for their use of performance evaluation is to provide information to employees about how they are performing (see Table 13.1). A substantive body of literature shows that feedback is "central to what we do on the job. Feedback guides, motivates, and reinforces effective behaviors and reduces or stops ineffective behaviors."[9]

6. **To Help Diagnose Organizational Problems.** While performance evaluation tends to be an individual-based process, data may be aggregated to help organizations see if there are problems with a unit or department. For example, if sales are down for a

particular company, performance evaluation data for all employees within a specific area may allow the company to find out if this problem lies in customer service, marketing, research and development, or some other unit.
7. **To Help Establish Objectives for Training Programs.** Should evaluations reveal any performance deficits, the organization may want to provide training to improve the skills of their employees. Data from performance evaluations can help shed light upon the specific areas that need improvement, and training programs can then be designed to address specific knowledge or skills. Chapter 14 will further elaborate upon how the need for training must be assessed.

Characteristics of good performance evaluation measures

While we hope that we have convinced you of the value of performance evaluations for both the organization and its employees, we now deliver the less enthusiastic news that accurately measuring performance is a very difficult task. By "measuring performance," we are referring mostly to the measures or forms that are used to rate employees. A typical measure is one that has several behavioral dimensions (e.g., "reliability" or "collaborative") with a numerical rating (usually on a scale of 1–5) and verbal anchors corresponding to each numerical rating (e.g., "3" = "meets expectations"). Drawing from decades of research that have gone into improving these measures, we present below a list of the characteristics that good performance measures should have, as well as some practical guidance on how to attain these characteristics.

Relevance. The contents of the measure should reflect the contents of the job. This is covered in Chapter 6. We can also refer to relevance as *job-relatedness*, in that the contents of the measure are relevant to the job. To increase the relevance of performance measures, a job analysis should be conducted to uncover the tasks and knowledge, skills, and abilities of the job. These specific contents should then be included in the performance measure.

Variance. In Garrison Keeler's radio show *Lake Wobegon*, all the women are strong, all the men are good-looking, and all the children are above average. On most performance measures, we often see this lack of variability. As discussed above, rating errors that often occur may limit the variability in ratings. In attempting to reduce rating errors, there have been lots of different approaches to designing rating formats. The one that has had the most influence is the Behaviorally Anchored Rating Scales (BARS) developed by Patricia Cain Smith, a delightful faculty member two of the current authors of this textbook had the pleasure to meet (Smith, 1963). Most performance ratings have some kind of vague labels attached to the ratings which might go from 1 to 5 or 1 to 7. Labels might be "One of the best in the company" or "Superior performance." Pat believed that these labels may be interpreted differently by different raters, thus introducing additional error into the ratings. She developed a system where psychologists would meet with subject matter experts (e.g., current incumbents or supervisors who know the job well) and have them generate critical incidents about behavior on the job. These critical incidents are detailed examples of a performance situation on the job and could describe good, average, or poor performance (the Critical Incidents Technique is also discussed as a method for job analysis in Chapter 3). For example, Zickar as the Department Chair might detail the performance of a faculty member who went beyond the expectations required to help a student resolve a problem involved in their honor's thesis data collection, or an incident of a faculty member who gave the same lectures year after year without changing any of the material (that doesn't describe any of us!).

After a series of these critical incidents are gathered, they are sorted into levels of performance (typically from 1 to 7). Incidents that are ambiguous and cannot be sorted reliably are discarded. Finally, incidents are distilled to essential qualities and a critical incident is assigned to each of various points on the scale. Therefore, 7 on the faculty performance scale might be "Helped a student collect honor's thesis data on the weekend," whereas the middle point 4 might be "Responds to emails within a 24 hour period" and 1 would be "fails to attend office hours and is hard to track down."

There has been a lot of research in evaluating the BARS format, as well as other formats. The research tends to suggest that BARS items tend not to provide much better (e.g., accurate) ratings than other formats, though the process of developing the BARS items can be useful for providing buy-in for employees in a company. In a sense, they have worked to create their own performance measure. Unfortunately, there is no magic way to solve the criterion problem even with such a fine system as the BARS.

Reliability. Reliability is one of the vital psychometric properties of any measure. Granted multirater feedback expects there will be differences in perspectives, it is still expected that evaluations of the same performance from the same employee would provide similar ratings.

Acceptability. One of the purposes of performance evaluation is to provide feedback to employees so they may develop. If they do not accept these ratings, there is lowered motivation to change. Acceptability is also important on the part of those who are evaluating the employees. If they feel that the form is confusing, time-consuming, or if they feel that the feedback they provide will not be taken seriously, they will not be motivated to provide honest, accurate feedback. One of the biggest drivers of acceptability toward the performance evaluation is whether those who are impacted think it is fair. Employees who feel that they are being unfairly evaluated are more likely to challenge and file a lawsuit against their employer.[10] Managers who perceive the performance evaluation to be fair report a greater ability to resolve work problems as well as being less likely to distort their employees' ratings in order to make themselves look better.[11]

As you may recall from Chapter 7, fairness refers to perceptions of fairness in outcomes (**distributive justice**) as well as in the process (**procedural justice**). In the context of performance evaluations, an employee would perceive high distributive justice if they were rated as "very good" in providing customer service and they agree that this rating accurately reflects their performance. However, if the employee, says, feels that they were evaluated based upon a different set of standards than their co-workers, or that they did not have an opportunity to appeal the ratings they were given, or that they were not treated with dignity and respect, they would perceive low procedural justice.

Practicality. As noted above, one of the reasons for the recent dismay about performance evaluations is how much time they take to administer. The extent to which both raters and ratees feel that the evaluation process is not a drain or burden on their time, they are more likely to provide valuable feedback to employees.

Judgmental measures of performance and rater errors

Recall what we had referred to in Chapter 6 as the "criterion problem" – the difficulties in conceptualizing and measuring performance constructs. In that chapter, we discussed that conceptualizing performance is complex as it is a multidimensional construct that entails broad components of task, citizenship, and counterproductive behaviors. In the current chapter, we focus more on the *measuring* aspect of performance. We focus on *judgmental measures* of performance, in which there is human judgment involved in the evaluation. DeNisi, Cafferty, and Meglino[12] (1984) proposed a model of performance rating that we think is fundamental to understanding how the rating process occurs.

As this model is complex, we want to highlight a couple of aspects here. First, the foundation of all judgmental measures are the behaviors of employees who are being evaluated. Performance measures should ultimately be based on behavior that was done by the person being evaluated. Memory processes of the person doing the rating are also important in the process. Employee behavior needs to be encoded, stored, and remembered and recalled when prompted by the performance measure. If a subjective item asks, "Does employee A work hard on a daily basis?," the supervisor may search his or her memory for instances of an employee working hard or slacking off. If employee behavior was never stored in the memory in the first place, this will be problematic.

As noted in the model, preconceived notions may bias the encoding. So if a supervisor really has a favorite employee, that supervisor may be more likely to encode positive work examples and neglect to remember negative experiences. In addition to storing information about employee behaviors, raters are likely to incorporate attributions about that behavior. Some employee behaviors may be judged to be due to an internal (personal to the ratee) factor or external (beyond the control of the rate) factor. In addition, the event may be viewed as something that is unstable (e.g., a rare occurrence) for the individual or very stable and a regular occurrence.

Finally, when asked to rate the employee, the context of the rating needs to be considered as well. If the rating is conducted purely for research purposes, the supervisor may be more likely to provide ratings of negative information. If the rating is also used for determining pay raises, the supervisor may be less likely to provide negative ratings thinking that the employee doesn't deserve to have their compensation suffer due to a minor performance problem. The key takeaways from this model are that judgmental measures are impacted by many factors *other than* the behaviors of the employee being evaluated. Because I-O psychology is a multidisciplinary area, researchers have drawn upon areas of social and cognitive psychologies in their efforts to understand the processes by which humans come to make an evaluation of other people. In sum, the culmination of research does not paint a flattering picture: human judgment is filled with fallacies. Here is but a partial list of these fallacies:

1. We tend to give higher evaluations of people who are similar to ourselves.
2. We tend to give higher evaluations to people who are physically attractive.
3. We allow race or gender to affect our evaluations.
4. We allow one positive characteristic of a person to color how we view his/her other characteristics. For instance, we may think that a person who is outgoing is also smart and responsible.
5. We seem to be unable to evaluate one person (or thing) at a time. In other words, we are always comparing and weighing persons against one another in order to make an evaluation of him/her. This is known as the contrast effect. For example, if we interact with a customer service representative who is merely mediocre – the person does his/her job but is neither friendly nor goes out of his/her way to help – we will evaluate this person even worse if we had first encountered a very helpful, friendly customer service representative. However, if we had encountered one who was outright hostile, the mediocre customer service representative would not seem so bad at all.
6. We tend to be unable to use anchor points in a rating scale evenly.
7. We tend to refer to only our most recent memories when making evaluations (i.e., recency effect).
8. We want to be right. That is, we tend to more strongly remember information about a person which is consistent with our current perceptions of that person, rather than information that may disconfirm our prior beliefs.

What do these fallacies mean? Essentially, they will result in evaluations or ratings that do not truly reflect the true performance of employees. This can then mean that organizational decisions to reward or reprimand employees are going to be wrong and unfair. So, what can be done? The most drastic step is to remove the human evaluator altogether from this process. This means relying on *objective measures* such as recording the number of days an employee has been absent or late, counting the number of things s/he has produced, counting the number of errors or accidents s/he has committed. While the objectivity of such data might be appealing, they do not give us the full picture of an employee's performance on a job. That is, there are more dimensions and requirements of a job than can be captured by countable measures. For example, by using objective measures, we may know that a waiter has served 400 tables, that they have made zero errors in giving orders to the cooks, and that they have dropped hot plates full of food twice in one month; however, we do not know via this information about one of the most important parts of being a restaurant server – how well does the waiter interact with customers? Are they friendly and helpful? We can only come to find out about this very critical dimension of the server's work by relying upon human judgment or evaluation, ideally from customers or from other observers, such as a manager or co-workers.

In essence, we cannot get away from the human element of evaluation. Fortunately, I-O psychology researchers have spent much time studying this topic in order to come up with ways to reduce errors in human judgment. There is a body of research looking at the types of errors and biases that raters tend to make. The first of them is *halo error*. The name comes from the idea that a child may have a symbolic halo in the view of a parent, in which that child can really do no wrong. In the context of performance ratings, it means that different performance dimensions tend to be much higher than you would conceptually think is true. For example, student ratings of the fairness in grading by a faculty member might be mildly correlated with the ability to provide inspiring classroom lectures, though the rating shouldn't be that high. With typical performance ratings, different dimensions that should have small correlations with each other tend to have much higher correlations than you would expect. What happens is that raters tend to form a general impression of a ratee (I like her or I dislike him) and let those general impressions cloud the judgments of all dimensions.

Other types of errors are *leniency* and *severity*. Some raters may be very tough, providing ratings that are lower in general than other raters, whereas others may have a leniency error and tend to provide more positive ratings than expected. Finally, there is *central tendency* error, where the rater tends to give all ratees average ratings. In these cases, the rating is not solely a function of the behavior of the ratee but also a characteristic of the rater. You all know this when you avoid the class of a difficult professor and choose a class of a professor who is known to be lenient when it comes to grading. These errors are problematic because, as mentioned previously, one of the characteristics required for a good performance measure is variance. Each of these three error tendencies – leniency, severity, and central tendency – fails to discriminate between employees with regard to their performance.

Rater training

There have been many attempts to try to minimize rater errors. Typically, this training explains the types of rating errors to raters and encourages raters to focus on individual behaviors before making individual ratings instead of relying on general impressions. While this type of training tends to be only moderately effective, the type of training referred to as *frame-of-reference (FOR) training*[13] has been shown to be most effective in increasing rater accuracy.[14] The primary goal of *FOR* training is to bring raters to a common conceptualization of what performance is as they observe and evaluate others. Raters are trained to understand the multidimensionality of performance, to define performance dimensions, and to provide behavioral incidents for each dimension. As discussed above, judgmental measures of performance are vulnerable to rater errors. Therefore, this type of training brings raters to the same reference point so that the evaluations given are based upon observed employee behaviors.

For decades, researchers have naively assumed that managers make a sincere attempt to be accurate when evaluating their employees. Researchers considered the inaccuracies of ratings provided by managers as the result of *errors*. Recently, however, I-O psychologists have come to recognize that sometimes managers or other evaluators will intentionally give undeserved good or bad evaluations of an employee. Take, for example, your life as a student, or if you have ever held a job, your experiences as an employee. Was there ever a fellow student or co-worker who did not really perform that well but managed to get high marks because this person was well-liked or friends with the instructor or boss? Most of the students whom we have asked this question have answered with a resounding "yes." The reverse can also occur. We have heard stories of poor employees who get high evaluations just because the manager wants to promote them out of his/her department! We have also heard stories of excellent employees who never get high evaluations because a manager wants to keep them from being promoted out of the department. Although these are merely anecdotes, they are consistent with some of the research on organizational politics. In an interesting study by Longenecker, Sims, and Gioia (1987),[15] the researchers surveyed 60 upper-level executives regarding their performance evaluation processes. A surprising number of these executives admitted to deliberately manipulating performance evaluations of their employees for political reasons. Some of the political reasons given for such manipulations were (1) to protect or encourage a low-performing employee because s/he was having personal problems; (2) to avoid hanging out dirty laundry; (3) to avoid a confrontation; (4) to get rid of a poorly performing employee; (5) to teach disliked employees a lesson; (6) to build a case against an employee; and (7) to send a message that would encourage an employee to leave the organization.

Abandoning performance evaluations?

Despite the abovementioned purposes of performance evaluations, some organizations have decided to abandon the formal annual review. Consider the below headlines from major news and business media:

- "Goodbye annual review, see ya performance ratings" – *CNN Money*
- "Microsoft and Dell are ditching employee performance reviews" – *Fortune*
- "In big move, Accenture will get rid of annual performance reviews and rankings" – *Washington Post*
- "Why More and More Companies Are Ditching Performance Ratings" – *Harvard Business Review*
- "Is the Annual Performance Review Dead? GE is latest company to reject time-consuming paperwork and yearly appraisals" – *SHRM*
- "More U.S. companies moving away from traditional performance reviews" – *Washington Post*

Given these obvious important purposes that performance evaluation could serve for organizations, why are some ditching them? Some of the commonly cited reasons are failure to deliver results, cost in money and in time, and demotivating to those being evaluated.[10]

Even with the commonly voiced complaints with performance evaluations, it is our opinion that evaluations should *not* be ditched given the many purposes they serve. Rather, organizations should rely upon what research has shown us to increase their utility. As discussed earlier in this chapter, performance evaluations serve a multitude of purposes for both the organization and its employees. In an aptly titled article *Getting Rid of Performance Ratings Genius or Folly?*[10] well-known researchers and practitioners in I-O psychology debate whether organizations should indeed abandon performance evaluations. While we fully acknowledge the difficulty in accurately evaluating performance and that human judgment is fraught with errors, we side with the camp which argues that performance evaluation systems need fixing but we cannot throw out the baby with the bathwater. To do so could (1) potentially leave organizations with no evidence to make promotion and pay decisions; (2) potentially leave organizations in danger of litigation as if they are unable to document performance in order to justify HR decisions; (3) reduce motivation of employees who expect to be formally evaluated; and (4) introduce more errors as decisions may be based on only informal conversations or narrative reviews.

Continuing with the restaurant server example from above, we can see how valuable a technique such as **multisource feedback** can be for gathering information about the employee's friendly and helpful behaviors toward customers. Although customers would be the key source of information in this example, perhaps it is also important that servers are friendly and helpful to their co-workers. Hence, co-workers can serve as an additional source of information. Multisource feedback allows organizations to gather performance information that a supervisor by themselves may not have. Because we know that individual biases can occur in evaluation, by relying on a number of different sources, we may be able to "water down" these biases and acquire a more accurate, three-dimensional evaluation of an employee.

Summary

Throughout this chapter, we have focused on the evaluation of performance, or how employee performance is measured and documented. It is important to note that evaluating performance is not the same as *managing* performance. Performance management, defined as "a process designed to monitor and enhance employee behavior in order to ensure it supports the mission and goals of the larger organization,"[16] involves management strategies that include providing meaningful and effective feedback, offering rewards that are motivating, and so forth. As we are focused on the *I* side of I-O in this textbook (see Chapter 1), rather than the *O* side, performance management is beyond the scope of our discussion. Nonetheless, the data obtained from performance evaluations are critical to effective performance management.

REVIEW QUESTIONS

1. What are the seven purposes for conducting performance evaluations?
2. Name and explain the five characteristics of effective performance evaluation measures.
3. Compare and contrast distributive and procedural justice.
4. What is frame-of-reference training?
5. What are some psychological fallacies that lead us to be inaccurate in our evaluation of others?

DISCUSSION QUESTIONS

1. Which of the purposes of performance evaluation do you think is most important? Why?
2. Which of the characteristics of effective performance evaluation measures do you think is most important? Why?
3. Why is perceived fairness of the performance evaluation process important?
4. Which of the rater errors do you think is most prevalent? Which do you think is most difficult to reduce via training?
5. How would you feel about being an employee in an organization that does not have formal performance evaluations?
6. Imagine you are the CEO of a company and have heard many other organizations similar to yours have decided to ditch formal performance evaluations of their employees. Would you do the same? Why or why not?

Notes

1 Barrett, G. V., & Kernan, M. C. (1987). Performance appraisal and terminations: A review of court decisions since Brito v. Zia with implications for personnel practices. *Personnel Psychology, 40*(3), 489–503.
2 Wingate, P. H., Thornton, George C., I.,II, McIntyre, K. S., & Frame, J. H. (2003). Organizational downsizing and age discrimination litigation: The influence of personnel practices and statistical evidence on litigation outcomes. *Law and Human Behavior, 27*(1), 87–108.
3 Katz, D., & Kahn, R. L. (1978). *The social psychology of organizations*. Wiley.
4 Gilboa, S., Shirom, A., Fried, Y., & Cooper, C. (2008). A meta-analysis of work demand stressors and job performance: Examining main and moderating effects. *Personnel Psychology*, 61, 227–271.
5 Eatough, E. M., Chang, C., Miloslavic, S. A., & Johnson, R. E. (2011). Relationships of role stressors with organizational citizenship behavior: A meta-analysis. *Journal of Applied Psychology, 96*(3), 619–632.

6 Örtqvist, D., & Wincent, J. (2006). Prominent consequences of role stress: A meta-analytic review. *International Journal of Stress Management, 13*(4), 399–422.
7 Fried, Y., Shirom, A., Gilboa, S., & Cooper, C. (2008). The mediating effects of job satisfaction and propensity to leave on role stress–job performance relationships: Combining meta-analysis and structural equation modeling. *International Journal of Stress Management*, 15, 305–328.
8 Lee, R. T., & Ashforth, B. E. (1996). A meta-analytic examination of the correlates of the three dimensions of job burnout. *Journal of Applied Psychology*, 81, 123–133.
9 London, M. (2015). *The power of feedback: Giving, seeking, and using feedback for performance improvement.* Routledge.
10 Martin, D. C., Bartol, K. M., & Kehoe, P. E. (2000). The legal ramifications of performance appraisal: The growing significance. *Public Personnel Management, 29*(3), 379–406.
11 Taylor, M. S., Tracy, K. B., Renard, M. K., Harrison, J. K., & Carroll, S. J. (1995). Due process in performance appraisal: A quasi-experiment in procedural justice. *Administrative Science Quarterly, 40*(3), 495.
12 DeNisi, A. S., Cafferty, T. P., & Meglino, B. M. (1984). A cognitive view of the performance appraisal process: A model and research propositions. *Organizational Behavior & Human Performance, 33*(3), 360–396.
13 Bernardin, H. J., & Buckley, R. M. (1981). Strategies in rater training. *Academy of Management Review*, 6, 205–212.
14 Roch, S. G., Woehr, D. J., Mishra, V., & Kieszczynska, U. (2012). Rater training revisited: An updated meta-analytic review of frame-of-reference training. *Journal of Occupational and Organizational Psychology*, 85, 370–395.
15 Longenecker, C. O., Sims, H. P., & Gioia, D. A. (1987). Behind the mask: The politics of employee appraisal. *Academy of Management Executive*, 1, 183–193.
16 Frear, K. A., & Paustian-Underdahl, S. (2011). From elusive to obvious: Improving performance management through specificity. *Industrial and Organizational Psychology: Perspectives on Science and Practice, 4*(2), 198–200.

14 Training

LEARNING OBJECTIVES

- Understand the purpose and necessity of training within organizations
- Recognize why the determinants of job performance are relevant to the training process
- Know what a needs analysis is and why it is important
- Know how the various training methods are applied within organizations
- Appreciate the contextual considerations relevant to the training process
- Understand how to evaluate the effectiveness of a training program

Think about the first time you drove a vehicle. Likely, you were nervously contemplating what you *should* do at any given moment: buckling up, checking your mirrors, anticipating when to speed up or slow down, signaling when appropriate, and so on. You probably also had a designated referee in the passenger seat – hopefully a seasoned SME – to guide you through the process, adjudicate when necessary, and ensure the safety of yourself and those around you. In other words, you did not go into the complex task of "operating a vehicle" blindly. You had already acquired preliminary knowledge through reading the driver's education manual, and you also received real-time guidance from an experienced driver as part of your driver's education course. As with first-time drivers, applicants entering a new job often receive training to prepare them for the task(s) at hand. **Training** refers to formal procedures designed to facilitate employee learning and development. Although applicants are selected as a result of their relevant KSAOs, work experience, and qualifications, it is often the case that applicants can benefit from job- or organization-specific training to help them perform a job successfully. In fact, organizations in the U.S. spend approximately $82.5 billion annually on training expenditures.[1] While the selection process provides a starting point for developing an effective workforce, training fills in the gaps in employee job-relevant KSAOs.

> **Training:** Formal procedures designed to facilitate employee learning and development.

Training purpose: Why is training needed?

The primary purpose of any training program is twofold: *learning* about job tasks and organizational procedures, and translating that learning into effective *performance* (i.e., on-the-job behaviors). Thus, training ensures that employees have the essential KSAOs to perform a job successfully. It is important to note that new applicants are not the only people who can benefit from training programs. As discussed in Chapter 3, one of the difficulties of job analysis is that jobs may change over time. With these technological and/or procedural changes, training may be necessary for incumbents to function effectively in their fluctuating work environment. Given that performance is the primary objective of training programs, understanding the determinants of performance is an essential first step in the training process.

Campbell (1990) proposes three determinants of job performance: declarative knowledge, procedural knowledge, and motivation.[2] **Declarative knowledge** refers to knowledge of facts or principles ("know what"). For example, a professional clarinetist must conceptually understand the meaning associated with different key signatures, time signatures, and tempos in a piece of music. **Procedural knowledge**, on the other hand, refers to the development of motor and technical skills needed to perform a task ("know how"). Just because a clarinetist understands the differences between two separate time signatures within a composition (declarative knowledge), this does not guarantee that s/he can play the notes within the piece of music properly (procedural knowledge). Finally, **motivation** simply refers to one's desire or willingness to engage in an activity. A musician may have sufficient declarative and procedural knowledge necessary to perform a piece of music, but that knowledge will not be put to use unless the musician has the desire to play. Because each of these determinants is uniquely important to the performance process, training programs may seek to develop one or all of these factors.

> **Declarative Knowledge:** Knowing conceptual information about a task or activity.

> **Procedural Knowledge:** Knowing how to actually perform a task or activity.

> **Motivation:** Desire and willingness to engage in an activity.

Needs analysis: What needs to be trained?

You may be wondering where to even start when developing a training program. This is where a needs analysis comes into play. A **needs analysis** lays the groundwork for an effective training program by assessing where training is needed within the organization, what topics or issues need to be taught, and who will be trained. Without addressing these concerns beforehand, developing clear and measurable objectives for a training program will be difficult, if not impossible. A formal needs analysis includes three separate analyses – organizational analysis, task analysis, and person analysis – to establish which specific determinants of performance should be addressed by the training program.[3]

> **Needs Analysis:** The process of gathering data to determine what training needs exist within the organization.

An **organizational analysis** examines features of the company that may impact the effectiveness of a training program. This includes organizational goals, available resources, and the general environment and culture within the organization. Each of these factors influences the feasibility of any given training program. For example, let's say a manufacturing facility is largely concerned with employee safety but not currently meeting their safety goals based on monthly reported accidents. This represents a ripe area for training. At the same time, however, the corporate budget constrains the company from developing an organization-wide safety training program. The organizational analysis may explore which specific departments or divisions within the company are the most at-risk for accidents. Using this information, the company can pinpoint specific work units where safety training would be most beneficial, and allocate resources accordingly. Another factor considered by the organizational analysis is the culture within the organization, as this may impact the intensity of the training needed.[4] If a workgroup does not take safety seriously (thereby exhibiting a weak safety culture), this environment will require more time, effort, and resources than a workgroup that already exhibits a strong safety culture but is simply not meeting their safety goals. In sum, the purpose of organizational analysis is aligning training programs with the organization's overall strategy.

A **task analysis** identifies the specific activities, duties, or competencies necessary for employees to do their job effectively. This process overlaps greatly with job analysis, focusing particularly on the required work tasks for each job and the associated KSAOs needed to perform them. Through task analysis, the organization can develop an understanding of which work activities employees can complete immediately upon being hired, and which tasks may require training. To assist in the task analysis, an organization may wish to survey incumbents to provide a sense of the complexity and difficulty of the tasks performed, and the specific KSAOs necessary for each task. The most complex tasks are often the focus of training efforts. If detailed job descriptions have been created through the job analysis process, this can greatly reduce the time and effort required for a task analysis in the training context.

A **person analysis** examines who, specifically, needs training and pinpoints the areas in which they need to be trained. A person analysis can be focused on applicants or incumbents. Regarding applicants, although new hires are selected for a position based on their expected competence, not all applicants are on an equal playing field when they begin a new job. Suppose an accounting firm has just hired two new accountants. One of the accountants has ten years of direct job experience and has used the same software program as required by their new employer. The other accountant is fresh out of college with no direct experience. The applicant with ten years of experience may not need any training, whereas the college graduate may need extensive training to become proficient in the software program used by the organization. As for incumbents, performance evaluation data may indicate specific employees who need to be trained, or retrained, in a specific area. For example, a receiving worker may receive high marks for the competencies of forklift operation, merchandise handling, and interactions with vendors. However, this same worker may make several mistakes when completing paperwork for the received merchandise. In this case, individualized training may be provided to improve the workers' capacity to complete necessary paperwork. Whether a person analysis examines applicants or incumbents, the primary focus is on identifying weaknesses that can be addressed through training.

> **Organizational Analysis:** Examination of company goals, resources, and problems to determine where training is needed.

Training

> **Task Analysis:** Examination of job tasks and the KSAOs required for employees to do their job effectively.

> **Person Analysis:** Examination of individual knowledge, competence, and performance to determine who needs to be trained.

A comprehensive needs analysis can go a long way in establishing the overall effectiveness of a training program.[5] Once a needs analysis has been completed, the organization can determine the most appropriate training method(s) to employ in order to meet their training goals.

Training methods: How can training be administered?

If you were trying to improve your physical health, what would you do? Would you read informational content regarding nutrition and exercise, ask someone who is exceptionally healthy for health tips and tries to mimic what they do, or jump right into a diet and exercise regimen? Any of these strategies may be effective, depending on your fitness goals. As with approaches to physical fitness, there are many strategies for improving employee job knowledge and performance. The most effective training approach will vary depending on the job in question, the skill/task to be trained, and the developmental purposes of the training program.[6] Although not an exhaustive review, this section will provide an overview of the various training approaches commonly used by I-O psychologists and HR professionals. While each method differs with regard to the implementation of training material, all serve the overarching purpose of enhancing employee learning and promoting job performance.

On-the-job training

On-the-job training (OJT) methods involve the learner being immersed in the job they are expected to perform. One of the most common OJT techniques is **modeling**. Stemming from the realm of social psychology, modeling occurs when employees learn simply by watching others perform the job. After watching others, individuals gain a better sense of how tasks should be done (declarative knowledge) and often seek to mimic the observed behavior when performing their own work tasks (procedural knowledge). A "good" model would be a high-performing SME. For example, Simone Biles would be a great model for a young gymnast with Olympic aspirations. While organizations may formally assign a model as part of a training program, it is often the case that employees can learn just as much by informally watching their coworkers and colleagues on a daily basis. Of course, not all models are created equal. For new employees, it is especially important that they be exposed to positive models early on in order to ensure the development of appropriate work habits and avoid the modeling of counterproductive behavior.

> **Modeling:** Learning through observation and imitation.

Although some form of modeling is used in almost any training program, modeling alone may be insufficient to learn the fine details of a particular job. Accordingly, **mentoring** may be used in combination with modeling. A mentor is an experienced employee who serves as a trusted advisor to a younger colleague. The mentor is responsible for helping the new employee adjust to their position and learn the ropes of the organization. Schools are a great example of mentoring in action. When a new teacher joins a school district, especially if it is their first job out of college, they may be assigned to a veteran mentor to assist them as they navigate their first year of formal teaching. The mentor is responsible for answering any questions the new teacher has, may provide advice regarding classroom management, and will help socialize the new teacher into the school district. Even if a new teacher is not assigned a formal mentor, the teacher may quickly develop an informal mentorship with a senior colleague whom they feel comfortable going to and asking for help. Whether formal or informal, mentoring has not only been shown to be a useful training technique but also beneficial for job and career satisfaction.[7]

> **Mentoring:** A relationship in which a senior colleague plays a supportive and advisory role for a new employee.

An apprenticeship represents a more intensive version of OJT. **Apprentice training** programs are designed to prepare workers for a profession through a combination of formal classroom instruction and in-depth on-the-job experiences.[8] A formal apprentice program requires a minimum of 144 hours per year of classroom instruction. An apprentice will typically shadow a SME for multiple years before gaining enough practical experience to branch out on their own. For example, an electrician apprentice may begin their apprenticeship by simply following a registered electrician to and from the work location, carrying tools, and watching the electrician complete his/her work. As the apprentice obtains more classroom knowledge and practical experience, he/she may take a more active role in job tasks, eventually completing all the activities carried out by the registered electrician. The apprenticeship culminates in the apprentice developing all the necessary KSAOs and practical experience required to become a registered electrician, at which point the apprentice can either become a full-time employee or start his/her own business. Although apprenticeships are often formal agreements and may be regulated by state or governmental agencies, apprenticeships can be less formal. For example, small family businesses often work this way, with a child taking on the role of an apprentice and the parent taking on the role of the supervisor. After many years of guidance, the child may take over the family business or strike out on their own to start an ancillary business.

> **Apprentice Training:** A system of training characterized by a combination of classroom instruction and on-the-job experiences.

Job rotation is another commonly used training technique. In this form of training, an employee performs several different jobs across multiple departments within an organization. Just as an athlete may engage in cross-training (performing exercises that are not part of her primary sport) to improve her overall physical fitness, employees may be trained across multiple jobs to improve their overall knowledge of the organization. This technique is popular for managerial training. In fact, one of the book authors witnessed job rotation first-hand during his college years while working part-time at Menards. As part of the training process to become a store manager, trainees were required to spend multiple weeks supervising each of the various departments within the store (e.g., hardware, plumbing, electrical, and floor coverings). This process was meant to ensure that all store managers were familiar with the inner workings of each department, providing a solid understanding of how the entire store functions effectively within and between departments. By providing a wide range of experiences, job rotations allow for the development of a broader collection of KSAOs than would be obtained from training in a single job. Moreover, job rotation allows potential managers to develop first-hand knowledge of the various tasks that their subordinates will be performing on a daily basis.

> **Job Rotation:** Moving employees between jobs and/or departments to promote experience and variety in skill development.

Finally, although easy to overlook, performance evaluation represents an important OJT method. Think about the many times in your life that a coach, teacher, or caregiver has provided you with a formal assessment of your behavior and tips for improvement. In the workplace, as in life, evaluating personal behavior and discussing strengths, weaknesses, and areas for development is one of the best ways to expand KSAOs and improve performance. As such, performance evaluation is not only important for making financial and promotional decisions but also a key mechanism for employee training and development.

Off-the-job training

While some form of OJT is typically necessary and beneficial for employee training and development, there are several approaches to developing job-relevant KSAOs without exposing employees to the actual work context. These would fall in the category of off-the-job training methods. One of the most common off-the-job training methods is the **lecture**, in which the trainer simply presents information to help trainees learn content knowledge relating to the job(s) they will be performing. Although lectures often get a bad rap, it is important to understand that lectures can take multiple forms. Specifically, lectures are not limited to one-way communication. Lectures that allow for interaction with the audience, in which learners may ask questions and provide feedback, will be much more conducive to learning than a traditional lecture in which only one person is allowed to speak. Furthermore, lectures may be supplemented with additional audiovisual information, such as printed handouts or video links, to highlight especially important information and provide a reference for employees to refer back to after the training session. When used appropriately, lectures are an efficient and effective way to present basic knowledge to a large number of trainees.[9]

> **Lecture:** Verbally presenting information to an audience.

A popular alternative to lectures is **computer-based training**, in which training material is presented through computer software in order to teach job-relevant KSAOs. While there are several ways of using computers in the training process, *programmed instruction* is one of the most popular techniques administered via computers. Programmed instruction employs learning principles to motivate and reward trainees for working through training material.[10] Specifically, trainees are usually expected to work through a series of modules, tested on the information presented in each module, and given feedback on how they performed. Trainees are required to meet a criterion standard for each module before progressing to the next stage of training. A primary benefit of this method, as opposed to lecture, is that it allows trainees to work at their own pace. Accordingly, fast learners and applicants with a large amount of experience will be able to progress through the training rather quickly, whereas slow learners and workers with no experience are afforded more time to work through the training modules. Because not all new employees come in with the same KSAOs, the self-directed pace of programmed instruction – paired with the flexibility allowed by computers – can greatly enhance the efficacy of a training program.

> **Computer-Based Training:** Presenting training material via computer.

Another method that allows for a great deal of flexibility is **distance learning**. This technique allows trainees to work through training materials electronically from a distant location, either synchronously or asynchronously. Synchronous distance learning administers training material to people across multiple locations at the same time. For example, if you have taken an online class with set meeting times for virtual lectures and discussion, this would be an example of synchronous distance learning. In this scenario, all students are receiving information at the same time. Asynchronous distance learning, however, allows employees to complete their training at the pace and time of their choosing. For example, an online course in which all lectures were previously recorded and posted on a course website would be an example of asynchronous distance learning, as students are able to access and work through the lectures as rapidly or slowly as they would like (within the confines of the semester). Distance learning is a valuable training option when trying to reach multiple groups of employees across different branches/locations within a company.

> **Distance Learning:** Training approach that allows learners to work through training materials electronically from a distant location.

In many situations, information-based methods such as lectures, computer-based training, and distance learning are simply not enough to prepare employees for the job at hand. In these situations, OJT methods are necessary and instrumental in employee development. However, some jobs are not conducive to OJT due to safety concerns, the costliness of errors, or the simple magnitude of the situation. For example, pilots cannot fully learn how to operate an aircraft simply by observing someone else. Similarly, they cannot be allowed to fly without some degree of practical experience, as the consequences of error are too costly. In these situations, **virtual reality** training is necessary. Virtual reality uses simulators to produce a training environment that mimics a real-world situation as closely as possible. For example, flight simulators are used to train pilots in basic and advanced flying skills. Through simulations, pilots can practice dealing with emergencies and high-risk situations without exposing themselves, or anyone else, to real danger. Virtual reality has also been highly influential in training astronauts, military personnel, and medical students. After trainees are exposed to a series of simulations, the hope is that they can then **transfer** their learning to successful performance on the job. Specifically, the concept of transfer includes both the generalization of learned material to the actual work environment, and the maintenance of the trained skills over time.[11] The ability of trainees to transfer what they learned in training to on-the-job behavior often hinges on the fidelity of the simulated experience.

> **Virtual Reality:** Training approach that uses simulators to mimic real-world situations as closely as possible.

> **Transfer:** Extent to which trainees can apply the knowledge, skills, and abilities acquired through training to their on-the-job behavior to improve performance.

Fidelity refers to the degree to which the training experience is similar to the actual job experience.[12] This encompasses both psychological and physical processes. If a simulation has psychological fidelity, the behavioral processes necessary for success in the simulation are similar to the behavioral processes needed for successful performance on the job. In other words, simulations with psychological fidelity develop the essential KSAOs outlined in the job analysis. For example, a firefighter training simulation may require the trainee to practice making a variety of real-time decisions that would be encountered in an actual fire emergency situation, such as managing multiple water sources, communicating with other firefighters over radio, deciphering the most appropriate rescue strategy given the size of the fire, and monitoring oxygen tank level during a rescue. Physical fidelity, on the other hand, refers to the extent to which the external conditions of the training simulation (i.e., equipment operation and physical surroundings) correspond to the real-world conditions on the job. In other words, does the simulation look, sound, and feel like the real thing? This would encompass aspects such as whether the firefighter is wearing all of the required gear to generate the physical fatigue that will occur during an actual emergency, whether there is substantial heat to replicate the intensity of an actual fire, and whether the simulated fire engine controls are the same as what would be available in a real emergency. To the extent that a simulation achieves both psychological and physical fidelity, the more likely transfer will occur.

> **Fidelity:** The degree to which the training experience is similar to actual, on-the-job experiences.

In summary, each training method has value in certain situations. When deciding which method to employ, practitioners should rely heavily on the needs analysis and the information generated by job analysis. For example, lectures may suffice for increasing knowledge pertaining to general departmental and organizational processes (e.g., declarative knowledge), whereas on-the-job modeling and rotation will be more effective for helping the employee effectively perform job-related tasks (procedural knowledge). Similarly, although OJT methods are often viewed as superior in that they provide hands-on experience, the consequences of error may greatly impact the feasibility of OJT efficiency. When OJT is not an option, virtual reality simulations help to fill the void and provide a valuable alternative to OJT.

Although each training method is implemented differently, all the aforementioned approaches have the potential to enhance trainees' motivation for the job by improving job-relevant KSAOs and facilitating an increase in trainee *self-efficacy*. Self-efficacy refers to one's belief in their ability to accomplish a task. To demonstrate the importance of self-efficacy for motivation, think about a task or activity in which you believe you are incompetent. Now think about a task or activity in which you believe you excel. When was the last time you engaged in each activity voluntarily? You're likely much more motivated to engage in activities when you have confidence in your abilities. In fact, people with higher self-efficacy are more likely to select difficult and challenging goals, show greater effort and persistence when working toward goals, approach tasks with better moods, and are better able to cope with stress and disappointment compared to those with lower self-efficacy.[13] Simply put, self-efficacy has large implications for employee motivation.

In summary, each of the described training methods strives to improve employee learning and performance by enhancing declarative knowledge, procedural knowledge, employee motivation, or all three.

Contextual considerations: What impacts the training process?

An integral part of the training process is understanding the many contextual factors that can impact the effectiveness of any given training program. These include learning principles, individual differences in trainees and trainers, and the organizational culture in which employees are being trained.

Learning principles

Learning is facilitated to the extent that learners are active and engaged in the learning process. **Active learning** includes hands-on activities – such as practice, reflection, problem solving, and social interaction – that aid one's ability to understand and integrate information. Suppose you were assigned to read a chapter of a textbook and will be quizzed on that chapter the next day. One possible strategy would be to read the chapter, then re-read the key terms and concepts time and time again to memorize the definitions and key ideas presented. Alternatively, you could read through the chapter, talk with other people about the content, play around with key ideas within the chapter in relation to your own life, and relate new information from the chapter to your previous knowledge and experiences. The second strategy is more active and will lead to a deeper understanding of the material. Applied to training, the more opportunities trainees have to actively interact with the information presented, the better. Active learning is especially effective when training is focused on developing procedural knowledge and when dealing with complex tasks.[14]

> **Active Learning:** A method of instruction that involves actively engaging learners through discussion, reflection, and problem solving.

Within training programs, a big portion of active learning is practicing work tasks. When employees are allowed to actually perform work tasks, whether that be through OJT or a simulation, this typically leads to more effective learning and retention than passive observation alone. When it comes to practice, the more the better. As contestants on *Dancing with the Stars* will surely tell you, just because they were able to perform a dance routine without any errors once during a practice session, that does not guarantee they will be able to do it again during prime time. This demonstrates that continued practice is highly valuable. Overlearning occurs when you continue practicing even after you have mastered a task. While this may seem like a waste of time, overlearning is beneficial in that it can lead to **automaticity** – being able to perform a task with little attention or cognitive resources.[15] This is particularly beneficial when it comes to complex tasks and high-pressure situations. To the extent that dancers overlearn their dance routine, this will go a long way in ameliorating the number and magnitude of potential mistakes that occur during their performance. Although overlearning does not guarantee perfection, it has been shown to positively impact long-term retention for both physical and cognitive tasks.[16]

> **Automaticity:** Being able to perform a task with little attention.

Another aspect to consider is the size and complexity of the task(s) to be learned. Will the employee learn an entire task all at once (**whole learning**) or will the training be broken down into separate sub-tasks, and then later combined (**part learning**)? If a complex task can easily be divided into smaller units, it is often useful to train different components of the task separately, mastering small bits before moving to the whole task. For example, if students were to be trained on how to navigate data analysis software, such as SPSS, it would be useful to first teach students the general layout of the SPSS interface, then demonstrate how to enter and import data, then cover the various analyses available within SPSS and what to look for in their associated outputs, and then cover the rules for using code or syntax with analyses. It would be very difficult to learn how to "analyze data" all at once. However, to the extent that the components of a task are interdependent, whole learning is necessary. For example, if someone were to be trained on how to operate a forklift, it would not make sense to train them how to use the foot pedals separately and independently from the hydraulic lift and tilt levers, as the foot pedals and hydraulic levers will be used and operated simultaneously when operating the forklift. For more complex tasks such as these, effective training takes time. This brings up the question of what training practice sessions should look like in terms of time and intensity.

> **Whole Learning:** Learning an entire task all at once.

> **Part Learning:** Breaking an activity into sub-tasks which are practiced separately, and later combined.

Massed practice occurs when training sessions are condensed into a few, long sessions where the trainee is continuously practicing without a break. **Distributed practice**, on the other hand, occurs when employees practice in shorter sessions, separated by breaks, and spaced over a longer period of time. Just as the habit of pulling an all-nighter before an exam (i.e., massed practice) is not as effective as studying for a few hours each day during the week leading up to an exam (distributed practice), the same is true for training. The research is clear in indicating that distributed practice is more effective for learning and retention than massed practice, as rest periods serve the purpose of reducing fatigue and also provide time for the learned content to sink in.[17] Even so, it is all too common for organizations to use massed practice for logistical purposes, sometimes even squeezing all of their training into one work day. Although this may save time, the learning and retention that results from massed practice is often inadequate.

> **Massed Practice:** Learners practice an activity continuously in a single session, without breaks.

> **Distributed Practice:** Learners practice an activity over multiple sessions, separated by breaks.

Finally, **feedback** is essential to the learning process. In order for an employee to improve and develop KSAOs, they need information about how they are performing. Some tasks provide direct and immediate feedback, such as when a basketball player shoots a free throw (either she makes it or she misses it). Other tasks are more ambiguous. A new secretary may be unsure of whether he is formatting excel spreadsheets correctly and/or unsure of which calls should be forwarded to his boss versus which should be summarized in a written message. In these situations, it is essential for the worker to receive some sort of indication (from a trainer or supervisor) of the adequacy of his behavior. Feedback is important not only because it directs proper behavior but also because it can enhance self-efficacy and motivation for the task.

> **Feedback:** Information about one's performance on a task, used as the basis for improvement.

Individual differences

Trainees

As previously mentioned, not all trainees are on an equal playing field when entering the job, as they may differ in their general capabilities, personality traits, and motivational strivings.[18] In other words, trainees differ in their **readiness** for training. Readiness refers to a person's general preparedness to learn. One factor that may influence readiness is job experience. Some applicants are hired with little or no actual work experience, whereas other applicants are hired because of their extensive work history. As a result, there can be large differences in trainee KSAOs. Similarly, trainees will vary greatly in their self-efficacy for the job, sometimes regardless of their standing on KSAOs. As a result, self-efficacy can have a substantial impact on the pace at which trainees progress through the training process, the confidence they exhibit after training has ended, and their general motivation. Related to self-efficacy, goal orientation represents another dimension on which trainees may differ. Individuals with a performance orientation are simply concerned about being evaluated favorably, whereas those with a mastery orientation are concerned with improving their competence for the tasks being trained. Mastery orientation has been shown to be more beneficial than performance orientation with regard to learning outcomes and the transfer of training.[19] Encouraging a mastery orientation among employees can help foster improved development of KSAOs, and, in turn, increased self-efficacy.

Trainee personality and general cognitive ability are also important to consider with regard to trainee readiness. Personality characteristics, such as the Big Five, may influence one's motivation to learn and impact training-related performance.[20] Moreover, trainee personality may interact with the type of training method(s) used, particularly in situations where there is a large amount of social interaction between a trainee and a specific trainer. While personality may impact one's motivation to learn, cognitive ability may influence the amount and speed at which information can be learned. In general, people with higher cognitive ability are able to learn and apply material more quickly than those with lower cognitive ability. In fact, cognitive ability has been shown to be one of the best predictors of job-related learning and performance in job training programs.[21] All of these individual differences should be considered when developing a training program and demonstrate the importance of conducting a thorough needs analysis to understand who, specifically, will benefit from training.

> **Readiness:** Being prepared and willing to learn.

Trainers

Just as trainees may differ in their readiness for training, trainers can vastly differ in their general competence. It should go without saying that a formal trainer should have expertise in the subject matter being taught. If you have ever been in a classroom with a teacher who did not know much about the subject h/she was teaching, it was likely a painful experience. Even when it is obvious that a teacher has content knowledge in the subject area being taught, the classroom setting can be just as painful if the teacher has no energy or enthusiasm when teaching. Thus, just because a person is a high-performing SME, this does not guarantee that they will make an effective trainer – they may not have the motivation to train others, they may not buy-in to the training process, or their personality may prohibit them from effectively interacting with trainees. Furthermore, trainers may not have sufficient knowledge of the learning process or an appreciation for the various learning principles discussed earlier. Good trainers will buy-in to the learning process and be motivated to help others learn.

Communication skills are perhaps one of the most important aspects of being an effective trainer. This includes being flexible in one's interaction style. Especially when working with multiple trainees, it is important to understand that different trainees may require different styles of communication. For example, in mentoring relationships, some trainees may simply request the essential knowledge to perform their job, whereas others strive for a more personal relationship in addition to formal guidance. An effective trainer will adjust their strategy to best suit the needs of each individual trainee. An example of this can be seen in the popular TV show *Kitchen Nightmares,* in which chef Gordon Ramsey seeks to revive failing restaurants. If you have watched this show, you will notice how chef Ramsey tailors his interpersonal style and management approach to the owner of each restaurant. In some episodes, chef Ramsey is seen screaming, yelling, and cursing at the restaurant owner (this seems to be his typical approach). In other episodes, however, he is seen sympathizing with owners, listening to their backstory, and empathizing in order to get his point across. It is plain to see that chef Ramsey changes his communication style, drawing on different aspects of his personality, based on the personality of the person he is working with and the surrounding situation. Although difficult to do, tailoring communication style to each individual trainee can pay dividends in developing rapport with trainees and facilitating the learning process. While not feasible in all jobs or training situations, the tailored approach to communication is more useful in situations where a personalized relationship is developed between the trainer and each trainee (coaches and individual athletes on a sports team, a mentor for multiple new teachers, etc.).

Organizational culture

Some organizations place a lot of value on learning and innovation, while others do not. Effective organizations often take on a culture of **continuous learning**, in which the company places value on learning new knowledge and skills on an ongoing basis.[22] Indeed, there has been growing interest in *learning organizations*. These are companies that promote continuous learning and value the process of learning and knowledge acquisition for its own sake. As an example of a continuous learning strategy, Adobe developed a program called "Kickbox" to encourage innovation among its employees. This program allows any staff member to request and receive a box containing all the materials needed to generate and test a new idea: instruction cards, writing materials, snacks, and, wait for it, a $1,000 pre-paid credit card! The credit card can be used on anything the employee deems appropriate, no questions asked. Whether the idea is eventually adopted by the company or scrapped entirely is of no concern – the point of the program is to promote innovative thinking among employees. While not all companies will be willing or able to provide $1,000 pre-paid credit cards, the key to developing a learning organization is being open to new ideas and valuing the learning process. Having an atmosphere that values and supports learning and development can go a long way in facilitating the effectiveness of training programs.

> **Continuous Learning:** Situation when employees are given the opportunity to learn while they work in order to become better at their jobs.

Evaluating training: Is the training effective?

After a training program has been designed and implemented, a crucial final step in the training process is to examine the effectiveness of the training program to determine whether it should continue. In many organizations, this step is neglected or glossed over relatively quickly. However, without evaluating the effectiveness of training programs, organizations are left in the dark as to the actual value the program provides to employees and the company as a whole. The most common framework for evaluating training effectiveness is Kirkpatrick's (1976) four "levels" of criteria: reaction, learning, behavioral, and results criteria.[23]

The first level of evaluation concerns trainee reactions. **Reaction criteria** evaluate employee perceptions about the training process. These criteria may assess whether trainees enjoyed the training, if they found the content engaging, and how satisfied they were with the training experience. Alliger and colleagues (1997) suggest that reaction criteria should not only assess affective reactions but also utility judgments.[24] For example, trainees may be asked for their impressions about how useful they perceive the training to be, whether the content had practical value, and whether it was job-relevant. This information is usually gathered through surveys or focus groups.

Level 2 examines the learning that has taken place during training. **Learning criteria** measure whether employees actually understood and absorbed the content of the training program. To assess learning, quantitative data is collected to determine if employee knowledge, skills, or abilities were improved as a result of training. This is accomplished by evaluating employees before and after the training has occurred, specifically looking for improvement in the second assessment. Learning criteria can be further broken down into immediate knowledge (assessed shortly after training has concluded), knowledge retention (assessed at a later date), and behavior/skill demonstration.[25] Written tests are commonly used to assess immediate knowledge and knowledge retention, often emphasizing the declarative knowledge of employees. Behavior/skill demonstration (i.e., procedural knowledge) can be demonstrated and assessed via work sample tests and simulations.

Behavioral criteria, level 3, assess if employees have changed their behavior as a result of training. The key question for behavioral criteria is whether employees can apply what they learned in training to their on-the-job performance (i.e., transfer of training). Behavioral criteria can be assessed with behavioral assessments, work samples, tests, and formal performance evaluation data. As mentioned previously, adequate transfer includes both the generalization of learned material to the actual work environment and the maintenance of trained skills over time.

Finally, **results criteria** determine the overall value of the training program to the organization, taking into account the company's goals and resources. Even if the training program demonstrated positive results with regard to reaction, learning, and behavioral criteria, the program may not be financially feasible for the organization to continue into the future. In other words, the organization must assess the *utility* of the training program. This can be determined through a careful cost-benefit analysis in order to examine a training program's return on investment (ROI). For a training program to have utility, the performance gains resulting from the training should outweigh the costs incurred during the development and implementation of the training program. If there is not a substantial ROI, the training program is usually deemed ineffective.

> **Reaction Criteria:** Measures employee perceptions about the training process.

> **Learning Criteria:** Measures how much was learned during the training program.

> **Behavioral Criteria:** Measures whether employee learning transfers to on-the-job behavior.

> **Results Criteria:** Measures whether training is valuable in relation to organizational goals, resources, and overall strategy.

While the Kirkpatrick model is the most common method of training evaluation, one criticism is that it is too simplistic. For example, other factors that may influence the effectiveness and outcomes associated with the training process include the learning culture of the organization, work unit goals and values, and the level of interpersonal/organizational support for skill acquisition and behavior change.[26] These are not included in Kirkpatrick's framework. Accordingly, practitioners may wish to supplement Kirkpatrick's model as appropriate based on the overall goals of the training program. For example, if learning culture and organizational support are deemed as significant factors to be improved by the training process, these should obviously be included in the training evaluation process.

Designs for evaluation

Training programs are developed to ensure that employees have the KSAOs required for their job. To be sure that training programs are, indeed, having an impact on employee KSAOs, formal research designs are used to test the effectiveness of the training program. Two designs lend themselves well to evaluating training effectiveness: the pretest-posttest design and the pretest-posttest design with a control group. To demonstrate the usefulness of each design, consider the following scenario:

> Suppose a large-scale window washing company is hiring 200 new employees. Before sending them off on the job, the company wants to ensure that all incoming employees have a thorough knowledge of the primary cleaning product used by the company. Specifically, employees are required to know the proper ratio of cleaning product to water for effective washing, directions for application and removal, and safety considerations associated with the product.

A **pretest-posttest design** allows for measuring employee knowledge both before (pretest) and after (posttest) training has occurred. Related to the scenario above, all 200 of the new employees would complete a pretest (before training occurs), be put through the training program, and then complete a posttest (after training occurs) on their knowledge of the cleaning product to be used. To the extent that employee knowledge about the cleaning product significantly improved on the posttest, the training program would be considered effective. Although this design is the most feasible for organizations to implement, the primary downside is that there is no control group. Because of this, one cannot rule out the possibility that other events happening between the pretest and posttest may have played a role in the improvement of their scores. Perhaps simply being around other employees and talking about the job may have improved their product-related knowledge. To ensure that training was the crucial factor in their knowledge development, a pretest-posttest with control may be used.

The **pretest-posttest with control design** follows the same general procedure as the pretest-posttest design, with the addition of a control group (which receives no training). So, applied to the scenario above, 100 of the incoming window washers would be assigned to the experimental group and receive training, whereas the other 100 would be assigned to the control group and receive no training. This method has stronger internal validity in that comparisons can be made between the pre- and posttests, and also between the experimental and control groups. If the posttest scores for the 100 that received training are significantly higher than the posttest scores for the 100 that received no training, this provides stronger evidence for the efficacy of the training program.

Pretest-Posttest Design: Design that measures employees on a criterion of interest both before and after training has occurred.

Pretest-Posttest with Control: Design that measures employees on a criterion of interest both before and after training has occurred, including a control group.

In addition to examining if training was effective in general, evaluative designs can also be used to assess which specific training delivery method is most effective. For example, suppose the window washing company is interested in determining whether a lecture, video, or computer module is most effective for training incoming employees. In this situation, 50 employees would be assigned to a lecture training group, 50 to a video training group, 50 to a computer module training group, and 50 to the control group. This design would allow the company to make comparisons between each training method *and* examine the effect of training versus no training. If all training groups perform better than the control group, this is strong evidence for the effectiveness of training in general. Further, if one training group performed better than the others, this may indicate that a certain delivery method may be superior for reaching their training goals. This design would also be useful for examining utility. If all training methods are roughly similar in their improvement of cleaning product knowledge, with similar employee reactions, the company may select the training method that consumes the least resources, as this would improve the ROI of the training program.

Once the organization has fully evaluated the training program, the resulting data can be used to make decisions on whether to retain the original training program, modify the methods of training used, or scrap the program altogether.

Summary

Through a comprehensive needs analysis, thoughtful method selection, careful consideration of contextual issues related to the training process, and a thorough evaluation, organizations can improve and refine their training programs over time. Training, in combination with a well-designed selection system, is an essential tool to develop and maintain a talented and successful workforce.

REVIEW QUESTIONS

1. What is training and why is it important for organizations?
2. How does training improve employee performance?
3. Why is a needs analysis necessary?
4. What are the various training methods used by organizations, and when/why might they be used?
5. What is transfer and why is it important?
6. What is fidelity and how does this play a role in training simulations?
7. What contextual considerations should be considered when designing and implementing a training program?
8. What are the various criteria used to evaluate a training program's effectiveness?
9. What research designs are used to test the usefulness of a training program?

DISCUSSION QUESTIONS

1. When might an off-the-job training method be more appropriate than an on-the-job training approach?
2. Have you been through any formal training programs? If so, what did you think about the process and procedures used?
3. If you were developing a training program, how would you deal with varying levels of readiness among trainees?
4. What do you think is more important to virtual reality training – psychological or physical fidelity? Why?
5. If you were the CEO of an organization, how would you foster a culture of continuous learning within your company?

Notes

1. Freifeld, L. (2020, August 19). *2020 training industry report*. Training. https://trainingmag.com/2020-training-industry-report/
2. Campbell, J. P. (1990). Modelling the performance prediction problem in industrial and organizational psychology. In M. D. Dunnette & L. M. Hough (Eds.), *Handbook of industrial and organizational psychology* (pp. 687–732). Consulting Psychologists Press.
3. Brown, J. (2002). Training needs assessment: A must for developing an effective training program. *Public Personnel Management, 31*(4), 569–578.
4. Bunch, K. J. (2007). Training failure as a consequence of organizational culture. *Human Resource Development Review, 6*(2), 142–163.
5. Goldstein, I. L., & Ford, J. K. (2002). *Training in organizations: Needs assessment, development, and evaluation* (4th ed.). Wadsworth.
6. Arthur, W., Jr., Bennett, W., Jr., Edens, P. S., & Bell, S. T. (2003). Effectiveness of training in organizations: A meta-analysis of design and evaluation features. *Journal of Applied Psychology, 88*(2), 234–245.
7. Kammeyer-Mueller, J. D., & Judge, T. A. (2008). A quantitative review of mentoring research: Test of a model. *Journal of Vocational Behavior, 72*(3), 269–283.
8. Noe, R. A., & Kodwani, A. D. (2018). *Employee training and development* (7th ed). McGraw Hill.
9. Arthur, W., Jr., Bennett, W., Jr., Edens, P. S., & Bell, S. T. (2003). Effectiveness of training in organizations: A meta-analysis of design and evaluation features. *Journal of Applied Psychology, 88*(2), 234–245.
10. Goldstein, I. L., & Ford, J. K. (2002). *Training in organizations: Needs assessment, development, and evaluation* (4th ed.). Wadsworth.
11. Baldwin, T. T., & Ford, J. K. (1988). Transfer of training: A review and directions for future research. *Personnel Psychology, 41*(1), 63–105.
12. Goldstein, I. L., & Ford, J. K. (2002). *Training in organizations: Needs assessment, development, and evaluation* (4th ed.). Wadsworth.
13. Bandura, A. (1994). Self-efficacy. In V. S. Ramachandran (Ed.), *Encyclopedia of human behavior* (pp. 71–81). Academic Press.

14. Bell, B. S., & Kozlowski, S. W. J. (2010). Toward a theory of learner-centered training design: An integrative framework of active learning. In S. W. J. Kozlowski & E. Salas (Eds.), *Learning, training, and development in organizations* (pp. 263–300). Routledge/Taylor & Francis Group.
15. Kanfer, R., & Ackerman, P. L. Motivation and cognitive abilities: An integrative/aptitude-treatment interaction approach to skill acquisition. *Journal of Applied Psychology, 74*(4), 657–690.
16. Driskell, J. E., Willis, R. P., & Copper, C. (1992). Effect of overlearning on retention. *Journal of Applied Psychology, 77*(5), 615–622.
17. Cascio, W. F., & Aguinis, H. (2014). *Applied psychology in human resource management* (7th ed.). Pearson.
18. Bell, B. S., Tannenbaum, S. I., Ford, J. K., Noe, R., & Kraiger, K. 100 years of training and development research: What we know and where we should go. *Journal of Applied Psychology, 102*(3), 305–323.
19. Ford, J. K., Smith, E. M., Weissbein, D. A., Gully, S. M., & Salas, E. (1998). Relationships of goal orientation, metacognitive ability, and practice strategies with learning outcomes and transfer. *Journal of Applied Psychology, 83*(2), 218–233.
20. Burke, L. A., & Hutchins, H. M. (2007). Training transfer: An integrative literature review. *Human Resource Development Review, 6*(3), 263–296.
21. Schmidt, F. L., & Hunter, J. E. (1998). The validity and utility of selection methods in personnel psychology: Practical and theoretical implications of 85 years of research findings. *Psychological Bulletin, 124*(2), 262–274.
22. Tannenbaum, S. I. (1997). Enhancing continuous learning: Diagnostic findings from multiple companies. *Human Resource Management, 36*(4), 437–452.
23. Kirkpatrick, D. L. (1976). Evaluation of training. In R. L. Craig (Ed.), *Training and development handbook* (pp. 18–27). McGraw-Hill.
24. Alliger, G. M., Tannenbaum, S. I., Bennett W., Jr., Traver, H., & Shotland, A. (1997). A meta-analysis of the relations among training criteria. *Personnel Psychology, 50*, 341–358.
25. Alliger, G. M., Tannenbaum, S. I., Bennett W., Jr., Traver, H., & Shotland, A. (1997). A meta-analysis of the relations among training criteria. *Personnel Psychology, 50*, 341–358.
26. Bates, R. (2004). A critical analysis of evaluation practice: The Kirkpatrick model and the principle of beneficence. *Evaluation and Program Planning, 27*(3), 341–347.

15 Summary and review

LEARNING OBJECTIVES

- Review and integrate information from previous chapters
- Know the major work activities completed by personnel psychologists
- Understand the many different job titles personnel psychologists can occupy
- Know the educational requirements necessary for a career in personnel psychology

How do you make the work experience fair, objective, efficient, productive, and enjoyable for employees (or at the very least tolerable) all at the same time? This is an extraordinarily complex question, and one that personnel psychologists grapple with in their daily work. After reading the previous 14 chapters, you now have a general understanding of the many strategies personnel psychologists use to address the question posed above. In this chapter, we will review and integrate the information presented in the previous chapters to summarize the type of work and career options available to those with an interest in personnel psychology.

Work tasks of a personnel psychologist

Personnel psychology has a long history of advocating for the application of psychology to the work setting. Whether working in academia or the applied realm, the goals of personnel psychologists remain the same. Specifically, personnel psychologists strive to apply psychological principles in order to (1) generate a better understanding of the work environment, (2) ensure fair and objective decisions across a wide variety of workplace issues, and (3) make the work experience better for all employees. In short, personnel psychologists endeavor toward a better workplace. To accomplish this goal, personnel psychologists engage in research and evidence-based practice across a wide variety of topics. Let us take a brief tour of the topics we have covered previously to paint a picture of the work activities involved in personnel psychology.

Job analysis

For the personnel psychologist, everything begins with job analysis. As discussed in Chapter 3, job analysis serves as the foundation for all other workplace personnel decisions. Because a thorough understanding of any given job is necessary to perform HR functions, many personnel psychologists spend their time developing job analysis materials and conducting job analyses. These analyses can be conducted for a variety of purposes – compensation, performance appraisal, and selection – but the overarching goal is to develop a detailed understanding of the day-to-day activities of the job. Regardless of the method used for job analysis, the process should result in a thorough job description which can be used for subsequent HR functions.

After a job description is developed, personnel psychologists can move on to their next task: recruiting a competent and diverse applicant pool.

Recruiting

Based on the results from the job analysis, personnel psychologists will strategically target potential job seekers in order to attract them to the organization. Taking into account the specific requirements of the position, as well as the organization's mission and values, personnel psychologists will determine the best approach for recruiting job applicants. As discussed in Chapter 4, person-organization fit represents a key determining factor in whether any given candidate will apply to (and stay within) a particular job or company. There are a variety of recruitment strategies organizations may employ, including advertisements, referrals, and social media. The most important factor for the personnel psychologist to keep in mind, regardless of the recruitment medium used, is to provide a realistic job preview to job applicants. Doing so will enhance the applicants' ability to self-select in or out of the application process, thereby expediting the process for both the applicant and the organization.

Once a suitable pool of applicants has been identified, personnel psychologists will shift their focus on the selection process.

Employee selection

Every company relies on their selection system to generate a competent workforce. Because of this, a large number of personnel psychologists specialize in developing, evaluating, and implementing selection systems for organizations. Indeed, employee selection is one of the largest areas of focus for personnel psychologists. Given that the importance of KSAOs will vary from one job to another based on specific requirements and work context (as outlined by a job analysis), the selection methods used, as well as their effectiveness, will vary across different jobs. It is up to the personnel psychologist to determine, based on the available evidence, which selection method(s) will be most appropriate for the job at hand.

Sound judgment and decision-making are integral to the selection process. Chapter 8 explores the various ways in which decisions can be made within the selection context. Despite our inherent tendency to rely on intuition and expertise when making decisions, the available evidence demonstrates that these tactics are not the most effective selection tools at our disposal. Given that formal tests and assessments consistently outperform intuition and expertise, personnel psychologists tend to place more emphasis on mechanical combinations of data when making selection decisions, as this leads to less potential bias in the hiring process.

There are a large number of selection tests available to organizations, each with pros and cons. These tests may be developed to assess ability, personality, behavior, or a combination of all three. Chapters 9 and 10 provide an overview of the many different types of ability and non-cognitive tests that may be used as part of the selection process. The job interview, along with several other commonly used behavioral and observational measures, is covered in Chapter 11. Finally, Chapter 12 explores some newer realms of assessment techniques while considering the increasing role that technology plays in the selection process. With all of these various assessments available for use, it is important to remember that no test – or combination of tests – is perfect. As a result, personnel psychologists must come to terms with the fact that predicting performance is a difficult undertaking with a large degree of inherent unpredictability.

Given the finicky nature of predicting performance, validity represents a key concept when it comes to the use and implementation of selection tests. Personnel psychologists and organizations must have sound rationale for the choices they make and the tests they include in the selection process. Chapter 5 explores the concept of validity as it pertains to the selection process and outlines the many different pieces of validity evidence organizations can draw upon when developing a selection system. However, just because a test has been shown to predict performance, this does not guarantee that the test is without potential problems.

Before a personnel psychologist even begins to think about which hiring methods to use, s/he must have knowledge of the legal context surrounding the selection process. Legal concerns, highlighted in Chapter 2, add yet another layer of complexity to an already difficult endeavor. The goal of any selection system is not only to maximize competence, but also to minimize discrimination against protected classes. Even if a selection method has been shown to be valid for predicting performance, one must be wary of the fact that the chosen method may still result in adverse impact. Accordingly, it is important for personnel psychologists to evaluate and monitor the selection system with an eye toward fairness in the selection ratios of protected classes. Moreover, although much legal precedent regarding employment discrimination has been in place for several years, a personnel psychologist must keep up to date on recent court cases and decisions regarding employment selection in order to ensure the utility and legality of selection tests.

Finally, personnel psychologists are not only concerned with the selection process itself, but also with applicants' reactions to the selection process and the subsequent selection decision. Organizations strive to implement procedures that are perceived as fair among both selected *and rejected* candidates. Chapter 7 identifies the implications that applicant reactions can have for both the individual applicant and the organization as a whole. The concept of organizational justice is of particular importance with regard to applicant reactions. Both structural and social factors of the selection process may contribute to the perceived fairness of the selection decision, and these factors should be taken into account when developing and implementing a selection system.

In sum, personnel psychologists have their work cut out for them when it comes to employee selection. A selection system must be deemed to be *appropriate* for a particular job based on the results of a job analysis, rely on *objective* decision-making processes, is *legal* in the sense that it maximizes competence among those hired (i.e., validity) while minimizing discrimination against protected classes, and is perceived as *fair* by the applicants who realize the consequences of the selection decision. It should be clear by now that employee selection is a complex and multifaceted process.

After a selection system is developed, implemented, and shown to be legal and valid, a personnel psychologist's work is not yet finished.

Training

Even the most qualified candidates may need some degree of assistance and preparation in order to be set up for success in their new job. Chapter 14 reviews the topic of training in relation to employee development. Personnel psychologists help organizations identify their training needs by performing organization, task, and person analyses to determine where, and how much, training is needed within the company. After discovering the organization's training needs, personnel psychologists can then select which training method(s) are most appropriate for the different jobs and departments within the organization. Finally, personnel psychologists will determine the utility of a training program by conducting pre- and post-tests on several important training criteria to determine if the training program transferred to on-the-job employee behavior. Although this final step – formal evaluation of the training process – is a step that is often overlooked in many companies, it is essential to determining the value and efficacy of any given training program.

Once employees have received the necessary training, they are ready to work!

Performance evaluation

After employees complete their training and possess the KSAOs necessary to perform required work tasks, personnel psychologists must determine how to objectively evaluate their on-the-job performance. Like employee selection, performance evaluation is an imperfect process. Personnel psychologists pride themselves on being aware of the criterion problem (i.e., the many difficulties in conceptualizing and measuring performance), and the potential sources of contamination and deficiency in performance data. The criterion problem is covered in-depth in Chapter 6. As part of the performance evaluation process, personnel psychologists may distinguish between several domains of employee performance: required tasks (i.e., task performance), going above and beyond (citizenship performance), and harmful employee behavior (counterproductive performance).

Although there are inherent problems associated with the measurement of performance, the goal for personnel psychologists is to limit measurement error in order to make the evaluation process as relevant and objective as possible. Armed with knowledge of the criterion problem and the various dimensions that contribute to employee performance, personnel psychologists set out to select the performance rating system best suited for the job at hand. Chapter 13 reviews the purposes of performance evaluation as well as the characteristics associated with effective performance evaluation systems. Although there are many rating formats and performance evaluation strategies to choose from, it is important to keep in mind that none of them provide a perfect or complete measure of performance. One simple strategy to reduce measurement error in any rating format is frame of reference training. To the extent that all raters are on the same page with regard to what constitutes "good performance," we can be more confident in the performance measurement process.

Data from a performance evaluation can be used for several purposes. For one, performance evaluations may highlight additional areas for employee training. Inevitably, in any given job, some employees will thrive and some will struggle. Thus, performance data can be used to further encourage employee development, either through further training and coaching and/or via self-reflection on one's strengths and weaknesses. Performance evaluations may also reveal top performers who are suitable candidates for promotion within the company. Accordingly, once performance data is generated, the job of a personnel psychologist starts over again, in the form of identifying employees to be promoted within the company. This process begins with a thorough understanding of the upper-level job within the company, proceeds through recruitment and selection strategies that are deemed most effective for that position, and progresses through training needs and performance evaluation of those who are selected.

There you have it, the primary work domains of personnel psychologists summarized in a few pages. Although it is not uncommon for some personnel psychologists to specialize primarily in one of the above areas, others may work as generalists engaging in all of these domains to some degree. One's degree of specialization may depend on their career goals and interests, employment status, and/or educational training.

Work activities and job titles

In order to accomplish the tasks outlined above, personnel psychologists engage in a variety of smaller-scale work activities. Below are several examples of the day-to-day work activities performed by personnel psychologists, taken from the O*Net job description for I-O psychologists[1]:

- Develop educational programs
- Conduct scientific research on organizational behavior or processes
- Mediate disputes
- Prepare scientific or technical reports or presentations
- Testify at legal or legislative proceedings
- Collect information from people through observation, interviews, or surveys
- Develop methods of social or economic research
- Review professional literature to maintain professional knowledge
- Administer standardized physical or psychological tests
- Confer with clients to exchange information
- Train personnel in technical or scientific procedures
- Advise others on business or operational matters

Given their extensive background and training in both science and practice, personnel psychologists can thrive in a variety of work positions and contexts. Some personnel psychologists will specialize in a particular sphere of interest (job analysis, selection, etc.), in either research or consulting, while others will perform a broader variety of HR applications. Regardless of specialization, you will find personnel psychologists in both private and public sectors, academic institutions, and non-profit organizations. Job titles for those with a degree in personnel psychology may vary extensively depending on educational level and experience. Below is a list of a variety of job titles (not exhaustive) that may be occupied by those trained in personnel psychology.[2,3,4]

Academic

- Professor (Assistant, Associate, Full)
- Department Chair
- Dean
- Provost
- President

Consulting and industry

- Organizational Consultant (Internal or External)
- Human Resource Management Specialist
- Talent Management Specialist
- Workforce Insights Analyst
- Organizational Effectiveness Manager
- Team Development Manager
- Change Management Professional
- Strategy Development Professional
- Staffing and Recruiting Manager
- Selection Systems Manager
- Behavioral Analyst
- Research Analyst
- Operations Research Analyst
- Training and Development Manager
- Labor Relations Specialist
- Executive Director
- CEO

As can be seen, there are many opportunities available to those with a degree in personnel psychology, and I-O psychology more broadly. Given that personnel psychologists are well-versed in a variety of workplace activities, they are well-equipped for positions at multiple levels within any given organization. Now that you know the various work activities and job titles enacted by those with a degree in personnel psychology, the only question remaining is "What are the educational requirements to become a professional in the field of personnel psychology?"

Educational requirements

To become a personnel psychologist, one must obtain an advanced degree – a master's or doctorate – in I-O psychology or a related field (e.g., organizational behavior, HR, business management). Academic positions will typically require a PhD, whereas a master's degree will suffice for a career in consulting or industry. Graduate programs in I-O psychology adhere to the scientist-practitioner model. Upon completion of a graduate program, graduates will have the skills to (1) develop their own research hypotheses and conduct original research, and (2) review the literature to develop evidence-based interventions. Although graduate program requirements and emphases will differ from one program to another, the general components of a graduate program will consist of coursework, research, and practical experience.

Coursework

To fulfill the requirements of a graduate degree in personnel psychology, graduate programs will require the completion of a certain number of academic credit hours. These credits will consist of in-depth courses on a variety of the topics covered within this textbook. For example, it is not uncommon for graduate programs to require a semester-long class on the topic of selection, one on performance evaluation, and so on. This is to ensure that students become subject matter experts in the field of I-O and develop a thorough understanding of the many topics within the field. The primary difference between a masters' program and a doctoral program is depth of training. Master's programs require less credit hours to complete, and therefore, typically will provide less depth in their coverage of personnel topics than a typical doctoral program.

Research

In addition to coursework on the content of I-O, graduate students are also trained in the research process and are often required to complete original research of their own. A **thesis** is typically (though not always) required to complete a master's program, whereas a **dissertation** is necessary to fulfill the requirements for a doctoral program. Both projects represent an original piece of scholarly work completed by the student. The primary difference is that a dissertation is expected to be more complex with regard to design, measurement, and analysis. Both projects allow students to demonstrate their mastery of the research process and showcase their knowledge on a particular topic within the field. In addition to the undertaking of a thesis and/or dissertation, it is not uncommon for students to be involved in multiple research projects – collaborating with peers and faculty members – during their time in graduate school. Although all graduate programs provide training on the research process to some degree, it is emphasized to a larger degree in doctoral programs. Even in programs where a thesis or dissertation is not required, students will be trained heavily in the areas of research design, data analysis, and data interpretation.

> **Thesis:** Original piece of research completed to fulfill the requirements of a master's degree.
>
> **Dissertation:** Original piece of research completed to fulfill the requirements of a doctoral degree.

Practical experience

Many master's and doctoral programs will provide the opportunity for students to apply their KSAOs in an organizational and/or consulting context. One way this may happen is through an in-house consulting group. For example, Bowling Green State University's graduate program has an in-house consulting firm – the Institute for Psychological Research and Application – where students and faculty collaborate to provide consulting services to outside organizations. Groups like these provide valuable hands-on experience for students while offering professional consulting services at a competitive price to outside organizations. Another way for students to obtain practical experience in graduate school is through the completion of an **internship**. As an intern, students may be asked to help design and organize research projects, assist in creating assessments, analyze and interpret data, and help in the development of evidence-based solutions to organizational problems.

> **Internship:** A short-term position within an organization designed to provide a student with meaningful work experience.

Although some graduate programs slant more heavily toward a research and academic focus, others are tailored more toward obtaining practical experience in preparation for a career as a practitioner. Whether a student takes a more academic or applied route, graduate programs will provide students with the KSAOs necessary to provide meaningful contributions to the field of personnel psychology.

The future of personnel psychology

In Chapter 1, we overviewed the top ten workplace trends reported by SIOP. Although some of these trends persist from year to year, others come and go with time. Regardless of which trends make the top ten list in any given year, the world of work is constantly changing, with new trends emerging every year. Whether it be the steady presence of technological changes, or the unpredictable upheaval that a global pandemic causes, the workplace will continue to evolve over time. The inevitability of change in the workplace, paired with the fact that the majority of adults will spend 40-plus hours per week at work, makes personnel psychology an interesting and necessary field. In fact, the U.S. News and World Report ranked Industrial Psychology as #3 in their list of best science jobs for the year of 2022.[5] It is an exciting time to be involved in the field of personnel psychology!

If you are interested in pursuing a career in the field of personnel psychology, be sure to revisit the "Personnel Psychology Today" section in Chapter 1. This provides recent workplace trends, a brief overview of career opportunities, and professional resources for those interested in the field. For more information on graduate programs and careers in personnel psychology, you can also visit the SIOP website (SIOP.org). Finally, if you haven't done so already, we encourage you to take a course in organizational psychology. While personnel psychology focuses on issues related to personnel selection and development, organizational psychology focuses more heavily on the surrounding work environment and issues related to maximizing employee well-being. Taking courses in both areas will provide you with a well-rounded perspective on the field of I-O and also a more detailed understanding of the various career opportunities available to those with a graduate degree.

Summary

We hope you enjoyed your tour of personnel psychology topics offered within this book. The world of work is a fascinating realm to explore, and one with many opportunities to contribute. Personnel psychology will continue to be a driving force in our understanding of the work environment for years to come. As the workplace continues to evolve, personnel psychologists will be eager to develop evidence-based solutions for any workplace issues that may arise. Now that you have an understanding of what personnel psychology has to offer, there is only one thing left to do – get to work!

Notes

1. https://www.onetonline.org/link/summary/19-3032.00
2. https://www.thechicagoschool.edu/insight/business/industrial-organizational-psychology-careers/
3. https://www.allpsychologycareers.com/psychologist-career/industrial-organizational-psychology-careers/
4. https://www.siop.org/Career-Center/I-O-Career-Paths/Consulting
5. https://money.usnews.com/careers/best-jobs/rankings/best-science-jobs

Index

Note: **Bold** page numbers refer to tables and *italic* page numbers refer to figures.

80% rule 22

academic job titles 241
acceptability 206–207
Acquisti, A. 72
active learning 224
actual criterion 107
ADA *see* Americans with Disabilities Act (ADA)
adverse impact 21
age discrimination 26, 31
Age Discrimination in Employment Act (ADEA) 26, 31
agreeableness 159
Alliger, G. M. 229
allocation rules 120–121
American Psychological Association 71
Americans with Disabilities Act (ADA) 26–27, 29–31, 151, 159, 176
anchoring 137
applicant reactions: individual outcomes 116–117; organizational outcomes 117–118
apprentice training 219–220
Army Alpha 8
Army Beta 8
Arvey, R. D. 40, 99, 150
assessment center 185–187
asynchronous video interviews (AVI) 198
Attraction-Selection-Attrition (ASA) model 80–81
attributions 117
automaticity 225
availability heuristic 136

background check 177–179
bad hiring 133

Barrett, G. V. 105
Bartels, L. K. 27
Bauer, K. N. 196
Bayerische Motoren Werke (BMW) 22
Begalla, M. E. 40
behavioral criteria 229–230
behavioral interview items 181
Behaviorally Anchored Rating Scales (BARS) 205–206
behavior tendency SJTs 166
benevolent 121
Bennett Mechanical Comprehension Test II (BMCTII) 150
big data 192–193
Big Five 123–124, 157–160, 162, 168, 194–195, 199, 227
Bingham, W. 5–6, 8–9
Binning, J. F. 105
biodata 167–168
blatant unfavorable treatment 21
bounded rationality 135
Bourdage, J. S. 198

Cable, D. M. 72
Cafferty, T. P. 207
Callan, R. C. 196
Campbell, J. P. 215
Campion, M. A. 59, 61
Cao, M. 163
Cattell, J. M. 5–6
central tendency error 209
citizenship performance 106–107
Civil Rights Act 20–21, 29
coefficient of determination 95–96

Index

cognitive ability 144–147, 227
cognitive task analysis 55
Colquitt, J. A. 120
Combination Job Analysis Method (C-JAM) 58
competency modeling **59**, 59–60
complementary fit 72
computer-based training 221
conceptual criterion 107
concurrent validity study 93–94, **94**
confirmation bias 23, 183
conflict-resolution 167, 181
conscientiousness 158
consistency 127
construct validity 87
consulting and industry 241
consulting firm 5
contamination 108
content-related validation **100**, 100–101
content validity 89–90, 125
context 49
continuous learning 228–229
convergent validity 89
Cooper, D. A. 168
core gameplay loop 195
Costa, P. Jr. 157
cost per new hire 78–79
counterproductive performance 107
coursework 242
COVID-19 pandemic 13, 197
criterion measures 92, 109–111
criterion problem 105–106
criterion-related validation 90, 93–98, **100**, 125
criterion terms 107–109
critical incident technique 55–56
cross validation 98
cybervetting 194

Dane, E. 138
Dark Triad 160–161
data scientists 192–193
decision 134
decision-making 134–135
decisiveness 181–182
declarative knowledge 215–216
deficiency 108
demand analysis 81
DeNisi, A. S. 207

descriptive model 135
Digman, J. 157
disability 26–27
discriminant validity 89
discrimination 19–23; age 26, 31; definition 19; disability 26–27; employment 20–22, 24–29, 31, 33, 238; gender 24–25; race 25–26; religious 26; sex 24–25, 27–28; weight 27
disparate treatment 21
dispositional attributions 117
dissertation 242
distance learning 221–222
distributed practice 226
distributive justice 119, 206
diversity 73
diversity management 34
Drasgow, F. 163–164
Drug-free Workplace Act of 1988 174
drug testing 174–176

emotional intelligence 165–166
employee referrals 75
employee selection 237–238
employment discrimination 20–22, 24–29, 31, 33, 238
Equal Employment Opportunity Commission (EEOC) 29–30, 32
equality 121
equity 120–121
equity-indifferent 121
equity sensitivity 121–122
essential functions 50
existing job information 52
expectations 122–123
expertise 138
external consultant 14
extraversion 158
extrinsic inducements 74

face validity 89, 124–125
faking 161–163
false positive 164
feedback 126–127, 204, 226
fidelity 223
Fleishman Job Analysis Survey 57
Fong, C. M. 72
Ford, H. 43

Index

four-fifths rule 22
frame-of-reference (FOR) training 209–210
French, M. T. 175
Functional Job Analysis (FJA) 56

game-based assessments 195–199
game-framing 195–196
gameful design 195
gamification 195
gap analysis 81
gender discrimination 24–25
gender role theory 25
general intelligence 145–147; popular measures of 146–148
Genetic Information Non-discrimination Act (GINA) 31–32
genetic screening 31–32
Gibby, R. E. 197
Gilbreth, E. 42
Gilbreth, F. 7, 41–42
Gilbreth, L. 7, 42
Gilliland, S. W. 127, 168
Gioia, D. A. 210
Google 75
Griggs versus Duke Power (1971) 21
Guion, R. 156

halo error 209
Harold, C. M. 123
Hawthorne effect 9
Hawthorne studies 9
heuristics 135–138
HEXACO model 160
Hickman, L. 199
Highhouse, S. 76, 138–139
hiring process 79–81
Hogan Development Survey (HDS) 160–161
Hogan, J. 150
honesty 127
Hsieh, T. 133
Huber, V. L. 134
Human Genome Project 31
Human Relations Movement 8–9
human resources (HR) 2–3
Hunter, J. 144

illusory correlations 23
impression management 164

inaccuracy 61, **62**, 63
in-basket exercises 186
incremental validity 96
individual differences 226–228
inducements 73–74
Industrial-Organizational Psychology (I-O) 2–3, 14, 22–23, 28, 33, 35, **49**, 51
information 126
informational justice 120
IntegrityFirst 168
integrity tests 168
intelligence: factors of 145–146
interactional justice 120
internal consistency reliability 88
internal consultant 14
International Cognitive Ability Resource (ICAR) 146
internet-based recruiting 77–78
internet testing 196–197
internship 243
interpersonal effectiveness 127
interpersonal justice 120
interviews 52, 179–181; biases 182–184
intrinsic inducements 74
intuition 137–138
involuntary turnover 111
ipsative measurement 162–163

job analysis 100, 217, 223, 236; art and science 47–48; and competency modeling **59**, 59–60; definition 40; history of 41–43; inaccuracy in 61, **62**, 63; information, collecting 48–59, **53**; purposes of 43–47, **44**; subject matter experts 60–61; tools 54–55
job classification 45
Job Components Inventory (JCI) 57
job crafting 43
job description 45
job design 46–47
Job Elements Inventory (JEI) 57
job evaluation 45
job performance 92, 106–107
job-relatedness 127, 205
job rotation 220
job titles 240–241
Joseph, D. L. 165
Judge, T. A. 72
judgment 134

judgmental measures 109, 111
judgment and decision-making (JDM) 134

Kahneman, D. 135
Kickbox 228
King, E. B. 27–28
Kirkpatrick, D. L. 229–230
knowledge SJTs 166
knowledge, skills, abilities, and other characteristics (KSAOs) 49–50, **51**, 58, 80, 91, 101, 126–127, 133, 176, 181, 183, 185, 198, 215, 217–221, 223, 226–227, 230, 237, 239, 243

Landers, R. N. 195–196
Landy, F. J. 5, 34
leaderless group discussion 187
learning criteria 229–230
learning principles 224–226
lecture 221
leniency error 209
lesbian, gay, bisexual, and transgendered (LGBT) 28
letter of recommendation 176–177
Levine, E. L. 40–41
local validity studies 98
Longenecker, C. O. 210
Lukacik, E. R. 198

machine algorithm 193
Magic 8 Ball 134
Marlowe-Crowne Social Desirability Scale 163
massed practice 226
mating strategy 69–70
Mayer, J. D. 165
Mayo, E. 8–9
McCrae, R. 157
McDaniel, M. A. 166
Meacham v. Knolls Atomic Power Laboratory 31
"measure" 91
mediator variable 10–11, *12*
Meglino, B. M. 207
mentoring 219
meta-analysis 99
modeling 218–219
moderator variable 11, *12*
Morgeson, F. 61
Mossholder, K. W. 99
motivation 216

multisource feedback 211
Munsterberg, H. 4–5

National Labor Relations Act 156
natural language processing (NLP) 193
Neale, M. A. 134
need 121
needs analysis 216–218
neuroticism 123–124, 159
Newman, D. A. 165
Nordstrom, C. R. 27
normative measurement 163
normative model of judgment and decision-making 134–135
Northcraft, G. B. 134

obesity 27
objective measures 109
observation 52
Occupational Information Network (O*NET) 52, 58–59
off-the-job training (OJT) methods 220–224
Olson-Buchanan, J. B. 167
on-the-job training (OJT) methods 218–220
openness to experience 157
organizational: analysis 216–217; culture 80–81, 228–229; justice 118–122; outcomes 117–118
overlearning 225

participation 126
participation/job performance 52
part learning 225
Paulhus, D. L. 160, 164
performance evaluations (performance appraisal) 239–240; abandoning 210–211; characteristics of 205–207; judgmental measures 207–209; purposes of 203–205; FOR training 209–210
performance management system **204**
Personality-Related Position Requirements Form (PPRF) 58
personality tests 156–157
personality traits 123–124
person analysis 217–218
Personnel Decisions International (PDI) 203–204
personnel psychologist 236–240
personnel psychology 2–3; career opportunities 13–14; definition 2; foundation of 40–43;

Index

future of 243–244; history of 4–11; professional organizations and resources 14–15; workplace trends 12–13
personnel selection 69, 87, *92*, 133–134, 146, 157, 167, 197
person-organization (P-O) fit 71–72, 78, 80–81
Phillips, J. M. 77
physical ability tests 150–151
physical fidelity 223
Ployhart, R. E. 123
Position Analysis Questionnaire (PAQ) 56–57
practical experience 243
practicality 207
Pratt, M. G. 138
predictive validity study 93–94, **94**
predictor 91
predictor construct 91
predictor measure 91, 95–97
pretest-posttest design 231
pretest-posttest with control design 231
procedural justice 119, 206
procedural knowledge 215–216
production data 109–110
programmed instruction 221
prospecting theory 69–70
protected class 20
Psychological Corporation 5–6, 8
Psychologically Healthy Workplace Award (PHWA) program 71

questionnaire 52

race 25–26
Ramsay Mechanical Aptitude Test (RMAT) 150
Ramsey, G. 228
range restriction 94
rationality 137
Raven's Advanced Progressive Matrices (RAPMs) 146
reaction criteria 229–230
readiness 226–227
realistic job previews (RJPs) 76–77
Recreational Equipment, Inc. (REI) 75
recruiting 236–237
recruitment process 46, 69–70; for applicant 70–73; employee referrals 75; for employer 73–74; evaluation 78–81; inducements 73–74; internet to 77–78; mating strategy 69–70; organizational values 76; prospecting theory of 69–70; realistic job information 76–77; strategic workforce planning 81–82
reference check 176–179
relevance 107, 205
reliability 87–88, 206
religious discrimination 26
remote interviews 197–199
representativeness heuristic 136
research 242
results criteria 230
role congruity theory 25
role play 186
Roosevelt, F. D. 156
Roulin, N. 198

Sackett, P. R. 148
Salovey, P. 165
Sanchez, D. R. 195
Sanchez, J. I. 40–41
Schmidt, F. 144
Schneider, B. 80–81
scientific management 6–7
scientist-practitioner model 2
Scott, W. D. 5–6, 8
selection process 133; information 127; plan 139–140; as prediction 134; procedural rules for 127–128; social components of 125–127; structural components of 124–125; tools 138–139
self-deceptive denial 164
self-efficacy 223
self-esteem 35–36
severity error 209
sex discrimination 24–25
sexual orientation 27–28
SHRM 79, 81, 203–204
similarity bias 182–183
similarity effect 24
Simon, H. 135
Sims, H. P. 210
SIOP *see* Society for Industrial-Organizational Psychology (SIOP)
situational attributions 117
situational interview items 181
situational judgment tests (SJT) 166–167
Skills Gap 193
Slaughter, J. E. 168

Index

social desirability scales 163
social media 32–33, 78, 193–195
social networking sites (SNS) 72–73
social psychology 24
social validity 126–127
Society for Human Resource Management 72
Society for Industrial-Organizational Psychology (SIOP) 2, 12, 14–15, 243–244
solution analysis 81
Spearman, C. 145
speeded test 149
Speer, A. B. 167–168
SPSS interface 225
stereotype threat 148
storification 196
Strategic Legal Solutions 31
strategic workforce planning 81–82
structured interviews 180–182, **182**
subclinical personality traits 160–161
subject matter experts (SMEs) 60–61
Subway 109–110
succession planning 81–82
supplementary fit 72
supply analysis 81
synthetic validity 99–100

task analysis 217–218
task inventory method 54–55
task-oriented approach 54
task performance 106
tasks 49
Tay, L. 195
Taylor, F. 6–7
Taylor, F. W. 41
"test" 91
test perceptions 122
test score banding 147
thesis 242
Thomson, S. 178
Threshold Trait Analysis 58
Thurstone, L. L. 145
time and motion study 7
Title VII of the 1964 Civil Rights Act 10
Tomeh, D. H. 148
Tovar, D. 178

trainee personality 227
trainees 226–227
trainers 227–228
training 215, 238–239; evaluation 229–232; impacts 224–229; methods 218–224; needs analysis 216–218; purpose 215–216
transfer 222
transparency 126
two-way communication 127

Uggerslev, K. L. 72
unequal status 24
unstructured interviews 179, **182**

validity/validation 87–90, 203; coefficient 95; content-related **100**, 100–101; criterion-related 93–98, **100**; generalization 98–100; shrinkage 98; sources of 88–90
Van Iddekinge, C. H. 168
variance 205–206
virtual reality (VR) 199, 222
Viteles, M. 41, 43
voluntary turnover 111

weight 27
Whetzel, D. L. 149
whole learning 225
Williams, K. M. 160
withdrawal behaviors 110–111
Wonderlic 106
Woodward, R. S. 156
work activities 240–241
work context 51
worker-oriented approach 54
work sample test 184–185
World War I (WWI) 8
World War II (WWII) 9–10
written tests 229
Wundt, W. 4–5

yield pyramid 79, 79–80
yield ratio 79

Zhang, D. C. 183–184
Zickar, M. J. 164

Made in United States
Cleveland, OH
24 May 2025